COMPETING FOR STOCK MARKET PROFITS

COMPETING FOR STOCK MARKET PROFITS

PAUL F. JESSUP

University of Minnesota

JOHN WILEY & SONS, INC.
NEW YORK   LONDON
SYDNEY   TORONTO

This publication is designed to provide accurate and authoritative information in regard to the subject matter covered. It is sold with the understanding that the publisher is not engaged in rendering legal, accounting, or other professional service. If legal advice or other expert assistance is required, the services of a competent professional person should be sought.

Library of Congress Cataloging in Publication Data

Jessup, Paul F.
    Competing for stock market profits.

    1. Investments. 2. Speculation. 3. Stock Exchange. I. Title.
HG4521.J46   332.6′322   73-15961
ISBN 0-471-44262-3
ISBN 0-471-44263-1 (pbk.)

Printed in the United States of America

10 9 8 7 6 5 4 3 2 1

To my parents
for their example and
quiet encouragement

Preface

This book is designed to challenge, persuasively, many conventional views of investment theory and practice. It is intended to encourage readers to examine carefully their personal views of stock market opportunities. It builds on extensive recent research in the areas of capital markets and portfolio management. I acknowledge my indebtedness to diverse researchers and writers, many of whom are referenced in this book.

Among the origins of this book is a set of lectures developed for my various classes in investment analysis and management. Astute comments and questions by many of my students have assisted me in refining my set of ideas and their style of presentation.

Colleagues and students of mine read early drafts of this manuscript. I acknowledge their assistance, in particular, that of W. Bruce Erickson, Per B. Mokkelbost, and Thomas W. Von Kuster, Jr.

The anonymous reviewers commissioned by Wiley gave me constructive comments. Their assistance was very helpful in preparing the final manuscript.

My wife, Johanna, provided important assistance and demonstrated patient understanding during my writing of this book.

I accept responsibility for any deficiencies in my presentation of a popular topic.

Paul F. Jessup

Contents

chapter 1
Objectives

Directed to many actual and potential investors, this book provides a useful new perspective for individuals anxious to build their capital by investing in common stocks.

A basic premise of this book is that many individuals are fascinated by the stock market. They now own stock, or they intend to purchase shares in the future. Therefore they want to know how to include stocks in their investment programs.

Many books and articles claim to inform investors about:

How to buy stocks.
Where to obtain investment information.
How to identify growth stocks.
How to select mutual funds.

Introductions to such topics conventionally offer general wisdom and describe accepted practice.

A willingness to challenge conventional statements and to consider new viewpoints is necessary for readers who want a practical understanding of their potential opportunities in the stock market.

The integrating theme of this book is that most stocks are bought and sold in public markets by investors aggressively competing for profits. This theme, developed more fully in the initial chapters, provides a consistent basis for examining many popular strategies for stock market profits.

Knowledge need not be stuffy. Common stock market fallacies are exposed in order to stimulate readers to examine their own assumptions and also some assertions of others. Thus, readers develop practical skills in evaluating stock market information.

Learning how to identify and avoid stock market fallacies is useful for individual investors. However these individuals want additional positive results, such as answers to the following set of questions:

What do I need to know about the stock market?

How well can I expect to do in the stock market?

How shall I evaluate common stocks?

Which investment strategies shall I use?

How can I decide when to buy or sell stocks?

How can new perspective about stock market opportunities be useful to me?

Therefore a principal objective of this book is to answer such questions with persuasive logic and evidence so that individuals personally can make informed investment decisions.

PART ONE

WHAT DOES AN INVESTOR NEED TO KNOW ABOUT THE STOCK MARKET?

chapter 2
The Stock Market:
A Forum for
Skillful Investors

A flood of details can swamp investors wanting to know about the stock market. Traditionally, books on basic investments provide detailed descriptions of the structure and principal procedures of the nation's largest stock exchange, the New York Stock Exchange. They portray how it is organized, how it operates, and how investors can participate.

However a proliferation of detail detracts from a central focus. What is needed, therefore, is a total perspective of how diverse features of the stock market are interrelated. A unifying perspective enables investors to understand better their place in the total market mechanism. Furthermore, it provides them with a basic outline to which they can later add extensive details to obtain an even fuller perspective of the stock market.

What Is a Competitive Market?

A comprehensive way of viewing the stock market is to compare it with the conceptual model of a *competitive market*. In summary, the following conditions are necessary for a competitive market.

1. There should be *many participants*. Although there can be diversity among the many, some should be generally talented and rational individuals seeking to maximize their long-run wealth.
2. There should be *ease of entry and exit* in the market. Thus skilled

individuals or people with new, untested ideas can readily enter the market. If they are effective, they are rewarded; if ineffective, perhaps having realized below-average rewards or substantial losses, they become discouraged and can leave.

To facilitate entry, market participants should have convenient access to capital. This does not mean that all participants have unlimited funds, but that those who demonstrate the quality of their skills or ideas should be able to raise funds, either by borrowing or by agreeing to manage, for compensation, the funds of others.

3. There should be *general availability of information* to market participants.

The above conditions need not hold at all times for all participants. As this book will develop more fully, these are standards against which to compare an actual market.

A stock market that in practice approximates the competitive model has important practical consequences. Basically, in a competitive market, there are no opportunities for consistent excess profits. Participants in such a market, over a period of time, will receive only a competitive rate of return on the resources they use in the market. Such a conclusion implies revision of many conventional views of stock market goals and strategies.

Placing One's Investment Skills in Perspective

Too many investors have a self-centered view of their place in the stock market. They are specifically involved in their periodic investment decisions, intermittent discussions with brokers, and occasional discussions with other investors. In addition to knowing of investment activities within their own circle, they are somewhat aware of the existence of other market participants. Periodically they read about institutional changes taking place in the Wall Street brokerage community or about the success stories of some investors or professional funds managers. On commuter trains or during coffee breaks they see many other persons turning to the market pages in the newspapers or hear them discussing investment aspects of various stocks. Yet, while generally aware that they are among the many participants in a large-scale market, most investors fail to examine the practical implications of having to compete for stock market profits. Instead they continue to concentrate on their personal day-to-day investment decisions, and they continue to search for investment strategies offering above-average opportunities.

Many participants in a market contribute to its being competitive. By a recent count there are about 18 million individual investors holding shares listed on the New York Stock Exchange.[1] Although some of these investors may be only small holders of shares in American Telephone or a local electrical utility, many others are active participants in the market. They spend long hours seeking and interpreting investment information from various sources. They have in-depth knowledge about various established and emerging companies, and they are skilled in analyzing financial statements. Examples of these devoted individual investors may be seen daily in the business sections of large public libraries or in the library areas of brokerage offices throughout the country. Thus, any one investor must compete against this set of devoted amateurs who are continually striving for stock market profits.

Many other individuals devote their careers to participating in the stock market mechanism. According to a recent count there are 577 member organizations of the New York Stock Exchange, many of which are brokerage firms that employ a total of about 53,000 registered representatives.[2] In addition, these firms often employ their own research staff of security analysts. Also, there are currently 13,000 members of the Financial Analysts Federation, a nationwide organization of analysts and managers who devote their skills to the search for investment opportunities.[3] Furthermore consider the number of professional portfolio managers who are making daily investment decisions for investment companies, bank trust accounts, insurance companies, pension funds, university endowment funds, and other such pools of capital. A recent study by the Securities and Exchange Commission estimates that the total pool of institutional investments in common stocks exceeds $300 billion.[4] In addition, there are the proverbial Swiss bankers and other international financiers who actively assess relative opportunities in the world's stock markets and invest in those American stocks they judge to provide above-average opportunities. These many professionals, domestic and international, are competing with each other in their search for attractive investment opportunities.

Of the many participants in the stock market can one confidently believe himself to be more knowledgeable or more talented than all the others? It is not adequate to compare one's perceived abilities only against some acquaintances who know little about the mechanics of

[1] *New York Stock Exchange Fact Book*, 1972, p. 47.

[2] *Ibid.*, pp. 58, 62.

[3] *Financial Analysts Journal*, January–February 1973, p. 6.

[4] *Institutional Investor Study Report of the Securities and Exchange Commission*, Vol. 2, (U.S. Government Printing Office: 1971), Table 2, p. 131. There are many footnotes detailing the estimation procedures and sources for this Table.

the stock market and who limit their investments to occasional small purchases of some stocks recommended by their brokers. Nor is it adequate to compare one's perceived abilities against the occasional cocky investment manager or security analyst who has his run of successes in a general upward stock market but whose star then falls. No, broad perspective and a dose of humility require that the realistic investor explicitly recognize that there are other talented individuals also competing for stock market profits. There are professionals who willingly forgo lucrative opportunities in business or other professions to devote full time to careers as security analysts, investment advisors, portfolio managers, and professional traders. Others become brokers, choosing to work with intelligent clients seeking to preserve and augment their wealth. Although there are bound to be some incompetent professionals—at least in the short run—there are others who conscientiously devote their time and talents in the quest to serve their clients and themselves by outperforming the market. With their continual dedication to this goal, they are likely to have an edge in knowledge and expertise over most part-time investors.

Is it likely that any one professional can have a consistent edge on others? Occasionally one security analyst, through superior information or skills, may select a stock that becomes a big winner. Such success stories make news and advance careers. But is he likely to be able *consistently* to select such winners? He is competing with other skilled analysts also working full time at other investment complexes with resources committed to thorough research. Similarly, consider a portfolio manager principally responsible for a large mutual fund. In any one year the fund under his supervision may have higher returns than other funds of its type. But is such a superior record likely to persist in subsequent years when he continues to compete with other portfolio managers some of whom also are intelligent, decisive individuals? If, as is likely, there are various skillful security analysts and portfolio managers all seeking exceptional opportunities, their very quest and competition help the stock market to approach the model of a competitive market. (Sportsmen should perceive analogies to various games where the score is likely to be close because the players or teams are evenly matched; furthermore, as the evenly matched contestants continue to play, each is likely to win about an equal share of the games played.)

What if one investor were very skillful and able to develop a strategy for selecting stocks that consistently outperformed the market by a substantial amount? He has three principal options. First, he can try to keep his skills to himself and over time multiply his own funds and those of close friends. (With his skills, his circle of "friends" may rapidly expand.) In so doing, however, he runs the risk that others will monitor his moves and try to benefit from his system. To illustrate, is this investor's broker, observing the client's continual success, likely to neglect to put himself, his family, and other clients into the same stocks purchased by the successful investor? Thus the investor is unlikely to be able to accumulate a large position in any one stock before its price moves upward, partly in response to the broadening circle of vicarious purchases. Furthermore, if the investor has a successful strategy, other investors, monitoring the stocks he buys, may perceive a pattern and decode his procedures. With this new information, they then can seek to *anticipate* his moves and, through their prompt actions, reduce or remove profit opportunities from his strategy. In summary, with intense competition for stock market profits, if one investor does develop a successful strategy for beating the market, it is improbable that he can long keep it for his exclusive use if his goal is to multiply his capital.

As a second principal option, the investor may choose to benefit from his successful strategy by selling his services to others. He may become an investment advisor, security analyst or, more likely, offer to manage, for appropriate compensation, a pool of money for other investors. Thus he can without much difficulty enter the ranks of professional money managers and, with his skills, attract capital to him. By entering the professional ranks, he may more quickly benefit from his system by immediate compensation for his skills. Nevertheless he runs the risk that his successful techniques will be monitored by other perceptive individuals who will eventually decode the system and, by adopting it themselves, begin to compete away its profit opportunities.

Third, instead of selling his professional services to clients, the skillful investor with his strategy may decide to sell it to the general public. He may publish newsletters to publicize stocks that, according to his strategy, have above-average potential.[5] As an alternative, he may decide to summarize his entire system and have it published as a popular book on how to beat the market or how to make big money in the stock market. Such books apparently sell well. But obviously, *even if* the author had a successful strategy, its mass distribution almost certainly eliminates any opportunities for investors to use it for consistently and substantially above-average profits. Since the many players knowing "the strategy" are competing with each other, any possible relative advantages are eliminated.

In summary, a sound perspective of the total stock market indicates that any one investor competes against many other investors. While

---

[5] For a provocative survey of the investment advisory industry, see John L. Springer, *If They're So Smart, How Come You're Not Rich?* (Henry Regnery Company: 1971).

some may be less competent, it involves substantial arrogance to believe that, compared to oneself, there are not many other investors at least as skillful and devoted to the quest for exceptional stock market profits. Not only do many skilled participants exist at all times, but new ones are continually being attracted to the market. It is comparatively easy to enter the market because brokerage firms are not known to reject promising new business, and commission charges seldom exceed two percent of the transaction cost. Furthermore, it is not particularly difficult to enter the ranks of stock market professionals, and demonstrated abilities can attract capital funds to be professionally managed. However, if an investor should develop a strategy to beat the market, it is not logical to believe that he can continue to use this procedure for long. Other skillful individuals are likely to perceive his strategy and begin to adopt it, thus removing the opportunity for exceptional profits. Skillful investors, competing for profitable investment opportunities, by their own actions eliminate opportunities for any one investor or small group of investors continually to have an edge on the market. Thus, the stock market—by not being a forum only *for*, but *of*, many skillful competing participants—may not depart substantially from the model of a competitive market. As developed in subsequent chapters, a growing body of evidence supports this initial conclusion.

chapter 3
The Stock Market Information System

Extensive information is available to most investors. Investments books traditionally focus on describing where to obtain investment information and how to analyze such information. Because investors thus learn that much of the detailed information available to them may be useful for personal investment decisions, they are encouraged to absorb more and more details about stocks in which they are interested.

Devotion to obtaining and digesting details too easily distracts investors from developing a comprehensive view of the stock market information system. What is needed is insight into the general process by which investment information is diffused among stock market participants. Although any investor can obtain more and more information, the principal issue is whether additional information is likely to provide benefits that will exceed the costs—both of money and time—of acquiring and analyzing such information. This framework of whether likely benefits will exceed the costs is relevant both for generally available information and "inside" information. Fresh perspective on the stock market information system enables investors to assess its practical consequences for their investment decisions.

Competing for Investment Information

How relevant information can be useful to investment decision making is suggested in statements such as:

If only I had known that the company's third quarter profits were going to be down. I would have sold my 500 shares before the earnings report was announced and the subsequent drop in the share price.

A friend told me that his firm was about to be acquired by a larger company. If I had bought shares in his company at that time, I could have made 10 dollars per share because of the attractive merger terms offered by the acquiring company.

This small new company began in a garage near my home. It developed an important new product in the area of computer peripheral equipment. Its shares, initially offered at three dollars, skyrocketed to 50. If only I had known about this company and its product sooner, I could have made a lot of money.

Variations of such statements are frequently heard or read. Although focusing principally on "what might have been," the statements also suggest the possibility of superior profits for investors with procedures for obtaining and properly evaluating new information.

There are many practical examples of how stock prices can be sharply influenced by new information. In February 1971 the Wm. Wrigley Jr. Company announced that it was increasing the wholesale price of its five-stick packages of chewing gum for only the second time in 53 years. Within two days the share price rose about $20, or 13 percent. This abrupt rise in the company's stock price apparently was associated with investor expectations that the new pricing policy would contribute to higher corporate earnings. Conversely, within one trading day after the Penn Central's announcement that its railroad affiliate was seeking protection from bankruptcy, the share price dropped over 40 percent from its closing price of the preceding Friday. Such episodes illustrate that new information can affect share prices.

Investors in search of promising opportunities generally strive to obtain potentially important information more promptly than other stock market participants. In addition, such invesors must strive to assess, rapidly and correctly, the probable impact of this information on future share prices. However, while such a strategy of acquiring and evaluating investment information sounds fine in theory, just how feasible is such a strategy in practice?

There can be two principal views about the process of information flow in the stock market and about how investors respond to relevant new information. The *market-opportunity* view is a popular way of considering the stock market. It recognizes that not all investors can have the resources or skills necessary to receive and evaluate promptly new information about many companies. If this is true, stock prices may respond slowly to new information. These conditions imply that investors who carefully analyze many stocks and who are committed to learning and evaluating new information about such stocks should be able to identify investments having exceptionally high profit opportunities. In this case, information can be valuable; therefore investors are well advised to spend long hours personally analyzing information about companies and reading professional analyses of various stocks.

However, there is a contrary view about the nature of stock market information flows and their investment consequences. This approach is called the *competitive-market* view. It recognizes that any investor is one among many. He could compare his probable resources and skills to those of a retired couple holding 100 shares of a local utility stock and conclude that he is better able to obtain and evaluate information about various investment opportunities. However such a comparison is incomplete. Competing with him for stock market profits are other resourceful individual investors and also professional teams of investment analysts, often with extensive resources of men and capital. If these competing investors and analysts, also with general access to market information, rapidly evaluate and act on relevant information, then persistent opportunities for some investors to make above-average profits cannot exist.

A competitive environment for stock market information does not prevent an investor from *at times* getting and correctly interpreting information more promptly than his competitors, in which case he can achieve above-average profits. However, at *other times* competing investors will more quickly recognize and profit from new information. *Over time,* however, no one investor or group of investors is likely to be able consistently to obtain information promptly and assess it correctly. Furthermore, having acted on new information, an investor sometimes will learn, too late, that he acted on misinformation. At other times, having received information, he will fail to recognize its relevance or will interpret it inappropriately. In such a competitive environment, the value of new information generally will be small and fleeting because it will be quickly perceived by some market participants, incorporated into their investment decisions, and thus rapidly reflected in share prices.

In summary, the practical value of investment information is linked to how information is transmitted and absorbed in the stock market. The market-opportunity view suggests that with long, careful study most investors periodically can identify unusual stock market opportunities. Therefore, over time, the value of their stock portfolios should grow more than that of other less-committed or less-talented investors. Paradoxically, however, by committing themselves to the market-opportunity view and therefore continuing to search for and evaluate information about various stocks, these very investors help create a competitive market for information about stocks.

Sources of Investment Information

Most investors are exposed to only several facets of the stock market information system. Their general awareness of daily investment events comes from reading the financial pages of their metropolitan newspaper and possibly also of *The Wall Street Journal*. On reading or hearing about a particular stock, an investor can ask a broker for further information. In response, the broker typically makes several general comments about the firm and its industry, and promises to send some research information. Often this follow-up information consists of a sheet from Standard & Poor's loose-leaf "Stock Reports," summarizing the company's past record, fundamental position, and future prospects. If, by chance, the brokerage firm's research department recently prepared a brief research report on the company, this also is likely to be sent to the inquiring customer. Such an information process, while typical, is but a small part of the total stock market information system. Therefore it is necessary to stand back and try to summarize the operations of this total system and, in so doing, answer whether it more closely approximates in practice: (1) an imperfect system conducive to major market opportunities, or (2) a competitive system limiting the persistence of unusual opportunities.

Published information about most stocks is generally available to investors. Most companies with publicly traded shares publish their financial statements, such as balance sheets and income statements. Such periodic reports are required as a condition of listing a company's shares on the nation's principal stock exchanges. These statements are prepared by accounting firms according to generally accepted accounting principles. Despite some notable exceptions, these statements generally provide the information necessary for an accurate and complete analysis of a company's recent financial condition.

Many large companies must file comprehensive, standardized financial reports with the Securities and Exchange Commission (SEC). These reports, which in detail go beyond even the published annual reports, are public information. They may be obtained by mail, at a relatively small charge, from the Commission. Furthermore, this detailed information filed with the SEC is available in comprehensive sets on microfilm or microfiche, with some libraries holding the information in this form. Not all investors have the time or skills to use this abundance of corporate financial reports. However, various investors and financial services do use the generally available reports of companies in which they are interested; therefore, indirectly, this information and its evaluation become available to many other investors.

Security analysts, working for various brokerage firms, securities research firms, and institutional investors managing large stock portfolios, draw on published financial information in searching for stocks that may provide above-average profits. In addition, by interviewing top managers of companies in whose stock they are interested, analysts try to evaluate from close range management's capabilities and the realism of its future corporate goals.

Corporate managers may at times meet only with an individual analyst or a team of analysts from one firm. However, other analysts similarly can arrange interviews, so that the company is monitored by competing analysts from various firms. Moreover, corporate managers also are invited to address groups of analysts from various firms. These meetings are attended by analysts competing for potentially useful information. While generally not open to the public, more and more of these meetings have been open to members of the press who can then report any information judged newsworthy for other investors and the public. Furthermore transcripts of some of these meetings are made available for publication, for example in *The Wall Street Transcript*, a weekly newspaper to which anyone can subscribe. In summary, most corporations are being monitored and evaluated by various security analysts who then prepare research recommendations for professional portfolio managers or for distribution to members of the investing public.

Research reports prepared by security analysts vary widely in their quality and distribution patterns. Most large brokerage firms have research departments preparing periodic reports on selected companies and industries, and these reports are generally available at no cost to customers and potential customers. Often these reports contain a brief review of a company's past history and provide some general comments about its future prospects. Individual investors will find it difficult to obtain directly a wide variety of brokerage-firm research reports over a long period of time. However, this hurdle can be overcome because *The Wall Street Transcript* and some other magazines publish a selection of various research reports, albeit with inevitable time lags for publication and distribution.

In-depth research reports also are prepared at times, but they are oriented more toward institutional investors or large private investors. However, even among these major clients competing for superior information, these reports can have comparatively broad distribution. These clients will therefore have an opportunity to assess any new insights relative to their alternative investment opportunities. Also, since no one institutional investor can maintain close ties with the many research-oriented brokerage firms, it is in no position to obtain consistently better reports more rapidly than competing institutional investors.

Strong negative statements about a company's shares seldom are contained in published research reports. Typically the reports contain "buy" or "hold" recommendations. This bias toward optimistic or neutral reports is related to analysts' valuing their continued assessibility to top corporate management. Such managers are unlikely to welcome back analysts who, being given the courtesy of management interviews, then prepare reports critical of a company's management record or potential. Thus, unless an analyst is positive or at least neutral about a company, he typically does not prepare a written research report; however his negative views may sometimes be transmitted orally to selected clients. This behavioral pattern, while understandable, can be disquieting for investors who buy a company's shares on the basis of a glowing research report but who subsequently may never receive a strong follow-up "sell" recommendation as the stock falls in price.

The major investment services also are an important element in the total stock market information system. Moody's Investor Services and Standard & Poor's both provide diverse publications concerning corporations with publicly traded shares. These publications range from comprehensive volumes containing extensive historical information about many companies to weekly surveys of the outlook for various industries and companies. The Value Line Investment Advisory Service also analyzes many companies on a continual basis, providing its subscribers with information about the past record and possible stock market prospects of various firms and industries. Building on the financial reports published by companies or filed with the SEC, these major investment services supplement these reports with information from other sources, coupled with their own analytical techniques.

These investment services are widely available to many investors. Interested investors can directly subscribe, or they can read them in many public and school libraries and in many offices of brokerage firms. Furthermore, many investors are indirectly linked to these sources of information because the comprehensive historical information published by the major services can be used as inputs to brokerage research reports written for broad distribution.

Financial newspapers, such as *The Wall Street Journal* and *Barron's*, report and analyze events relevant for investors. They review national and international economic and political events. Periodically they focus on new products, changing industries, and changing consumer interests. They summarize corporate earnings reports and other major corporate announcements. Staff writers sometimes dig deeply and analyze particular corporate activities and statements, often with a skepticism that provides new insights. In addition, they periodically provide information about current research reports of various brokerage firms and about the investment transactions of mutual funds and corporate insiders, such as managers and large shareholders. Thus these newspapers, drawing on many sources and summarizing and analyzing many events, play a pivotal role in the stock market information system. They alert all interested readers to recent and contemporary events. (Even more contemporary is the widely monitored Dow Jones news ticker service.) But since there are many readers— *The Wall Street Journal* recently had 1,300,000 subscribers—information published in these newspapers is widely distributed and promptly read for its probable investment consequences.

Financial magazines, such as the *Financial Analysts Journal, Forbes, Fortune,* and *Institutional Investor,* perform some investor-information functions similar to those of financial newspapers. However their relative emphasis is on in-depth analysis in contrast to the reporting of daily events. Readers of such magazines are kept informed of major trends that can affect investment strategies. Furthermore, since anyone can subscribe to these journals or read them in various libraries, their information is available for many competing investors to incorporate in their investment decisions.

Computerized files of investment information have recently become popular. Subscribers can readily obtain tapes containing extensive accounting data of firms with broad investor interest. Basically these computerized data files are nothing more than convenient, accessible summaries of the accounting data provided in corporate financial reports. Sometimes, the services constructing the tapes try to standardize the reported accounting figures in order to provide some degree of comparability among the financial data. In addition to accounting data, other available computer tapes summarize past prices and trading activity in various stocks.

Most investors do not have the hardware and software computer resources to use computerized data files. However, at a price, they are available to any interested subscriber. Analysts employed by many institutional investors and also researchers in many universities have ready access to these tapes, and they can extensively analyze them in search of superior information or superior techniques for processing information. If successful in their quest, they can prepare research reports and recommendations; in this way, the new information is communicated to various investors. However, since these tapes seldom are the exclusive property of one group of analysts, they are competing with other talented analysts who also are trying to derive superior information from the tapes. With such competition, what is the likelihood of any one group of analysts being able consistently to derive superior investment information from computerized data files?

Five principal points can be summarized from the preceding brief survey of the total stock market information system:

1. The information system is based principally on the financial reports of publicly held companies. These reports, examined by major accounting firms, are required by the SEC and the New York Stock Exchange to provide full and fair disclosure.

2. Many competing investors have direct and indirect access to many sources of investment information.

3. The various sources of investment information are interrelated, often monitoring each other. Analysts read each other's research reports. Brokerage reports derive information from major investment services and standardized computer tapes. Financial newspapers and magazines summarize and review various research reports. In this type of environment, there is frequent cross-checking of sources of investment information.

4. New information is rapidly transmitted to market participants, by news services and newspapers and, indirectly, via brokers and other investors.

5. Importantly, most information is past or contemporary, with future estimates being based on the generally available past information.

These five points indicate that, in practice, the stock market information system approaches the competitive-market view.

What are the practical consequences of this competitive-market view for most investors? Much information about events linked to stock prices is rapidly transmitted to many competing analysts and investors. In constantly seeking superior information, these many participants— often monitoring each other—reduce the possibility that any unusually valuable information can long remain undetected. For the sensible investor this means that the research recommendations, investment reports, and news articles he reads are unlikely to be based on information or insights not already available to other investors who also use it in their investment decisions. In such a competitive environment, spending long hours and costly resources seeking investment information is unlikely to be very rewarding, if at all.

Many investors may be willing now to accept the competitive-market view concerning information about large publicly held companies that are continually monitored by many analysts. Can one really believe that through extensive reading and research he can hope to gain unique information—not available to some other talented analysts— about companies such as American Telephone and Telegraph, General Foods, IBM, Proctor & Gamble, or Texaco? Yet what about smaller companies whose shares are less widely held, for example, many of the companies not listed on the New York Stock Exchange? To illustrate, in contrast to the many followers of IBM, fewer analysts and investors monitor and investigate each small company in the computer area. Also, for these small companies the published financial information, the number of research reports, and the news coverage generally are less comprehensive than that of the larger companies. Nevertheless some other analysts and investors are following the fortunes of small companies. Some investment advisory services concentrate their resources in searching for what they believe to be above-average opportunities from shares of less-publicized companies. Many professional analysts, paid to identify shares of smaller companies judged to have above-average potential, can visit with the corporate managers to learn more about their plans and capabilities. Thus, although the information system concerning smaller, less-known companies is less formal and comprehensive, an investor must ask himself whether it departs substantially enough from the competitive market view in order for unusual opportunities to persist. With investors and analysts also competing for superior information about various less-publicized regional firms, any potential rewards are unlikely to warrant the input of much time and financial resources by most investors.

Heretical as the preceding conclusions may first appear, they do not depart sharply from the mainstream of investment analysis. A classic volume on this subject is Graham, Dodd and Cottle's *Security Analysis: Principles and Technique*. This is an excellent book for serious investors; according to a recent survey, it is the one most used by professional security analysts. Careful readers of this book will observe, however, statements such as the following:

"The real accomplishment of the many thousand analysts now studying not so many thousand companies is the establishment of proper relative prices in today's market for most of the leading issues and a great many secondary ones.

"But insofar as stock prices are relatively 'right' on the basis of known and foreseeable facts, the opportunities for consistently above-average results must necessarily diminish."[1]

Financial analysts, as a group, by their own capable work and rivalry, help the stock market to approach the model of a competitive market that seldom provides exceptional profit opportunities.

Using Inside Information

The *malevolent-market* view is a third possible way of analyzing the stock market information system. It sees the market as interlaced with —if not dominated by—insider information, tipees, touts, and special information channeled in response for special favors. If true, perceptive investors will have to evaluate their chances in such a system.

"Inside information" is not generally available to most investors. It is usually passed on verbally, instead of more formally in published documents. If such information is useful for predicting profits from a stock, then this information can be valuable to early recipients who proceed to incorporate it in their investment decisions. Variations of the following statements illustrate the transmittal of inside information:

My golf partner tells me that his small company is about to sign a major sales contract that will substantially boost future earnings. He and is family are buying more shares in the company.

A family friend tells me that he has heard about a small oil company drilling in a new area. The initial results, while not yet confirmed or publicized, are extremely promising.

A buddy of mine works in the financial planning department of a company that has been reporting rapidly growing earnings. Now, however, because the company has run into major operating and legal problems, it will shortly be announcing a sharp drop in its third-quarter earnings.

Seeing the probable impact on share prices when the news is publicized, recipients of such inside information can see the possible rewards from their making rapid investment decisions that will exploit such opportune news. Too often, however, they fail to recognize explicitly the hazards involved.

[1] Benjamin Graham, David L. Dodd, and Sidney Cottle, *Security Analysis: Principles and Technique*, 4th ed., (McGraw-Hill Book Company: 1962), pp. 707–708.

Three principal hazards in trying to exploit inside information can be specified. An investor can reduce the effects of two of these hazards, but the third is largely outside his control.

Misinformation, or incorrect interpretation of valid information, is the first hazard. What is transmitted in good faith, or otherwise, as inside information can sometimes be erroneous. (The extent to which information can become distorted as it is transmitted by word of mouth is revealed in party games where participants are to pass on to other players an initial verbal phrase.) People who acted promptly on what turns out to have been incorrect information are often reluctant to discuss their errors. Yet at times investors can be heard to say how their greatest losses are from stocks in which they believed themselves to have had inside information.

The hazard of acting on misinformation can be reduced by a detailed evaluation of the probable credibility of the source and by seeking independent confirmations of the information from other sources. However such actions to reduce the hazard add delays to the investment decision and increase the number of people who learn about the inside information. If they act promptly to exploit it or if they publicize it, then by their actions they will effectively remove further opportunities for the information to be exploited.

The second hazard is that the inside information, while valid, is received too late. Although not yet generally available to most investors, the information already has been informally transmitted among a broadening circle of "insiders" and the people who know the insiders. These individuals, competing for superior information, already have incorporated the advance news into their investment decisions; in this way they help the stock price to adjust to reflect this special knowledge. In such cases there will be few, if any, potential rewards to subsequent recipients of this inside information.

To reduce this second hazard, an investor must try to assess realistically where he probably stands in the flow of a specific piece of inside information. He can try to learn whether others have already heard it; but, if they have not, they now are alerted to the news. Also, he can examine the recent prices of the stock to try to estimate whether there has already been an adjustment reflecting the inside information. As with misinformation, attempts to reduce the hazard of being a latecomer involve delays and possible broadening awareness of the information, such that the opportunity then passes.

The third hazard of using inside information is new and particularly important. Benefits from the use of inside information have become much less certain because of recent court cases and regulatory decisions. Specifically, the SEC has ruled that investors may violate the law by acting on nonpublic stock tips. "A person acting on a tip received either directly from a corporate insider or from an intermediary would violate the law if he had reason to know that the information would be a material factor in an investment decision."[2] The SEC outlines four tests:

1. "Is the information material?
2. Is it nonpublic?
3. Does the person receiving the information have reason to know that it is nonpublic and obtained improperly by 'selective revelation,' meaning that it isn't generally available?
4. Is the information a factor in the tipee's investment decision?"

"If the tests are met, a tipee, to avoid breaking the law, must either refrain from acting on the tip or get the information made public."[3]

This amounts to a major revision of the rules of the game concerning use of inside information.[4]

Because recent regulatory and legal decisions are broadening the range of actions that constitute illegal use of "inside information," an investor tempted to use inside information must recognize the probable consequences of his actions. On receiving such information, he can act promptly to exploit it; but then he accepts hazards one (misinformation) and two (too late). Attempts to reduce these hazards lessen the possible value of the information. If his investment decision turns out to be inappropriate, he most likely loses. What happens, however, if the decision turns out to be appropriate so that he profits? After the fact, he may be found to have violated the law and have to accept penalties, such as returning the investment profits to the company. On this basis, with the new legal environment, investors choosing to exploit inside information now enter a game in which the apparent odds favor their losing.

In conclusion, even if inside information were useful in some past investment decisions, the new legal and regulatory rules are designed to restrict its future use. A goal of the new rules is to have market information publicly available to competing investors. Such a policy moves the real-world information system even closer to the competitive-market view.

[2] As reported in *The Wall Street Journal*, July 30, 1971, p. 26.

[3] *Ibid.*

[4] Commentary about recent legal and regulatory events concerning "inside information" is presented in a published transcript, "Loomis on Inside Information," *Financial Analysts Journal*, May–June 1972, pp. 20–21 ff.

REVIEW OF PART ONE

Question: What do I need to know about the stock market?

Answer: What one does *not* need to know are extensive details, if attention to details detracts from the development of a comprehensive viewpoint.

What one basically needs to know is whether there is a realistic *general framework* by which to understand the stock market. Three possible frameworks were presented in Part One:

The market-opportunity view

The competitive-market view

The malevolent-market view

When one recognizes that selected examples can be found to illustrate each of these three views, the practical issue is which one of the three is most *generally representative* of the stock market.

What one also needs to know is whether additional details generally support acceptance of the competitive-market viewpoint, or whether additional details indicate rejection of the competitive-market viewpoint and acceptance of another framework. Knowing additional details about the stock market is useful for testing the competitive-market viewpoint. Toward this end the following types of additional reading are suggested.

* * *

These materials basically describe various features of the stock markets and report recent developments affecting these markets:

Engel, Louis, *How To Buy Stocks* (Little, Brown & Co.: 1971).

National Association of Securities Dealers Inc. The annual reports of this association focus on developments involving the over-the-counter markets.

New York Stock Exchange Fact Book. This booklet, published annually by the New York Stock Exchange, Inc., provides a useful, timely introduction to the Exchange Community.

Regan, Donald T., *A View from the Street* (New American Library, Inc.: 1972).

Zarb, Frank G., and Gabriel T. Kerekes (editors), *The Stock Market Handbook: Reference Manual for the Securities Industry* (Dow Jones-Irwin, Inc.: 1970).

Because of the rapid pace of change in the structure and practices of the stock markets, investors who want to keep informed of new developments must regularly read financial periodicals such as *The Wall Street Journal.*

PART TWO
HOW WELL DO INVESTORS DO IN THE STOCK MARKET?

chapter 4
Keys to Successful Investment: An Evaluation

In this chapter investors are alerted to some common fallacies of investment communication. Instances of stock market success are evaluated, showing why and how many such success stories are generally irrelevant.

Only by developing a tough, questioning approach can investors objectively evaluate various investment opportunities. By insisting on the facts and by placing such information in perspective, astute investors can themselves evaluate the practicality of successful investment episodes.

How to Identify Profitable Stocks

How are stocks that show substantial price appreciation over time usually identified? The answer is alarmingly simple—by hindsight.

The stock of International Business Machines often is cited as a premier investment. Fortunes have been made by families and institutions that were sufficiently astute or lucky to have purchased shares of IBM 20 or 30 years ago, and held all their IBM shares for a long time. This past success of IBM not only has contributed to the financial well-being of some investors, but has provided a major input for stories of Wall Street success. Ask yourself, how frequently has the stock of IBM been cited to show what might be achieved in the stock market?

Other stocks, such as American Hospital Supply, Avon Products, Eastman Kodak, Polaroid, and Xerox, also have shown above-average price appreciation in recent years. Although such stocks are often mentioned by investors, brokers, and financial writers, these same authorities generally neglect to use similar skills of hindsight to highlight information about the many stocks that have shown only average price appreciation over past decades or to compile lists of stocks that have performed poorly. Stories of successful stocks typically dominate stock market discussions and writings, unless there is a newsworthy stock market debacle, such as the recent collapse in the shares of Penn Central.

To test this thesis of a persistent bias toward success stories, the practical reader should reflect on the discussions of the stock market he has heard and the articles he has read. What proportion consists of stories about successful stocks, and what proportion describes investor experience with routine stocks and stocks that have collapsed in price? The answer to this question should enable the reader himself to assess how comprehensive is most discussion of the stock market.

Also it is imperative to recognize that examples of past winning stocks focus only on the *past*. The key, practical issue is the need to identify stocks that promise above-average price appreciation in the *future*. This critical gap between revewing the past and predicting the future is developed more extensively later in this book.

How to Develop Astute Investment Timing

No doubt financial rewards await investors who successfully implement the conventional Wall Street strategy statement of "Buy low and sell high." However, from the viewpoint of a realistic investor, the key issue is how practical is such a self-evident strategy statement? Can one really expect to put such a maxim consistently into practice? If such a strategy, or its variants, cannot be realistically implemented over a long period of time, then it is nonoperational. Such nonoperational statements, while partially true in theory, are trite in practice.

Conventional support of investment timing generally rests on the convenient use of hindsight and selected case examples. In listening to individuals discuss their investments, how often are heard statements such as:

If only I had bought Syntex in January 1971 when the price was around 38. I just knew at the time that the price was too low. Shares purchased then would have been worth around 74 within five months.

Also how often are heard variants of the following statement: "If only I had sold my shares of American Telephone years ago when the price was in the 70s. Now the price is around 50." Such retrospective statements not only assume that one ought to have foreknowledge of *which* stocks to buy or sell, but also *when* to do so.

Retrospective statements of successful timing typically focus only on what is shown by hindsight to be the correct outcome. An investor who looks back and says, "If only I had bought this stock at 10 and held until it was 40," should ponder that *even if* he had bought at 10, is he not likely to have become impatient and decided to take his profits when the stock first hit 15 or 20? Furthermore, is there any more reason to believe that the funds from such a sale, if reinvested, would have been used to buy a stock that subsequently went up, rather than down?

Many investors at times must think if only they had bought shares of Control Data or McDonald's Corporation when they first were publicly traded. Certainly the theoretical profits are large, but consider that, in practice, there must have been invstors who did buy such shares at low initial prices, quickly doubled their money, sold out, and reinvested in some of the many other stocks that subsequently had only mediocre performance. Thus, although some investors may wish that they had bought a certain stock at a certain time, there are likely to be those on the other side of the equation, who regret having sold that stock at that time.

In summary, to look at what "might have been" must always be conjectural. Therefore, if one chooses to indulge in this pastime, it is only practical to consider a broad sequence of possible actions and their related outcomes—not just the one that, by hindsight, emerges as the most opportune. Also, in moving from conjecture about the past to reasonable predictions about the future, investors must explicitly recognize a broad range of possible events, some within their control— but most of them outside it. Investment realism requires departure from the narrow consideration of "what might have been" to careful consideration of "what is likely to be."

How to Double Your Money

Statements about doubling one's money are common to investors. For example, one investor may assert that the value of his stocks has doubled. At first this statement sounds excellent—until it is recognized as potentially incomplete. As such, it is without practical value.

First, there is no *time dimension* in the assertion. It is necessary to know over how long a time period this doubling of value has occurred. Was it in less than a year, over several years, or over many years? There is little sense in trying to compare directly stocks that double over time periods of various length.

The time dimension within which stocks double also is important because of the time value of money. Money today can be placed at interest such that the compounding process will enable the initial sum to grow over time. For example, money placed in a deposit account compounding at the rate of five percent will double in about 15 years.

Second, the assertion that the investor's stocks doubled neglects to consider *alternative opportunities.* Stocks in general, as measured by popular stock market averages, may have doubled or even more than doubled during the same time interval. If so, the investor's success of doubling his value is not particularly noteworthy. Furthermore, within the same time interval the investor may have had other investment opportunities, such as in real estate, that also would have at least doubled in value.

The time value of money and a comparison with alternative investment opportunities are generally neglected in the reports of many mutual funds, which, as explained later, are vehicles for indirect investment in common stocks. Typically these reports contain a graph portraying the growth over time of a hypothetical initial investment in the fund. A graph for the decade of the 1960s may look approximately as follows:

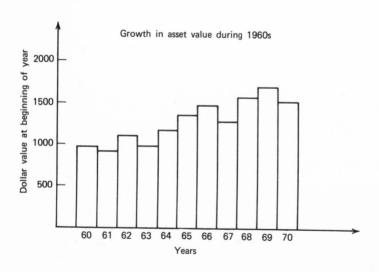

One thousand dollars invested at the beginning of 1960 is shown to have grown to $1600, excluding dividends, by the beginning of 1970.

Now to illustrate the time value of money and the importance of recognizing alternative investment opportunities, the same graph is reproduced below with one addition. It is assumed that the investor could have put $1000 in a deposit account at four percent interest in early 1960. This initial sum would have grown through the decade as portrayed by the dotted line.

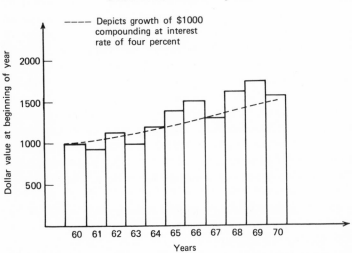

Growth in asset value during 1960s

By 1970 the value of this deposit growing with compound interest is about $1480.

In summary, realistic investors cannot place much weight on examples or graphs that portray only how certain investments have grown. They will explicitly recognize how the process of compound interest can make any initial sum grow over time, and they will understand the need to examine alternative investment opportunities.

How to Magnify Investment Success

An investor, asserting how he recently held a stock that doubled within six months, is likely to find a receptive audience. Such success can be expected to reflect on the investment prowess of the speaker, who is tacitly encouraged to explain how he was able thus to double his investment.

Such a success story of investment prowess is potentially misleading. Often it rests on the fallacy of the incomplete statement.

First, it focuses only on one successful stock held by the speaker. The logical question is: What happened to the other stocks he held over the same time interval? If he held stocks in 10 different firms, and only one stock doubled while the others stagnated or declined, then the total price performance of this group, or *portfolio*, of stocks may have been similar to that of many other investment portfolios. Isolated examples of success are virtually worthless; the practical question is how does the *total* performance of the investor's portfolio compare to that of others?

Second, such a successful investment can be quite small in absolute amount and a small part of the total portfolio. Consider an investor with a $50,000 portfolio of various high-quality stocks. At times, to "shoot craps," he may purchase $250 worth of a new stock issue that rapidly doubles in price, at which time he takes his profit. Although this investment indeed has doubled, the amount is inconsequential relative to his total portfolio, the performance of which is likely to have approximated that of the general market. Yet it is the doubling that is judged worthy of mention, not the small amount of the investment or the average performance of the overwhelming part of his portfolio. Also, the speaker may conveniently neglect to note that some of his other small speculations have been much less successful, at times resulting in write-offs for tax purposes.

The realistic investor hearing a tale of investment success often is in a dilemma. Conventions of polite conversation indicate that he should not ask the speaker too many potentially embarrassing questions, such as:

What was the dollar amount of the particular investment?

What was the relative proportion of this investment in the speaker's total portfolio?

What was the total performance of the portfolio, and how did it compare with alternative investment opportunities?

Even if this investment episode was comparatively successful, does it merely offset the losses or mundane performance of previous, similar investments?

Trying to obtain answers to such questions may result in the loss of friends. However, unless he can obtain satisfactory answers to this checklist of practical questions, the realistic investor should take such episodes of investment success with the proverbial grain of salt.

How to Broaden Your Perspective

Skillful communication bolsters many statements about successful investments. Careful examination of such statements demonstrates how they are often incomplete, resting on fallacies, such as:

1. Reliance on hindsight, especially without recognizing the complexities of possible past outcomes.
2. Selection of case examples, particularly of past winning stocks.
3. Emphasis by investors on their several stocks that have done best, instead of on the total performance of their portfolios.
4. Failure to consider the time value of money.
5. Failure to recognize alternative investment opportunities.

Alerted to such fallacies, perceptive investors now can critically examine conventional statements about achievement of investment success. Statements of others can be analyzed as to their completeness and realism. At the same time self-examination is important because other practical investors may no longer accept your "success stories" without asking some hard questions, or at least looking rather unconvinced, if not uninterested. Thus to those who enjoy presenting tales of investment success, a certain joy may be forever lost. Tough questions are likely to follow.

chapter 5
Realistic Measures of Investment Results

Successful businessmen insist on records to assist them in making decisions. Profit statements, balance sheets, and budgets are necessary tools for guiding a business and measuring its long-term success. Similarly, many families measure their financial wealth and income flows by such devices as elementary budgets, balance sheets (such as the size of their bank accounts), and the income statements prepared at least once a year before April 15. Thus most well-managed businesses and households measure their income and wealth. While such measures vary widely in their complexity, they should be reasonably accurate, and appropriate for their management objective.

Practical measures of investment returns also must be easily understood and used. They must avoid major measurement errors, and they must be generally appropriate to goals of realistic investment management. *Rate-of-Return (ROR)* measures basically meet these practical criteria.

Returns from Single Stocks

If an investor buys a share of stock at $40 near the beginning of one year, receives a $2 cash dividend from the stock during the year, and sells the stock at the end of the year for $48, what is the rate of return? The answer is 25 percent. This is calculated as follows.

$$ROR = \left[\frac{D_1}{P_0} + \frac{P_1 - P_0}{P_0} \right] \times 100$$

where

$ROR =$ rate of return for one year (in percent)
$D_1 =$ cash dividends received from the share of stock
during the year, and not reinvested
$P_0 =$ initial share price
$P_1 =$ ending share price

and

D_1 and P_1 are adjusted where necessary for
changes in the firm's number of outstanding shares.
Share prices are net of transaction costs,
such as brokerage fees and transfer taxes.
The value of 100 is necessary to convert the
numerical fraction to a percentage figure.

Now, to return to the example:

D_1, the cash dividend received during the year, is \$2.
P_0, the initial share price, is \$40.
P_1, the ending share price, is \$48.

These concrete numbers are placed in the preceding equation as follows:

$$ROR = \left[\frac{2}{40} + \frac{48 - 40}{40}\right] \times 100$$
$$ROR = [.05 + .20] \times 100$$
$$ROR = .25 \times 100$$
$$ROR = 25 \text{ percent}$$

Effectively summarized in the above figures are the two principal components of the rate of return on a stock. The *cash dividend yield* is .05, or 5 percent; and the *capital gain* of eight dollars from the stock going from \$40 to \$48 is .20, or 20 percent. Thus the rate of return is a comprehensive measure that includes both (1) a stock's dividend yield, which is zero from a stock paying no cash dividends; and (2) its capital gain, or loss. Conveniently, also, since the above calculation is on a per-share basis, no matter what the actual number of shares in the transaction, the rate of return on the total number of shares is 25 percent.

The rate of return from a single stock is an easily understood, comprehensive measure of a stock's performance. In the above example of a 25 percent rate of return, the time interval is stated to be approximately a year, such that the 25 percent is an annual rate of return. Similarly, annualized rates of return can be calculated for stocks held longer than a year, but these calculations require more complex formulas.

Annualized returns facilitate direct comparisons of investments in stocks held for time intervals of different length. For example, a stock that doubles in 15 years and pays no cash dividends during the interval has an annualized rate of return of about 5 percent. This figure can be compared with annualized returns from other stocks, and also from alternative assets, such as money invested in bonds or deposited in a savings account. Thus the time value of money and the process of compounding interest are not disregarded by rate-of-return measures that facilitate comparisons between alternative investments over time.

Returns from Portfolios of Stocks

In addition to measuring returns from single stocks, it is important to use appropriate techniques for measuring the total return from a portfolio of stocks. To learn that an investor had a one-year rate of return of 100 percent on a single stock still leaves open the possibility of the selected case example. The questions yet to be an answered are: What was the return on his *total* portfolio? and How does this portfolio return compare with alternative investment opportunities?

Rate-of-return measures, as used for single stocks, can be directly extended to measuring the total return from a portfolio of stocks.

To provide practical examples of measuring total portfolio returns, Exhibit 2–1 summarizes important investment information about an illustrative portfolio of three different stocks.

The one-year return from *each* of the three stocks in the portfolio is presented in the Exhibit. The return from Old Line Chemical Company is 25 percent, the same figure calculated earlier to illustrate the return from a single stock. The returns from New Breakthrough Computer Company and Big Volt Utility Company are 90 percent and −10 percent, respectively. With these three different returns in a portfolio, is not an investor most likely to talk about his computer stock that almost doubled in one year? But now the sensible investor is likely to inquire tactfully about the return from the total portfolio.

One way of measuring total portfolio return is similar to calculating returns from single stocks. The equation becomes:

$$PROR = \left[\frac{TD_1}{V_0} + \frac{V_1 - V_0}{V_0} \right] \times 100$$

Exhibit 2-1. Measuring Returns from an Illustrative Three-Stock Portfolio

Stock	Number of Shares Owned	Price per Share at Beginning of Year (P_0)	Value at Beginning of Year	Cash Dividends Received per Share During the Year (D_1)	Cash Dividends Received During the Year	Price per Share at Year-end (P_1)	Value at Year-end	One-year Rate of Return $\dfrac{D_1}{P_0} + \dfrac{P_1 - P_0}{P_0} \times 100$
1. Old Line Chemical Company	100	$40	$ 4000	$2	$200	$48	$ 4800	$25\% = \dfrac{2}{40} + \dfrac{8}{40} \times 100$
2. New Breakthrough Computer Company	200	$10	$ 2000	0	0	$19	$ 3800	$90\% = \dfrac{0}{10} + \dfrac{9}{10} \times 100$
3. Big Volt Utility Company	200	$20	$ 4000	$1	$200	$17	$ 3400	$-10\% = \dfrac{1}{20} + \dfrac{(-3)}{20} \times 100$
Total	500		$10,000		$400		$12,000	

where

$$PROR = \text{portfolio rate of return for one year (in percent)}$$
$$TD_1 = \text{total amount of cash dividends}$$
received during the year, and not reinvested
$$V_0 = \text{total value of the portfolio}$$
at the beginning of the year
$$V_1 = \text{total value of the portfolio}$$
at the end of the year

and

similar conditions to those summarized for
the single-stock rate of return

To illustrate, from Exhibit 2-1, the following information is available:

TD_1, the total cash dividends received during the year, is $400
V_0, the total value at the beginning of the year, is $10,000
V_1, the total value at year-end, is $12,000.

Placing these numbers in the preceding equation yields:

$$PROR = \left[\frac{400}{10,000} + \frac{12,000 - 10,000}{10,000} \right] \times 100$$
$$PROR = [.04 + .20] \times 100$$
$$PROR = .24 \times 100$$
$$PROR = 24 \text{ percent}$$

This total portfolio return can be decomposed into its two components: the cash dividend yield of 4 percent and the capital gain, on the total portfolio, of 20 percent.

Of principal interest to the realistic investor is the total portfolio return. While the rate of return from the shares of New Breakthrough Computer Company is 90 percent, this is offset by the two other stocks returning only 25 percent and −10 percent. Furthermore, these other two stocks carry more weight in the total portfolio return, because at the beginning of the year the investment of $4000 both in the Old Line Chemical Company and the Big Volt Utility Company is twice that of the $2000 investment in New Breakthrough Computer Company. Thus, as fractions of the total initial portfolio value of $10,000, the value of the investments in the three different stocks is as follows:

Old Line Chemical Company	.4
New Breakthrough Computer Company	.2
Big Volt Utility Company	.4
Total	1.0

These fractions, called the *portfolio weights*, can be directly linked to the rates of return from the different stocks in order to calculate the total portfolio return. Here is the equation:

$$PROR = w_1 ROR_1 + w_2 ROR_2 + w_3 ROR_3$$

where

> $PROR$ = portfolio rate of return for one year (in percent)
> w_1, w_2, and w_3 = the initial portfolio weights of the first, second, and third stocks
> ROR_1, ROR_2, and ROR_3 = the one-year rates of return from the first, second, and third stocks (in percent)

and

> the equation can be expanded to include additional stocks

The illustrative figures are as follows:

	Initial Weights (Calculated from Exhibit 2-1)	Rates of Return (from Exhibit 2-1)
Old Line Chemical Co.	$w_1 = .4$	$ROR_1 = 25$
New Breakthrough Computer Co.	$w_2 = .2$	$ROR_2 = 90$
Big Volt Utility Co.	$w_3 = .4$	$ROR_3 = -10$

Solving for the total portfolio return

$$PROR = .4(25) + .2(90) + .4(-10)$$
$$PROR = 10 + 18 - 4$$
$$PROR = 24 \text{ percent}$$

This, of course, is the same total portfolio return previously calculated. But it provides important additional information by focusing on the individual rates of return of the component stocks in the portfolio and by focusing on their relative weights in the total initial portfolio. Thus, in the illustration, the 90 percent return from the computer stock is somewhat dampened in the total portfolio return because the other two stocks have lower returns, *and* they carry larger weights in the initial portfolio.

Portfolio return measures overcome many potential stock market fallacies, such as overemphasis of selected examples. Measuring the *total* return from a portfolio of stocks recognizes the relative weights of all the component stocks. In this way a stock that doubles or triples can be recognized for what it often is, the one notable stock among other less-distinguished stocks in a portfolio. Return measures also can avoid other fallacies, such as neglect of the time value of money and of alternative investment opportunities. Annualized portfolio returns can be directly compared with returns from assets other than common stocks, such as deposit accounts, bonds, or real estate. Portfolio rates of return thus are comprehensive measures that can provide relevant information for practical investors.

Criteria for Beating the Market

"Beating the market" is the objective of many investors who enter in the competition for stock market profits. At times this goal is explicit, as when investment managers have contracts providing additional compensation if their portfolios have higher returns than popular stock market indicators, such as the Dow Jones Industrials Average or the Standard & Poor's Industrial Index. Other investors similarly focus on how well their portfolios do in comparison with general stock market indicators. One hears or reads statements such as:

> Last year my stocks increased 20 percent in value while the Dow Jones Industrials Average was up only six percent.

or,

> The list of stocks recommended by our firm early last year increased in price by, on average, 25 percent. During the same year the Dow Jones Industrials Average was up six percent and the Standard & Poor's Industrial Index was up 12 percent.

Such "success statements" must be fully considered by investors who insist on straight talk and hard evidence.

To measure whether an investor is "beating the market," one requires a measure of market performance to serve as a basis for comparison. Various stock market price indexes often are used as the comparative standard. Widely reported are such indexes as: (1) the Dow Jones Industrials Average; (2) the Standard & Poor's Industrial Index; and (3) the New York Stock Exchange Composite Index. Less widely reported are other price indexes of stocks traded on the New York Stock Exchange and in other markets. Although some of their technical features have been criticized, these indexes serve as useful indicators of general movements in stock market prices. Note, however, that these indicators focus only on price changes and are not total return measures.

Comprehensive measures of stock market returns recently have been developed. In a major undertaking, the Center for Research in Security Prices (sponsored by Merrill Lynch, Pierce, Fenner & Smith, Inc.) at the University of Chicago developed an extensive, computerized file of information about all stocks traded on the New York Stock Exchange from 1926 through 1965. Drawing on this new information, Professors Fisher and Lorie have published a series of articles analyzing returns from investments in common stocks listed on the New York Stock Exchange.[1] In their initial study they report as follows:

"During the entire thirty-five-year period, 1926–60, the rates of return, compounded annually, on common stocks listed on the New York Stock Exchange, with reinvestment of dividends, were 9.0 percent for tax exempt institutions; 8.2 percent for persons in the $10,000 income class; and 6.8 percent for persons in the $50,000 income class. These rates are substantially higher than for alternative investment media for which data are available."[2]

In addition to calculating rate-of-return measures over extended time periods, the Fisher and Lorie studies provide measures of returns from NYSE stocks on a year-by-year basis, 1926 through 1965. Thus these studies provide comprehensive indicators of past returns from NYSE stocks.

"Beating the market" implies having a portfolio of stocks that either increases more, or declines less, in value that does a general market

[1] L. Fisher and J. H. Lorie, "Rates of Return on Investments in Common Stocks," *The Journal of Business*, January 1964, pp. 1–21. Also by the same authors, "Rates of Return on Investments in Common Stock: The Year-by-Year Record, 1926–65," *The Journal of Business*, July 1968, pp. 291–316; and "Some Studies of Variability of Returns on Investments in Common Stocks," *The Journal of Business*, April 1970, pp. 99–134.

[2] L. Fisher and J. H. Lorie, "Rates of Return on Investments in Common Stocks," p. 9.

measure. Although appropriate indices of stock prices can be used, measures of the market rate of return provide more comprehensive standards against which to compare the return from a stock portfolio.

For example, assume that in one year an investor holding various NYSE stocks has a total portfolio return of 30 percent. In order to evaluate whether this return is exceptional, it must be compared to returns from other portfolios of NYSE stocks in the same year. If the year is one of generally rising stock prices, many other investors also are likely to have returns of at least 30 percent from their portfolios of NYSE stocks. In this case a return of 30 percent is not unusual. On the other hand, what if the year is one when stock prices generally do not change much? In such a market environment many investors are likely to have only small positive or negative portfolio returns, in which case a portfolio return of 30 percent can indeed be exceptional.

If an investor's stock portfolio has a higher return than does the general market in any one year, should this be attributed to skill or to chance? Possibly the investor is very adept in selecting stocks providing above-average returns, or he is following a strategy that gives him a continued advantage over most other investors. However, it is also possible that he invests a large part of his portfolio in one or two stocks that, by chance, provide above-average returns. Because of these different possibilities, an investor's return in excess of the general market return in one year is insufficient evidence of an investor's skill.

What evidence is necessary for concluding that an investor is "beating the market"? First, it is necessary that he *frequently* outperform the market. This requires that his portfolio returns be compared to market performance over a series of years. To illustrate, if, over many years, an investor's portfolio returns are intermittently higher and lower than those of the general market, this is not a very consistent record of success. It can be categorized more as: "win a few, lose a few." Second, "beating the market" also requires that an investor have portfolio returns *substantially* above general market returns over an extended period of time. To illustrate, if, over a long time period an investor's annualized return is 10 percent and the general market return is $9\frac{1}{2}$ percent, this is not particularly newsworthy. In contrast, if during the same time period an investor's annualized return is 20 percent, this is news! In summary, "beating the market" requires evidence of frequently having portfolio returns substantially above market returns. How frequently and how substantially cannot be precisely specified. However, in evaluating assertions about "beating the market," investors will now ask penetrating questions, focus on relevant measures and market comparisons, and insist on a reasonable amount of hard evidence.

REVIEW OF PART TWO

Question: How well can I expect to do in the stock market?

Answer: Expectations based on stock market "success stories" are unlikely to be achieved. An objective of Chapter 4 was to identify basic fallacies that frequently underlie uncritical use of episodes of past success. Broadened perspective enables the practical investor to enjoy the personal satisfaction of dissecting such success stories. When judged appropriate, he can also ask precise questions of speakers and writers who use various forms of the syndrome of selected success.

Knowledge of appropriate measures of market returns provides a basic foundation for evaluating how well investors do in the stock market over time. Principal benefits of rate-of-return measures are their comprehensiveness in including both dividends and price changes and their applicability to time periods of various length and to single stocks and portfolios of stocks. Such benefits are achieved from calculations that need not be unduly complex or costly. Popular stock market indices are not expressed as rates of return, and their results are affected by varying technical construction, such as sample selection and weighting technique. Thus, while useful for providing general indications of how well investors do in the stock market, the potential limitations of such indexes must be recognized.

New information about rates of return from investing in common stocks are provided by the comprehensive studies by Professors Fisher and Lorie. Their published articles can provide a broad perspective to investors wanting a general answer to how well investors could have done by investing in stocks listed on the New York Stock Exchange. Although these studies report comprehensive measures of *past* outcomes, they provide a comparative basis against which to judge whether specific investors or investment strategies have been successful in "beating the market." To "beat the market" requires the demonstrated ability of frequently having portfolio returns above general market returns. In a competitive market a key issue is whether a practical investor realistically should expect to beat the market.

Introduced to fallacies of incomplete measures and to merits and potential usefulness of rate-of-return measures, investors are encouraged to involve themselves in further readings.

* * *

The following articles provide basic information about rates of return from stocks listed on the New York Stock Exchange.

Fisher, Lawrence, and James H. Lorie, "Rates of Return on Investments in Common Stocks," *The Journal of Business,* January 1964, pp. 1–21.

————, "Rates of Return on Investments in Common Stock: The Year-by-Year Record, 1926–65," *The Journal of Business*, July 1968, pp. 291–316.

————, "Some Studies of Variability of Returns on Investments in Common Stocks," *The Journal of Business*, April 1970, pp. 99–134.

The following book provides new information about rates of return from stocks quoted in national and regional over-the-counter markets.

Jessup, Paul F., and Roger B. Upson, *Returns in Over-the-Counter Stock Markets*, University of Minnesota Press, 1973.

PART THREE

EVALUATING COMMON STOCKS

chapter 6
Estimating Corporate Earnings

Earnings figures often are cited as critical inputs for estimating relative values of various stocks. Emphasis on earnings is illustrated by the following types of frequently heard statements:

> Our research department likes this particular soft drink stock for possible price appreciation. The company has aggressive management. In addition its shares are selling for only 15 times last year's earnings. Shares of other soft drink companies are selling closer to 25 to 50 times their last year's earnings.

> For a stock with above-average potential, I like this small computer company. Although it had losses in previous years, my analysis suggests that it will break even this year, and then its growth in earnings will be rapid. In fact the stock is selling at 30 times my estimate of next year's earnings but at only 15 times my estimate for two years from now.

Such statements, focusing on a company's past reported earnings and/ or on estimates of future earnings, imply that analysis of earnings is a key to the selection of promising investments.

A principal objective in buying a company's stock is to sell it later to someone else at a profit. In addition, a purchaser may look forward to the dividends he is planning to receive on the stock until he sells it.[1]

---

[1] As demonstrated in Chapter 5, rate-of-return measures include both of these components, capital gain (or loss) and dividend return, in a way that facilitates comparisons with returns from alternative investments.

Now if an investor buys a stock with the intention of later selling it to another investor at a profit, he must have some beliefs as to why other investors will later want to buy the stock at a higher price. He cannot know or predict the motivations of all investors, some of whom may sometimes buy a stock because, for example, they like the company's products or advertising; they work for the company; or they respond to rumors. Nevertheless, he must have some knowledge about what rational investors, competing for above-average returns, must usually look for in a company in which they are considering an investment. A critical element is future earnings, which (1) may be retained by the company for direct reinvestment intended to provide longer-run benefits to shareholders, or (2) partly distributed, at some time, to stockholders as dividends. These investors also may consider a company's management, labor relations, assets, and debt structure, but principally as such factors are related to estimates of the company's stream of earnings that eventually will be available to common stockholders. Estimated earning streams of various companies can then be compared, with the intention of identifying unusual investment opportunities.

Broad perspective provides new insights about reported past earnings and estimates of future earnings. A hallmark of security analysis is a detailed examination of reported figures in order to compare past financial results of various companies. Professional analysts commit substantial resources to recasting past earnings information in ways judged useful to predict future earnings. Their specialized skills usually are developed through intensive study and extensive experience. One measure of this professionalism is that recently there were 3200 Chartered Financial Analysts. To become a CFA an individual has to demonstrate specialized skills under test conditions and to meet qualifications of practical experience. Recognizing this level of professionalism, aspiring investors should question whether they will achieve benefits that are likely to outweigh the costs to them of striving to become *part-time* security analysts.

Interpreting Earnings Reports

What are a company's earnings? This question can be examined at three principal levels:

1. Nonanalytical acceptance.
2. Aspiring analyst.
3. Competing analysts.

Most books on investments encourage investors to move from level one to level two. However, the practicality of many investors moving to level two (aspiring analyst) is doubtful. Furthermore, such a move can be unnecessary once investors consider the investment consequences of level three (competing analysts).

Level one (nonanalytical acceptance) is where investors uncritically accept reported earnings statements. For example, on learning that a company earned $1.26 per share last year, a level-one investor accepts this figure without question. A level-one investor also unquestioningly accepts a company's reported sequence of past earnings per share, such as the following:

Three years ago	$ .60
Two years ago	.90
Last year	1.26

Furthermore, he will compare these figures directly with those reported by other companies.

Not many investors stay at level one very long. As soon as they read several earnings statements in greater detail, they realize that reported earnings per share (EPS) are, within limits, just what a company wants to report as its per-share earnings. Alternative accounting procedures can lead to different possible figures for a company's EPS. Thus, on the basis of "generally accepted accounting principles," the reported EPS figure of $1.26 could as well have been anywhere between, for example, $1.10 and $1.40. Furthermore, since the boundaries of generally accepted accounting principles are not rigorously defined, with some imagination the range of possible figures for reported EPS can be expanded beyond $1.10 to $1.40.

Although corporate management has some discretion as to what it chooses to report as its EPS for a particular period, it cannot arbitrarily shift its accounting procedures. Its accountants usually insist that accounting procedures be consistently applied and that any major changes be noted in the company's published financial reports. However, since such changes often are presented in the footnotes to the complete earnings statements, they can be overlooked by investors or summarized—if not omitted—in the editing process when a company's EPS is reported in newspapers or put on a computer data file. Recognizing such possibilities, thoughtful analysts realize that footnotes to financial statements, along with the accompanying accountant's statement, are not only "an integral part of the statement," but often provide the most interesting reading.

Challenge

Scan the "Digest of Earnings Reports" in several recent issues of *The Wall Street Journal*. Observe the number and diversity of footnotes in these summary earnings reports. Recognize that these notes often represent only some of the extensive footnotes in the complete report.

Level-two investors (aspiring analysts) are aware that level one involves too simple a view of reported earnings figures. Level-two investors are encouraged by most investments books to learn the intricacies of financial analysis. They read about how to interpret corporate reports and how to become skillful at adjusting a company's reported accounting information in order to make it reasonably consistent over time and comparable with accounting information reported by other companies. It is such level-two investors who carefully read footnotes to financial statements to understand and adjust reported figures.

In learning about the general framework of financial statements and the techniques for analyzing them, level-two investors begin to recognize the many stages at which different accounting procedures can affect reported EPS. Consider the following *schematic summary* of an earnings statement:

$$
\begin{array}{l}
\text{Operating Revenues} \\
- \text{Operating Expenses} \\
\hline
= \text{Operating Earnings}
\end{array}
$$

$$
\begin{array}{l}
+ \text{Nonoperating Income} \\
- \text{Nonoperating Expenses} \\
\hline
= \text{Net Earnings before Income Taxes}
\end{array}
$$

$$
\begin{array}{l}
- \text{Income Taxes} \\
\hline
= \text{Net Income}
\end{array}
$$

Furthermore,

$$
\frac{\text{Net Income}}{\text{Number of Common Shares}} = \text{"Earnings per Share"}
$$

The final "Earnings per Share" is specifically placed in quotation marks to emphasize that, in actual earnings statements, this reported figure is the outcome of many previous steps, many of which could have been done somewhat differently. In most cases the issue depends on how a company chooses to *time* the reporting of the various income and expense components of its earnings statement.

Reported revenues basically reflect only how a company chooses to time its selling activities. Consider these practical examples.

1. Computer manufacturers basically can sell or lease new computers. If they sell, then the revenues are recorded at the time of sale. If they lease, then the revenue from the same equipment is recorded over the period of the lease. In comparing two computer companies one of which sells while the other leases, the seller will show greater current revenues but less certain future revenues than the second with its lower current revenues but with the contractual stream of future revenues from the leases.

(a) A company that has leased in the past now decides to sell. Suddenly it reports a sharp increase in its revenues during that transitional period.

(b) A company with many computers already leased decides to sell the lease contracts to another company. Reported revenues from this sale of past leases can be substantial in the time period when the sale occurs.

2. Land development companies can time the sale of property in various ways. Assume that two such companies typically sell lots for $5000 each, with $500 paid down and the balance to be collected equally over 10 years. One company may choose to see itself as making a sale of $5000, although only $500 has been collected, with the balance of $4500 represented by a note receivable. Thus it reports most of the $5000 as revenue at the time the sales contract is signed. The second company reports the revenue only as received over the 10-year period of the sales contract. Thus the revenues reported by these two companies can vary sharply in various time periods even if they sell the same number of lots.

Although many variations of the preceding examples can be cited in these and other industries, the common theme is how the timing of reported revenue can vary among companies and for the same company over time.

Reported operating expenses also reflect management decisions concerning the timing of outlays. Depreciation is a major component of operating expenses, and it rests on assumptions concerning an asset's estimated useful life and its terminal scrap value. Furthermore the Internal Revenue Service permits companies to select from among straight-line depreciation and different forms of accelerated depreciation. This latitude of depreciation procedures among companies and the possible revising of procedures by any one company should alert investors to the discretionary aspects of this item of operating expenses. Investors can pursue this topic in greater detail in articles such as "Depreciation Manipulation for Fun and Profits."[2]

Managerial discretion also can affect the timing of other components of reported operating expenses. Inventory can be valued on the basis of either last-in-first-out (LIFO) or first-in-first-out (FIFO). Which procedure is used has different effects on a company's reported cost of goods sold in various time periods. Also, within limits, the labor component of reported operating expenses can be varied by the timing of pension fund contributions. Differences in the timing of reported expenses also result from management's decision either to charge off research-and-development (R&D) expenses as incurred or to defer such expenses until the R&D begins to contribute to the company's revenues. The preceding summary statements only highlight *some* of the ways in which reported operating expenses are subject to accounting assumptions about their timing.

Nonoperating income and expenses are additional elements in a final EPS figure. Basically nonoperating items are judged not to arise from a company's normal selling activities. For example, an oil company owns a block of another company's stock for investment purposes. Dividends received from this investment typically are treated as nonoperating income. Even though the oil company expects to continue receiving dividends in future years, it separates this investment income from the operating revenues from its ongoing petroleum operations. However, there continues to be a gray area in trying rigorously to distinguish between some "operating" and "nonoperating" activities. To illustrate, although commercial banks regularly buy and sell marketable securities, many have treated the gains or losses from such banking activities as "nonoperating" items. More recently the federal banking agencies and the accounting profession have required that banks be more explicit in their reporting about such ongoing securities transactions. Various conglomerate companies have shown creativity in their distinctions between nonoperating and operating items in the accounting treatment of the sale of movie libraries, dividends from acquired companies, and profits from their holdings of marketable securities.

Net income follows from the preceding array of accounting assump-

[2] John H. Myers, "Depreciation Manipulation for Fun and Profits," *Financial Analysts Journal*, November–December 1967, pp. 117–123. Also a follow-up article by the same title in the same journal, September–October 1969, pp. 47–56.

tions and adjustments. Furthermore at least two other major reporting procedures also can influence what is finally reported as net income.

Extraordinary gains and losses are judged to be unique and nonrecurring. Examples are a manufacturing company's income from the sale of one of its old plants (not a usual occurrence) and substantial noninsured losses from fire or flood. Write-offs of various nonrecurring actual or probable losses, such as from antitrust penalties, initial merger costs, and errors of preceding management, have led some companies to create reserve accounts that may be used to adjust the timing of subsequent streams of income. Also tax credits from a company's preceding losses can be treated as extraordinary gains.

Merger accounting is the second major reporting procedure that allows corporate management some additional flexibility concerning what it will report as net income. If one avoids the many details, the issue depends basically on whether an acquiring company chooses to prepare its financial statements on assumptions of "pooling" or "purchasing." Furthermore, in choosing one of the two basic procedures, additional flexibility remains concerning the timing of the merger for reporting purposes. Level-two investors are already aware of some of the intricacies of merger accounting, but as refreshers they can consult articles such as, "The Earnings Per Share Trap" and "The 'Funny-Money' Game."[3]

Earnings per share intuitively should flow directly from the calculation "Net Income" (after any preferred dividend requirements) divided by the company's total number of common shares outstanding. Thus, for example, if a company has net income of $2 million and has 1 million shares of common stock outstanding, then its reported EPS is $2.00. However, for many corporate reports the solution is not so direct. Creative financial practices have generated many variations of financial instruments that derive some present or potential value from their linkage to a company's common stock. Such instruments include warrants, convertible debentures, and convertible preferred stock (Chapters 13 and 14). Furthermore, potential increases in a company's outstanding common stock are associated with stock option programs and acquisition agreements contingent on subsequent performance. If one avoids complex details, the key point is that there are estimation problems in determining just what is "the number of outstanding shares" for companies with such commitments. Should this be only an average of the number of shares outstanding during the accounting period; or

[3] Marvin M. May, "The Earnings Per Share Trap," *Financial Analysts Journal*, May–June 1968, pp. 113–117. Abraham J. Briloff, "The 'Funny-Money' Game," *Financial Analysts Journal*, May–June 1969, pp. 73–79.

should it recognize potentially outstanding shares, in which case how should such potential be estimated? In trying to cope with such issues, the accounting profession has developed various guidelines so that some companies now report several EPS figures, such as (1) primary EPS, and (2) fully diluted EPS. Level-two investors are encouraged to learn more about these different concepts that are changing over time. One source is the article, "New Rules for Determining Earnings Per Share."[4]

Level-two investors, recognizing that reported EPS can be affected by many accounting procedures, can view a company's EPS basically as only one figure from a range of possible EPS figures. However, to understand these various intricacies of accounting practices, level-two investors aspire to become capable financial analysts. Not only must they learn an initial set of skills, they must stay current with rapid changes in the accounting area and in corporate financial management. To do so entails a substantial commitment of resources, especially time. How many individual investors realistically *can* commit such resources to financial analysis? Furthermore, by moving to an understanding of level three (competing analysts), it is practical to question whether most individual investors *should* commit much of their personal resources to trying to develop the skills of security analysis.

Level three explicitly recognizes that at any time there are many competent individuals analyzing corporate earnings reports. Many of these people are professional analysts devoting their chosen careers to interpretation of accounting reports and other financial information. In addition to analyzing the derivation of a company's reported EPS, these analysts examine other measures of past corporate performance, such as balance sheet items, sources and uses of funds statements, and many ratios derived from reported financial information.

Competing analysts strive to understand reported financial data and, when necessary, they deploy skills to recast reported information to make it reasonably consistent over time and comparable among companies. Their analyses, often published as research reports, advisory services, or in-depth financial articles, become part of the stock market information system. In this way other investors are alerted to various appraisals of a company's reported financial information. Not that the various analysts are consistently correct, but in the competitive flow of information and ideas, it is difficult for any corporation or industry to avoid, for long, careful scrutiny of its reporting practices by some skilled analysts whose views are then publicized among market participants. To illustrate, in recent years the reporting practices of some

---

[4] James E. Parker, "New Rules for Determining Earnings Per Share," *Financial Analysts Journal*, January–February 1970, pp. 49–53.

conglomerates, computer leasing companies, franchising firms, and land development companies have been subjected to professional scrutiny, resulting in publicized skepticism of some of their reported EPS figures. If, based on such new information, some investors conclude that the reported EPS of some companies are unrealistic, they will focus on what analysts judge to be more realistic estimates of EPS and use these as factors in their investment decisions about such stocks. In this way the share prices will adjust to reflect this new information.

Recognizing level three, the role of competing analysts and how share prices can adjust to new, generally available information about reported EPS, it is doubtful that most individual investors should remain at level two (aspiring financial analysts). In a competitive market, the probable benefits for most investors are unlikely to warrant the costs, in financial resources and time. Furthermore they can begin to consider alternative investment strategies appropriate for a competitive stock market.

Predicting Future Earnings

Investors can obtain predictions of corporate earnings from various sources such as brokerage reports and investment advisory services. Also they can read or hear about estimates of future earnings made by some company officials, for example, at security analyst meetings or shareholder meetings. Such publicly available estimates can range from precise figures to more general statements, such as, "The company is expected to continue its recent 10 percent growth rate in earnings per share." In addition to obtaining earnings estimates from diverse sources, investors can develop their own predictions of various companies' EPS. However, two critical questions arise concerning various predictions of future EPS:

1. *Can* investors be confident that the predictions of future corporate earnings available to them are consistently more accurate than those available to competing investors?
2. *Should* most investors try to commit much time and talent to trying to predict streams of future earnings?

Answers to these questions follow directly from practical examination of the complexities of prediction and from viewing the stock market as a competitive system.

Predictions of the future can be derived only from past experience (or from a vivid imagination). In developing predictions of any company's future earnings stream, investors can use various analytical tools ranging from simple extrapolation of past trends to computerized predictive models. Nevertheless past information is the common base of all such predictive devices.

Since past and contemporary corporate information is generally available, competing investors are basing their predictions on similar information. Any principal difference in predictions must therefore arise from different interpretations of the available information base or from novel insights provided by various analytical techniques. However, in placing one's investment skills in the perspective of many capable competitors, can any one investor or analyst realistically be confident that his interpretations of, or insights from, similar investment information are consistently better than his competitors? At times his predictions may prove uncanny, but such successes must be viewed in relation to his incorrect predictions. What is critical is the *total* predictive record over a long time period.

Over various time periods some companies establish enviable records of past earnings. For example, the following illustrative companies have reported consistently higher earnings per share each year from 1965 through 1970, and for some the record is longer:

Avon Products

Coca–Cola

International Business Machines

Johnson & Johnson

Minnesota Mining & Manufacturing

Xerox

Competing analysts, monitoring such companies, are paid to report on the quality of the reported earnings figures. In addition, through the stock market information system, past earnings records of various firms are generally known to many investors. Brokerage reports, investment advisory services, and news stories periodically comment on the past earnings records, particularly successful records.

How can past information about earnings growth be used to predict the future? At one level investors can extrapolate past growth rates into the future and use this as their best estimate. For example, a company's EPS, based on consistent reporting, has grown at 10 percent a year for the last 10 years. Therefore, a best estimate is that the company will continue to report such annual earnings growth of 10 percent. Variations of extrapolation procedures, using statistical procedures such as regression analysis and curve-fitting techniques, can also be used with the hope of developing a more accurate distribution of predicted values of future earnings growth. But such statistical techniques still build on past information; and, while not known to all investors, they are known to at least some competing analysts and investors.

Extrapolation techniques are most appropriate for companies with reasonably consistent records of past earnings. Thus an investor has some confidence about using extrapolation procedures for a company having a history of earnings growth that consistently has been between, say, four to six percent a year. Such consistency is common to some electrical utility companies. But other investors and analysts can also see such consistency in the past records of some companies and use this information for developing their estimates of future earnings. Furthermore, for companies having inconsistent records of past earnings, various investors and analysts are likely to have reservations about using extrapolation procedures as a basis for predictions of future earnings.

Other predictive techniques go beyond extrapolation of past EPS figures. For example, investors can examine many measures of a company's performance, such as sales growth, various cost ratios, and profit margins. These performance measures can be examined for consistency, trend, change in trend, or other patterns. To illustrate, a company's past ratio of profits to sales can be inspected to see if it is stable over time, gradually increases over time, or recently increases after major management changes. Similarly, many other measures can be analyzed in detail. But all such information is past history and is available to other stock market participants as inputs into their predictions of future earnings.

Investors can also develop estimates about how a company's past financial relationships, such as sales growth, wage costs, and interest costs, *may change* in the future because of, for example, changes in consumer demand, competition from new products, new labor contracts, revisions of bank lending rates, or new management. However, three principal aspects of thus developing complex predictions of a company's future financial relationships must now be recognized.

First, careful specification and analysis of past relationships are necessary for understanding possible future relationships. Unfortunately, frequently advocated procedures of ratio analysis generally are inadequate to answer why and how various aspects of a company's operations are functionally related to a company's earnings performance.

Second, even if a complete model of past financial interrelationships can be developed, how confident should one be about its predictive qualities? Even if one can specify the major factors contributing to a company's past performance, there are many interrelated factors that can shift in the near future, because of, for example, a competitor's announcement of a major competing product, a failure of a major supplier, a prolonged transportation strike, or overseas events such as nationalization and devaluation. Although subjective probabilities can be attached to such events, no investor can be confident whether they will occur and, if they do, how they will affect the company's future performance. Even corporate management, with the information and internal power available to it, cannot be very confident about its predictions and control of corporate performance in a competitive economy. Despite careful corporate planning, constant monitoring of its environment and internal operations, and prompt but thoughtful management decisions, corporate managers recognize their vulnerability to events that cannot be predicted with much accuracy. Thus, if these officials cannot afford to be too confident, then how confident should investors and analysts be who are outside the company and separated from its internal information and control procedures?

Pause to Reflect

Think back to instances where some corporate managers or analysts made confident predictions about future EPS.

Remember the episodes of subsequently revised estimates—downward as well as upward.

Third, assume that somehow an investor does develop analytical skills or complex models that enable him to make reasonably confident predictions of a company's performance. In any case, the predictions must be derived from past or contemporary information that is available to other analysts and investors who also devote resources to developing their predictive skills. Thus, in a competitive system, is any small group of investors or analysts likely to develop insights or techniques capable of generating predictions that are consistently better than those of others? Even, if they do for awhile, how long will they be able to maintain this competitive advantage? (Remember Chapters 2 and 3.)

In conclusion, investors must explicitly recognize the limitations of all estimates of future corporate earnings.

1. All predictions are basically derived from past or contemporary

information that is generally available to other analysts and investors competing for superior information.

2. All estimates remain subject to unpredictable future events.

3. Estimates in which an investor can be reasonably confident, for example, the future EPS growth of many electrical utilities, also can be perceived with similar confidence by other stock market participants.

4. In contrast, realistic investors can have little confidence in estimates about companies for which unpredictable future events are critical to actual future EPS, if any. For example, substantial skepticism should be applied to any estimates of EPS growth of a small new company in a competitive technological industry. However, in such cases the practical uncertainty of future outcomes is shared by competing analysts and investors.

In summary, realistic investors cannot be confident that predictions of future corporate earnings available to them are consistently more accurate than those available to competing investors. Furthermore, even if they commit substantial time and other resources to trying to predict future earnings streams, most, if not all, investors are unlikely to be able to develop predictive methods that will provide them a consistent edge over competing analysts and investors.

chapter 7
Identifying Undervalued and Overvalued Stocks

How much should an investor pay for a company's stock? This basic question continually confronts individual investors, security analysts, and professional portfolio managers. Answers to this basic question are indicated by the following types of statements that comprise much of stock market communications.

Our research department believes the shares of this grocery chain to be particularly undervalued. The firm has good management, and its shares currently are selling for only 10 times the company's last year's earnings per share.

That stock clearly is overvalued. No stock is worth 40 times its reported EPS when high-quality, dividend-paying stocks can be purchased at 15 to 18 times their EPS.

Logically the only way to tell whether a stock is overvalued or undervalued is to discount the future stream of dividends expected from the stock.

Such statements indicate that various stocks can be identified as undervalued or overvalued at particular points in time.

To say that a stock is undervalued or overvalued implies that, at any point in time, the stock can have a "value" other than its current market price. Terms such as "intrinsic value," "real value," or "relative value" are used to represent this concept. For example, to say that a stock is undervalued can only mean that its market price is less than the stock's current "value." Furthermore such a statement implies that the value can be objectively estimated by using skills and techniques of financial analysis, or else by some indescribable "feel" for values.

Identifying an undervalued stock has little relevance for an investor unless he also believes that the stock's market price soon will approach the estimated value. To illustrate, consider a stock that is selling in the market for $30. After careful analysis an investor estimates this stock's value to be $60. Purchase of this stock is unwarranted unless the investor further believes that other investors subsequently will also recognize the stock's value to be around $60 and therefore will "bid up" its market price toward this value. Unless such an adjustment occurs, the investor may buy for $30 an undervalued stock that continues to have a market price of around $30 in future years while stock prices in general are rising. In this event higher returns from alternative investments are precluded while the investor waits for the stock price to go up. In summary, little is accomplished by identifying and investing in undervalued stocks unless an investor is confident that other investors soon will perceive and remove the undervalued condition. Similar reasoning applies to selling overvalued stocks.

Proponents of stock selection typically specify various methods for identifying whether stocks are undervalued or overvalued. Widely publicized methods include use of price-earnings ratios and use of techniques to discount future streams of dividends. Therefore, investors seeking a full perspective will welcome an examination of both the logic and usefulness of popular valuation methods.

Using Price-Earnings Ratios

Price-earnings (P-E) ratios often are suggested as measures for valuing the common stocks of various companies. Therefore they are key elements in such stock market statements as, "The stock of this paper company is selling at only five times earnings, while other paper company shares are selling between 10 to 15 times their earnings." Implied conclusion: the stock selling at five times earnings is undervalued relative to other paper shares.

Unfortunately, P-E ratios are too readily accepted by stock market participants. Therefore it is necessary to examine: What are P-E ratios? and How can they be used? This examination is done at three different levels:

1. Description.
2. Valuation.
3. Competition.

New insights about the practicality of P-E ratios result from such an assessment.

As *description*, a P-E ratio is merely a mathematical relationship requiring precise definitions of the component elements: price, and earnings. The formal relationship is:

$$M = \frac{P}{E}$$

where

> M is the P-E ratio
> P is Price per share
> E is Earnings per share (or EPS)

Once P and E are specified, the resultant M follows directly. The key issue, therefore, is the need for precise specification of P and E.

To illustrate, to be told that a stock's P-E ratio is 10 is to be told nothing directly useful. By implication, the stock currently is selling at 10 times the company's earnings per share (EPS). What is missing, however, is a precise specification of the EPS figure being used in the relationship. Since EPS can represent various estimated figures, a realistic investor cannot unquestioningly accept the P-E ratio of 10. His logical question is: "This ratio of 10 represents *which P-E ratio* for this stock?"

P-E ratios thus are largely dependent on which EPS figure is used in calculating the ratio. Basically EPS can represent at least three different figures, each of which itself rests on estimation procedures:

1. Reported EPS.
2. Normal EPS.
3. Future EPS.

As developed in Chapter 6, reported EPS can be visualized as one of several possible EPS figures that could have been reported within the boundaries of generally accepted accounting principles. However, recognizing this flexibility, if a stock is said to be selling at 10 times the company's last year's reported EPS, the EPS component of this P-E ratio is comparatively unambiguous. The ratio is a meaningful descriptive statement.

Normal EPS is an estimated figure dependent on: (1) judgment concerning what are normal or abnormal events; and (2) the procedure used for deriving the normal EPS figure. Thus it is less objective than reported EPS. To illustrate, assume that the reported EPS of a major chemical company ranges between $2.00 and $5.00 between 1960 and 1969, with some observable uptrend in the reported EPS over the 10-year period. In 1970 the company earns $1.00 per share, this relatively low figure being associated with major strikes. Many analysts and investors would see the $1.00 reported EPS for 1970 as unrepresentative of the company's normal earning power. For example, within the historical range of $2.00 to $5.00 statistical techniques may indicate that a good estimate of normal EPS is $4.00. Thus at a current market price of $40, the stock's P-E ratio is 40 times the reported EPS of $1.00 for 1970; but it is 10 times the estimated normal EPS of $4.00.

Future EPS is linked to predictions, with their surrounding uncertainties. Thus, for a small technological company that last year had a reported EPS of $0.25, an analyst may estimate next year's EPS at $1.00. On this basis, with a current market price of $25, the stock's P-E ratio is 100 times last year's reported EPS ($0.25) but 25 times the analyst's estimate of next year's EPS ($1.00). (If, instead of the best estimate of $1.00, next year's estimated EPS ranges between $0.50 and $2.50, then the P-E ratio ranges between 50 and 10, indicating the uncertainty surrounding the estimates of next year's EPS.) Of course, estimates of future EPS also can be made for beyond one year but, for many companies, not with much confidence.

In summary, realistic investors cannot uncritically accept statements about P-E ratios, even at the level of description. They must make certain *which P-E ratio* is being described, because this is dependent largely on the EPS figure used to calculate the ratio.

P-E ratios also can be used at a second level, *valuation*. Here investors and analysts often use P-E ratios as guides for determining undervalued or overvalued stocks. These relative relationships usually are based on: (1) comparisons among current P-E ratios of various stocks, and (2) comparisons of current P-E ratios with historical precedents.

Recall one of the introductory statements of this chapter:

"Our research department believes the shares of this grocery chain to be particularly undervalued. The firm has good management, and its shares currently are selling at only 10 times the company's last year's earnings per share."

If the shares of other grocery chains are generally selling at P-E ratios of 15 to 20 times last year's EPS, then the implied conclusion is that the shares with the P-E ratio of 10 are undervalued compared to similar stocks. Furthermore, if the company's shares previously have had P-E ratios of 13 to 17, then the current ratio of 10 suggests undervaluation on an historic basis. Dangers, however, are attached to this conclusion of undervaluation.

1. Are the EPS figures reported by the various chains for last year based on similar reporting practices? For example, the grocery chain with shares selling at 10 times last year's EPS may have some unusual income in last year's EPS or may have shifted to relatively less conservative reporting practices.

2. If the one chain's shares still are believed to be relatively under-valued, is there any reason that the share price will increase to bring the P-E ratio more in line with that of the other chains? Undervaluation is relevant only if it will soon be removed by a pre-dictable adjustment in share price.

3. Before concluding relative undervaluation, perceptive investors must ask themselves *why* other competing investors are willing to pay only 10 times the chain's last year's EPS. These competitors, many of whom are skillful, are currently valuing the company at only 10 times last year's EPS, based on all the information avail-able to them, including the relatively low P-E ratio. Why??

Thus, in learning about a P-E ratio that is relatively low, based on comparative or historical relationships, realistic investors must not accept this apparent discrepancy but, instead, must focus on how such a discrepancy can arise in a competitive market. In seeking to answer this key question, many undervalued stocks, as measured by relatively low P-E ratios, will be found to be illusions.

What about stocks that are selling at comparatively high P-E ratios? To illustrate, recall another introductory statement of this chapter:

"That stock clearly is overvalued. No stock is worth 40 times its re-ported EPS when high-quality, dividend-paying stocks can be purchased at 15 to 18 times their EPS."

Again the P-E ratio is used as a valuation guide. The statement focuses on the high P-E ratio compared to those of some alternative invest-ments. Also, by implication it draws on historical experience according to which not many stocks have sustained P-E ratios of 40 or greater over time. Conclusion: a stock with such a high P-E ratio must be overvalued. But why are some competing skillful investors, also aware of its P-E ratio, currently willing to buy the stock at around 40 times its reported EPS? Among the possible explanations are the following:

1. Last year's reported EPS was abnormally depressed, for example, by strikes or unusually heavy start-up costs. In this event the investor is alerted to the need to specify an estimated normal EPS. The P-E ratio using normal EPS is likely to be less than 40.

2. Some investors are expecting a rapid increase in future EPS for this company. While the exact magnitude of future EPS is uncertain, these investors are reasonably confident about future growth in EPS such that they are willing to pay a current market price that results in the P-E ratio of 40 based on reported EPS.

Thus, as with stocks having comparatively low P-E ratios, sensible investors seeing high P-E ratios should ask *why* such ratios appear in a competitive stock market. Often the explanation is associated with investor expectations about rapid future growth in EPS. (See Chapter 10 for a further discussion of growth stocks.)

Level three, *competition*, provides additional insights into the practicality of P-E ratios. As description (level one), P-E ratios require precise specification of terms, especially EPS; but they cannot provide any predictive insights. As description, a stock's P-E ratio, once defined, is just a number, nothing more. Only as guides to valuation (level two) can P-E ratios be considered as predictive. At this level P-E ratios are compared among stocks and over time to try to identify stocks that are relatively undervalued or overvalued. However, consideration of competition (level three) casts major doubt on whether P-E ratios can have predictive value.

A stock's price, determined in a competitive market, summarizes investor expectations about that stock, based on information available up to that time. (Among all the information available to competing investors are the stock's various P-E ratios.) Over time the price will adjust to new information and revised expectations about this stock and alternative investment opportunities. This competitive process determines the price. The P-E ratio is merely derived from the competitively determined price and some EPS figure. Viewed in this way a P-E ratio can have no inherent predictive power; it can only be a descriptive mathematical relationship.

To illustrate, in 1973 the stock of IBM opened at about $400 on the New York Stock Exchange. This price was determined by competing investors. At the time IBM's last reported annual EPS was $9.38. Thus, the P-E ratio derived from these two figures is around 43. (By using other EPS figures, such as estimated 1973 EPS, one would obtain a different P-E ratio.) But note that the P-E ratio of 43 is derived from a specified P (market price) and a specified EPS figure. It describes the relationship between these two figures, but there is no logical basis for assuming that it can be used to predict the future market price of IBM, or future changes in the price of IBM shares relative to future changes in market prices of other stocks.

In conclusion, by focusing on the fact that stock prices are determined in competitive markets, new insights can be gained into P-E ratios. First, unusually low or high P-E ratios must be closely examined to understand why they appear different. Using this approach, one sees that apparent differences often will disappear because of closer focus on factors such as: which P-E ratio, differences in reported information, and investor expectations about future EPS. Clear specification of terms will reduce confusion. Second, there is no logical basis for P-E ratios, however specified, to be predictors of subsequent changes in share prices or subsequent rates of return. Some analysts will cite case examples or limited studies showing how some low P-E ratio stocks subsequently had higher returns than stocks in general and examples of stocks with high P-E ratios that subsequently collapsed in price, resulting in adverse investment returns. But realistic investors go beyond selected examples and ask *why should* P-E ratios be *generally* predictive of subsequent investment returns? Without logical reasons and/or convincing empirical evidence, perceptive investors will remain skeptical of valuation statements based on P-E ratios.

Discounting Future Streams of Dividends

A logical method does exist for estimating a stock's value. By comparing the estimated value to the stock's market price, a decision can be made on whether the stock is undervalued, overvalued, or appropriately valued.

A stock's value logically should be the discounted stream of future benefits that the stock will provide to its owner. Expected future dividends basically comprise the stream of future benefits. Therefore any stock's estimated value can be summarized by the following equation:

$$P_v = \frac{D_1}{(1+k)^1} + \frac{D_2}{(1+k)^2} + \frac{D_3}{(1+k)^3} + \cdots + \frac{D_n}{(1+k)^n} \qquad (7\text{-}1)$$

where n approaches infinity and where:

P_v = estimated present value of a stock

D = cash dividend expected in each year 1 through n and appropriately adjusted for capital changes, such as stock splits

k = an appropriate rate at which to discount the future stream of dividends

A summary form of the preceding equation is:

$$P_v = \sum_{i=1}^{\infty} \frac{D_i}{(1 + k)^i} \qquad (7\text{-}2)$$

Each form of the basic model equates a stock's estimated present value to its appropriately discounted stream of future dividends. For convenience this basic equation will be called the P_v model.

Objections to the P_v model arise at two levels: (1) the conceptual and (2) the practical.

Objection one is to the model's focus on future dividends, not future earnings. A stockholder has residual claim to both components of a company's total earnings available for common stockholders, the part distributed as dividends and the undistributed part retained by the firm. Therefore is not the P_v model incomplete because of its apparent failure to include total earnings? The P_v model does incorporate total earnings by recognizing that earnings retained by a firm affect the firm's future dividend stream. To illustrate, a company that believes itself to have excellent investment opportunities will likely retain much of its earnings and invest them in expanding the firm's operations. The proportion of the company's earnings paid out as current dividends then will be low. Over time, however, this policy is expected to result in future dividends that will be higher than they would have been without the current high level of retention and reinvestment. Thus management decisions about current dividend payout and earnings retention will affect the *pattern of future dividends*. The P_v model is capable of valuing any pattern of future dividends and therefore is broadly applicable.

Objection two poses the question: Why does not the P_v model focus on future earnings directly instead of indirectly by way of the pattern of future dividends? The best reply to this question is the following illustration:

Imagine a company that is showing credible EPS growth of about 10 percent a year. This earnings growth is confidently expected to continue far into the future. The company's management asserts that the firm will never pay a dividend, but will keep retaining the growing stream of earnings. Furthermore the company has an unusual charter prohibiting its ever being liquidated or its being taken over by new owners or managers wanting to revise the stated policy of perpetual reinvestment of a growing stream of earnings.

Question: What price should a rational investor be willing to pay for a share of this company's stock?

Answer: Zero

Accepting the conditions of the question, there is no logical basis to believe that a shareholder will receive future benefits from holding stock in such a company. Willingness to pay a price above zero rests on belief that: (1) some loophole will be found in the policy of zero future cash distributions; or (2) that such stock can later be sold at a higher price to another investor. The latter strategy of buying now to sell later to a "bigger fool" is a fragile basis for investment decisions.

While the preceding illustration pushes the issue of earnings or dividends to a logical extreme, it effectively demonstrates that future dividends—not earnings—are what a stockholder can expect to receive and therefore dividends, not earnings, logically should be discounted in estimating a stock's present value.

Objection three observes that some stocks pay no cash dividends. How can shares of nondividend-paying companies be valued in the P_v model? The P_v model focuses on future dividends. Thus it is applicable to stocks currently paying no dividends but expected to do so in the future. A company currently paying no dividends is likely to be following a policy of reinvesting its current and near-future earnings in expectation of subsequently paying out a higher level of dividends. As demonstrated, decisions to reinvest current earnings basically affect only the pattern of future dividends. Unless he believes that no future dividend will ever be received from a stock such that it has no rational value, an investor must believe that dividends will begin being received at some future time. Thus the basic P_v model is applicable to any pattern of future cash dividends, including many years of zero dividends preceding receipt of the initial dividend of a subsequent stream. Similarly it is applicable to the stock of a declining company that pays no current dividends but that will eventually be liquidated to provide some terminal cash distributions to its stockholders.

Objection four notes that the P_v model focuses on dividend streams that approach infinity. Why should investors be concerned with infinite time horizons when neither individuals nor institutions have infinite lives? Logically it is the total stream of future benefits (dividends) that should be discounted in calculating a stock's present value. In practice, relative to dividends expected in the nearer term, dividends expected in the distant future have minor impact on a present-value calculation. For example, an expected dividend of $10 to be received 30 years from now has a present value of $0.99 when discounted back at a rate of eight percent. Although sensitive to the rate of growth of future dividends and the rate at which future dividends are discounted, most present-value calculations assign little current value to dividends that will not be received until far in the future. Thus focus by the P_v model on all future dividends is logically valid and need not lead to nonsensical results in practice.

Objection five observes that in practice most investors buy a stock intending subsequently to sell it at a profit. Emphasis is on capital gains, and not on holding a stock principally to participate in its future stream of dividends. Can concern for capital gains be recognized in the P_v model, which focuses on future dividends? The key issue is how an investor estimates the future price at which he intends to sell a stock for a profit. To illustrate, today an investor interested in capital gains is considering buying a stock with a market price of $30. The stock currently pays no dividends and is expected not to do so for at least another five years. He wants to sell the stock about three years from now at a profit. How can he estimate the price at which the stock will sell three years from now? He can guess at any figure, such as $40 or $50. He can try to estimate the psychology of other investors three years from now and judge that some of them will be willing to pay $40 or $50 for the stock. Such estimations by guess lack a logical basis. In contrast, the solution can be stated in terms of the P_v model as follows:

The investor is considering buying a stock. No dividends are expected in the next several years. The investor wants to sell the stock at the end of 3 years.

$$P_v = \frac{D_1}{(1+k)^1} + \frac{D_2}{(1+k)^2} + \frac{D_3}{(1+k)^3} + \frac{P_3}{(1+k)^3}$$

Since, in this example D_1 through D_3 are zero, the present value depends on the estimate for P_3 (the price at the end of the third year) and on the rate (k) at which this future expected sale price is discounted.

Today's estimate of the price three years from now can be explicitly part of the P_v model whereby,

$$P_v = \frac{0}{(1+k)^1} + \frac{0}{(1+k)^2} + \frac{0}{(1+k)^3} + \frac{P_3}{(1+k)^3}$$

where

$$P_3 = \frac{D_4}{(1+k)^4} + \frac{D_5}{(1+k)^5} + \cdots + \frac{D_n}{(1+k)^n}$$

or

$$P_3 = \sum_{i=4}^{\infty} \frac{D_i}{(1 + k)^i}$$

The mathematical notation merely summarizes that, in the P_v model, today's estimate of a stock's price three years from now is explicitly based on today's estimate of the future stream of dividends beyond the third year. In this way, the P_v model can logically be used by investors focusing on capital gains.

The conceptual framework of the P_v model stands firm against major objections. Practical application of the model is vulnerable to criticism. Such criticism focuses on how investors, especially those without access to elaborate computer facilities, can realistically expect to specify the inputs necessary for solving the P_v model.

Valuation techniques building on the P_v model theoretically should enable investors to discriminate effectively among stocks and to identify those that are relatively "undervalued" or "overvalued." Extensive tables, detailed to the second decimal place, and elaborate computer programs are available to assist investors in their investment decisions.[1] The various valuation tables usually depend on certain key assumptions about: patterns (usually linear) of future growth in dividends per share; investor planning horizons; and investors' desired returns from risky assets. Computer programs can be more flexible; but they, like the tables, require *projected* growth rates of dividends or EPS for various time intervals and, specified returns desired from risky assets. Given these necessary inputs, a precise number can be calculated showing a stock's "value." (A numerical estimate of the uncertainty surrounding this estimated value also can be generated.) If the estimated value is substantially above the current market price, this implies that the stock is "undervalued." The use of such techniques is supposed to enable investors to identify the most "undervalued" stocks that should then provide above-average future returns.

Before most investors commit much time and talent applying these P_v techniques to individual stocks, they should recognize that the precise estimated values basically depend on *necessarily imprecise* estimates of future events. Furthermore, how confident should one be

---

[1] For examples of stock valuation tables, see Nicholas Molodovsky, Catherine May, and Sherman Chottiner, "Common Stock Valuation: Principles, Tables and Application," *Financial Analysts Journal*, March–April 1965, pp. 104–123. For an example of a computer program, see David K. Eiteman, "A Computer Program for Common Stock Valuation," *Financial Analysts Journal*, July–August 1968, pp. 107–111.

about applying such techniques to a stock traded in a competitive market? Example: after careful study and thoughtful estimates an investor's computerized valuation program indicates that the "value" of a share of IBM is $600 when its competitively-determined market price is $400. Conclusion: the stock is "undervalued." However, should this investor assume that his procedures for selecting undervalued stocks are superior to those of many competing analysts and investors? In facing this question openly, the investor will probably check carefully his computer program and his various estimates of future relationships before he proceeds to commit substantial investment resources to this seemingly "undervalued stock." It is one investor's valuation estimate against the collective valuation of the market. He may be correct at times, but consistently? It is necessary to place one's skills in the context of a market having many skillful participants.

Finding Undervalued or Overvalued Stocks in a Competitive Market

In a competitive market a stock's price is a best estimate of its value at any point in time. The stock can be bought or sold only around this market price, which effectively summarizes the value of the stock to various investors at this point in time. For example, it represents the value to actual and potential buyers and sellers who have tried to assess the stock's future potential relative to alternative investment opportunities. Their estimates, by necessity, are based on past or current information that is generally available to stock market participants. Thus in a competitive market a stock's price represents a concensus of the value of the stock to investors at any particular point in time.

Over time the price of a stock will change. Investors who focus on intrinsic value can then assert that the market price is moving toward or away from the stock's intrinsic value, which may later be subject to revision. In contrast, investors who reject the concept of intrinsic value can assert that the market price is continually adjusting to *new* information and to *revisions* in some investor expectations concerning the potential of that company's shares relative to alternative investment opportunities. On this basis the stock's market price over time continues to be a best estimate of its value to various investors.

Hindsight provides much of the basis for popular acceptance of the concept of intrinsic value. There are episodes where a stock that had been traded in a narrow price range, say between $25 and $30, suddenly jumps toward $50 and then continues to be traded between $45 and $55 for an extended time period. In retrospect, it can be inferred that the stock must have been undervalued when it was in the range of $25 to $30. But could the subsequent price change have been confidently predicted at the time? It is more likely that new information, such as new management or a major new product, became known to various analysts and investors, leading to revisions in some investor expectations about the stock. Based on the actions of various competing investors, the stock price then rapidly adjusted to these revised expectations.

In a similar way, there are case examples of stocks that have fallen rapidly in price, say from $70 to $30. After the fact, it can be asserted that the stock was clearly overvalued at $70 and that careful analysis would have indicated that the stock was worth only around $30. But again, much of the price decline probably resulted from new information and revision of investor expectations that could not have been confidently predicted when the stock's market price was $70.

In valuing their stock portfolios for periodic financial reports, institutional investors must use a stock's market price to measure its value on the day of the portfolio valuation. For marketable securities the institution cannot report, for example, an intrinsic value of $30 for a stock that it purchased at $25 and that now has a market price of $20. The best estimate of the stock's value is its market price, not some intrinsic value that is based on analysis or judgment that is independent of the market price. Even for large blocks of stock or stocks that are inactively traded, the market price is still usually seen as the best estimate of the stock's value, recognizing that an unusually large buy or sell order can contribute to a change in the stock's market price. But because the magnitude of the hypothetical price change cannot be unambiguously forecast, the market price continues to be a best estimate of a stock's value.

What evidence is necessary to support the concept that stocks can have values that differ from their market price? It would require that some analysts or investors specifically identify these differences so that they can predict undervalued or overvalued stocks, such that over time portfolio returns from their selected stocks substantially exceed general market returns. Without such evidence realistic investors must question the feasibility over time of searching for gaps between "value" and current market price as a means of identifying undervalued or overvalued stocks.

chapter 8
Risk of Owning a Stock

To evaluate stock market opportunities, investors must consider both returns and risk. Yet the term "risk" is used in diverse—potentially confusing—ways. To illustrate, consider the following types of statements common to investment communications.

In my judgment this stock provides an excellent opportunity for achieving capital gains. Its price is likely to double in the coming six months, and its risk is limited.

In analyzing this stock, I believe the reward-risk ratio to be greater than three to one. Thus, in my judgment, the stock is a good buy around its current market price.

This airline stock has a Beta of 1.52 while this utility stock has a Beta of .70. Thus the airline stock is more than twice as risky as the utility stock.

Review how often you have heard or read statements that refer to a stock's risk. By examining how various stock market participants thus use the concept of risk in practice, realistic investors will gain new insights into investment opportunities—and pitfalls. Competitive markets also provide a unifying framework for analyzing investment risks.

Why Is a Stock Risky?

What is the risk involved in investing in a common stock? The principal risk is the uncertainty of its future return. This can best be illustrated

73

by contrasting the uncertain future return from a common stock to the certain future return from some alternative assets.

If an investor puts $1000 in a federally insured bank at a stipulated interest rate of 4 percent for one year, then he is certain to receive a 4 percent annual return from his deposit. The interest return is certain, as is the fact that he will still have his initial $1000 deposit at the end of the year. Similarly, if an investor pays $980 for a marketable U.S. government bond that is scheduled to be redeemed at $1000 in one year and that will also pay $30 in interest during the year, then he is certain of a one-year return of $50 ($20 capital gain plus $30 interest) on his initial investment of $980. This expected return is approximately 5.1 percent. Even if he sells the bond before maturity, he will receive around $1000; so that his expected return from this investment remains around 5.1 percent. Because an investor can thus be exceptionally confident, almost certain, about future returns from such assets, these are classified as *riskless assets*.

Now, contrast expected returns from riskless assets to the degree of confidence that investors can have about *future* returns from common stocks. Expected returns from a common stock involve uncertainty about both components of a stock's total rate of return: (1) future dividends and (2) the capital gain or loss associated with the stock's future change in price. Furthermore the period of time an investor will hold the stock is also uncertain, in contrast to the previous examples of the bank deposit and the marketable U.S. government bond having one-year maturities.

To illustrate, an investor may today buy the stock of a major utility company for $40. He expects the stock to continue paying a $2.00 annual cash dividend for at least the next year, but he realizes that the dividend can be reduced, omitted, or increased. Thus, although he is reasonably confident of an expected dividend return of 5 percent, he must be less confident of this return than he would be if he deposited the money in a bank account at 5 percent. Furthermore, in his judgment the stock will be selling at $48 at the end of one year. Thus his expected capital gain is $8 on the initial investment of $40, for a percentage capital gain of 20 percent. Although $48 is his best estimate of the stock's price after holding it for a year, he cannot be as confident about this as he can be about the dollar value of his bank deposit or government bond after one year. The possible stock price after one year may realistically range from $30 to $60 per share, so that the possible one-year capital gain or loss on the $40 initial investment can range from −25 to +50 percent. (Theoretically the range of possible values is −100% to + infinity, but it is necessary to focus on a plausible range of possibilities for the shares of a major utility company.) Thus, if there is a low probability that the dividend will be cut within one year, then the possible total one-year returns from this stock range between −20 percent (25% capital loss + 5% dividend yield) to somewhat over 55% if there is some probability of a modest dividend increase (50% capital gain + 5% dividend yield + small percentage from modest increase in cash dividend). Note, moreover, that the total range of possible future returns from this stock is about 75 percentage points (from −20% to somewhat more than +55%). This range of possible values surrounds the investor's "best estimate" of 25 percent, based on an expected dividend return of 5 percent and an expected capital gain of 20 percent. Furthermore, all of this is based on a one-year holding period, which is less definite when an investor buys a stock than when he makes a deposit or buys a bond with a stipulated maturity.

Uncertainty about future returns from a stock usually increases as investors try to look further into the future. Although many corporate officials are reluctant to reduce or omit cash dividends to common stockholders in the short run, in the longer run such a downward revision of the cash dividend is likely to occur if a company has persistent financial difficulties or unusually attractive investment opportunities. Conversely investors may anticipate that a company's cash dividend will be increased periodically in future years; but the rate of any such increases is less certain in longer-run predictions. To illustrate, consider an electrical utility with a record of periodic increases in its cash dividends to common stockholders. (Other competing investors also are aware of this past record.) Investor confidence about the cash dividend within the coming year or two can be high, approaching certainty. But five years in the future? 10? 20? Now consider a small technological company currently paying a token cash dividend. Uncertainty of this firm's future dividends is greater than the uncertainty of future dividends from the electrical utility. Thus future dividends from common stocks all involve some uncertainty, with some much more uncertain than others.

Capital gain or loss is the other principal component of the future total return from holding a stock. Such a gain or loss is determined by the future prices of the stock. Major uncertainty surrounds predictions of future prices. Investors cannot be confident about any prediction of a company's stock price five or 10 years from now, even for a mature company almost certain to expand in the future. For example, predict the prices of the following companies one, five, and 10 years from now:

Aluminum Company of America
General Motors
International Business Machines

Proctor & Gamble

Sears, Roebuck & Company

Westinghouse Electric

Even if one asserts that the national economy will most likely expand in the next 10 years and that each of these companies will most likely expand with the economy, this only implies that their stock prices will be higher sometime in the future than they are now. Even if the economy does expand over time, it will expand at an uneven rate, and not all companies will participate equally, or predictably, in the general expansion. Thus recognizing the uncertainty surrounding predictions of future stock prices of mature companies, realistic investors readily acknowledge the relatively greater uncertainty surrounding estimates of future share prices of small new companies in competitive technological industries. For any such company the share price within the next 10 years may range from zero to a large positive number. Therefore, the possible capital gain or loss from owning such a stock is very uncertain, as is the future stream of dividends. Consequently the total expected return from such a stock also is very uncertain. On this basis such a stock is more risky than that of a mature company with a relatively more predictable future. However, while individual stocks vary in their relative risk, all stocks are risky compared to riskless assets.[1]

How practical is it to define or measure rigorously the future risk of any common stock? With precise specifications of returns and time periods, analysts can readily calculate a stock's *past* risk, as measured, for example, by the variance of a distribution of past returns. A precise numerical answer emerges. However, can investors be confident that any precise measure of past risk can be extended to predict a stock's future risk? Also, even if this past information is a useful guide to the future, various investors can use this information in developing their stock market strategies.

As an alternative, a precise numerical estimate of the future risk of

---

[1] Investments textbooks often detail various sources of investment risk. These books typically classify "risk" into subcategories, such as:

Purchasing power risk.
Interest rate risk.
Business risk.
Financial risk.

Basically, the many possible combinations of such sources of risk affect the uncertainty and/or valuation of future returns from various assets. For further details, see Steven E. Bolten, *Security Analysis and Portfolio Management: An Analytical Approach to Investments* (Holt, Rinehart and Winston, Inc.: 1972), pp. 151–276; or Jack Clark Francis, *Investments: Analysis and Management* (McGraw-Hill Book Company: 1972), pp. 258–265.

holding a stock can be calculated directly from estimates of possible future returns from the stock. For example, an investor can thus calculate the variance of expected future returns from a stock in a coming one-year holding period. Paradoxically such an estimate of future risk depends on predictions of future returns; and, as previously shown, predictions of future returns from common stocks necessarily are uncertain. In summary, attempts to define and measure rigorously a stock's future risk are unlikely to surmount the fact that the future predictions about returns from common stocks are themselves uncertain. Although astute investors demand precision, they are skeptical of "precise" measures derived from necessarily imprecise estimates.

Risk, which cannot be precisely measured, surrounds an investment in any stock. Stock prices generally are determined in competitive markets, so that at any point in time a stock's price is a best estimate of that stock's value to investors, based on available information, analyses, and expectations about possible future returns. Thus a stock's price also reflects its risk as perceived by various competing investors.

With this framework of the hazards in prediction and of competitive markets, reconsider one of the introductory statements of this chapter.

"In my judgment this stock provides an excellent opportunity for achieving capital gains. Its price is likely to double in the coming six months, and its risk is limited."

On close examination, such a situation is unlikely to exist in a competitive market. How confident should an investor be about the speaker's prediction of the stock's doubling? Other skillful analysts and investors with access to information also are monitoring this stock's potential relative to that of alternative investments. If today's competitively determined stock price is, for example, $40, how confident should be any one investor of the price going to $80 within six months? The expected return from such a price change is one of many possible future returns. The fact that other investors currently will buy and sell the stock at about $40 indicates the low probability of a price of $80 within six months. Furthermore the probability of negative returns, or low returns relative to alternative investment opportunities, cannot be readily dismissed. Occasionally predictions of high short-run returns from specific stocks prove accurate; but not often. Realistic investors insist on looking at the total record of returns over an extended period of time.

The risk of investing in an individual common stock is seen to involve uncertainty about future returns. Such risk, common to all stocks, varies over different time horizons and among stocks. Since risk can vary among stocks, it is necessary to go beyond single stocks to analyze risk as it is related to portfolios comprised of individual stocks (Chapter 9). Also it is instructive to examine the use of reward-risk ratios as applied to individual common stocks.

Using Reward-Risk Ratios

Reward-risk ratios are used by some investment managers to summarize their views of a stock's potential. Such ratios combine numerical estimates of reward and risk into a summary figure, as illustrated by the following statement:

"In analyzing this stock, I believe the reward-risk ratio to be greater than three to one. Thus, in my judgment, the stock is a good buy around its current market price."

What is the basis for such an assertion?

Reward in reward-risk (R-R) ratios is defined typically as upside potential as measured by the projected increase in price from its current market level. To illustrate, if a stock that sells today for $20 is expected to go to a target price of $35, its upside potential ("reward") is $15. "Risk" in such ratios is defined as downside risk, as measured by the maximum probable decline of a share price from its current market price. To illustrate, if the $20 stock is expected to go no lower than a floor price of $15, then its downside risk is $5. Thus the R-R ratio in this example is 15/5 or 3-to-1, a concise summary figure. Such R-R ratios rest, however, on unusual definitions and on precise estimates of uncertain future outcomes.

Reward focuses only on price appreciation, instead of on the total rate of return from holding a stock. It has no explicit time dimension, as does an annualized rate-of-return measure. For example, an assertion that a stock's upside potential is $15 from its current price is incomplete without stating whether this will occur in six months or six years. Reward (upside potential) is derived from a numerical estimate of a future price ($35 in the example), but investors cannot be very confident about such a precise prediction of a stock's future price. Yet a precise estimate is necessary for the numerator of a R-R ratio.

Risk in R-R ratios is notably different from risk defined as uncertainty of future returns. Instead of focusing on uncertainty, it requires a precise estimate of the lowest price to which a stock can fall. Hazards are involved in predicting this theoretical floor of a stock price. Such "floors" can easily collapse from an onslaught of unpredictable adverse events. Also no time dimension is usually specified for such downside risk. Ambiguities and hazards thus surround the denominator of a R-R ratio.

The combination of reward and risk into a summary ratio only leads to additional practical problems.

How should R-R ratios be used in selecting among stocks? Should investors focus only on stocks with R-R ratios of 5-to-1, 3-to-1, or just what? If such ratios for various stocks are calculated with a similar time horizon, such as one year, then the answer appears simple: invest in those stocks with the highest R-R ratio. For example, if the highest ratios are 5-to-1, why settle for lower odds? However, such a choice highlights a principal weakness of R-R ratios—their oversimplification of possible outcomes.

Consider the following R-R ratios:

Stock A		
(current price $20)	Reward (target price of $45):	$25
	Risk (floor price of $15):	$ 5
	R-R Ratio:	5
Stock B		
(current price $20)	Reward (target price of $35):	$15
	Risk (floor price of $15):	$ 5
	R-R Ratio:	3

Both ratios are based on similar quality estimates and on one-year time horizons.

The ratios fail to show the *probabilities* of these projected outcomes. If it is equally probable that Stock A will hit $15 or $45, this is generally preferable to Stock B if that stock is equally probable to hit $15 or $35. Downside risk is the same ($5), but the upside potential for Stock A is greater. However, what if both stocks have floors of $15; but with a 90 percent probability of Stock A hitting $15 but only a 10 percent probability of Stock B hitting $15? Similarly, the probability of Stock A hitting $45 is now 10 percent, while the probability of Stock B hitting $35 is 90 percent. On this basis Stock B is likely to be the better choice, although its R-R ratio is lower than that of Stock A. In summary, by considering only target and floor prices and by implicitly assuming equal probabilities, R-R ratios neglect distributions of possible outcomes and thus can lead to inappropriate choices among stocks.

Not only are the construction and use of R-R ratios potentially misleading, their logical basis is suspect in a competitive market. In such a market a stock's price reflects the information, analyses, and expectations available to competing investors until that point in time. Captured in this price are investor expectations about the stock's future returns in relation to alternative investment opportunities and uncertainties about such possible returns. Over time the stock price will adjust to new information and to revised analyses and expectations. Thus the market price itself reflects a concensus of investor views concerning future returns from a stock. To create a reward-risk ratio from this competitively determined price is redundant unless an investor believes that his estimates of future stock prices are consistently better than those reflected in market prices.

In summary, a statement about a stock's reward-risk ratio initially sounds authoritative. Seemingly it expresses much information in one useful number. Unfortunately both the logical basis and numerical construction of a R-R ratio are questionable, at best. Uncritical use of such ratios for selecting among stock can lead to inappropriate investment decisions.

Using Beta to Measure Risk

Beta now is offered to investors as a new method of specifying and measuring "risk." Increasing numbers of articles and investment advisory services proclaim Beta, as illustrated by the statement:

"This airline stock has a Beta of 1.52 while this utility stock has a Beta of .70. Thus the airline stock is more than twice as risky as the utility."

What is Beta, and how useful is it to investors?

Beta is a measure of relative volatility. It rests on the assumption that a stock's risk basically can be defined and measured as the volatility of returns from the stock *relative* to the volatility of returns from the general market. By definition the general market has a volatility of 1.00. Therefore a stock with a Beta of 2.00 is twice as volatile as the market, while a stock with a Beta of .51 has about one-half the volatility of the general market. Furthermore the stock with the Beta of 2.00 is almost four times as volatile as the stock with a Beta of .51.

Understanding how Beta is calculated enables investors better to understand how it is interpreted. The following series of numbers are the one-year rates of return from Hypothetical Stock A over a recent 10-year period.

Year$_1$	55
Year$_2$	−16
Year$_3$	44
Year$_4$	35
Year$_5$	26
Year$_6$	−19
Year$_7$	50
Year$_8$	25
Year$_9$	−20
Year$_{10}$	1

Alongside the series of one-year returns from Hypothetical Stock A one can list the one-year rates of return from the general market, as represented, for example, by the returns on the NYSE Common Stock Index. This index is referred to as a "market portfolio."

One-Year Rates of Return From:

	Hypothetical Stock A	Market Portfolio[a]
Year$_1$	55	28
Year$_2$	−16	− 8
Year$_3$	44	21
Year$_4$	35	18
Year$_5$	26	13
Year$_6$	−19	− 9
Year$_7$	50	26
Year$_8$	25	13
Year$_9$	−20	− 9
Year$_{10}$	1	0

[a]Estimated from *New York Stock Exchange Fact Book*, 1972, pp. 23, 78.

In the first year Hypothetical Stock A (HSA) provided a return of 55 percent while the return on the market portfolio was 28 percent. Thus HSA provided a return nearly twice that of the market portfolio. In the second year, HSA provided a return of −16 percent while the return from the market portfolio was −8 percent. Thus in the second year, the return from HSA was more than twice as adverse as that from the market portfolio. Similarly the return from HSA can be compared with that from the market portfolio in each of the other eight years.

Each year's returns from Hypothetical Stock A and from the market portfolio can be plotted on a graph, as shown in Figure 8-1. On the graph one can plot a "line of best fit" that summarizes the relationship between the returns from HSA and from the market portfolio in each of the 10 years.[2]

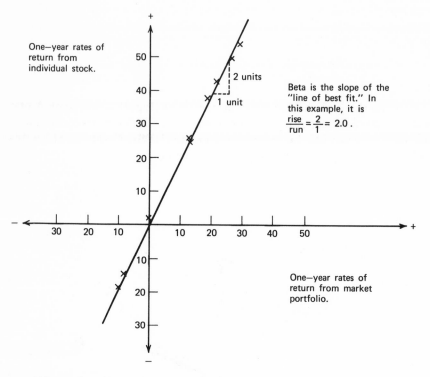

X Returns from Hypothetical Stock A (HSA) plotted against returns from market portfolio.

Figure 8-1. A graphic example of Beta: one stock

The "line of best fit" portrays the *average* relationship between the two sets of returns. For example, in none of the 10 years did the market portfolio provide a return of +10 percent. Yet by observing the line on the graph, if the return from the market portfolio were +10 percent in

[2] More formally, this line of best fit is a least-squares regression line. Also a numerical measure of the "goodness of fit" is the R^2 value calculated for the regression line. Many investors are introduced to the logic and numerical calculations of regression data when they take a basic course in statistics. For a primer on Beta (and Alpha) see Chris Welles, "The Beta Revolution: Learning to Live with Risk," *Institutional Investor*, Sept. 1971, pp. 21–27 ff.

a year, then a best estimate of the return from HSA in that year would be +20 percent. Conversely, when the market return is −10 percent, HSA is likely to return −20 percent. Returns from HSA thus are estimated to be twice as volatile as returns from the market portfolio.

The general relationship between returns from HSA and from the market portfolio also can be estimated by calculating the slope of the "line of best fit," which in the example is 2.0. *Beta* is the summary term used to refer to this slope. In sum, the stock of HSA is said to have a Beta of 2.0, indicating that, on average, returns from HSA are twice as volatile ("risky") as returns from the market portfolio, which by definition has a Beta of 1.0.

Returns from a stock with a Beta of less than 1.0 are less volatile, on average, than the returns from a market portfolio. Portrayed in Figure 8-2 is the "line of best fit" for Hypothetical Stock B that has a Beta of 0.5.

Returns from Hypothetical Stock B not only are less volatile than

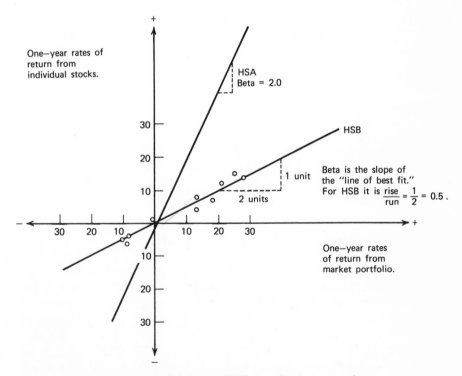

o Returns from Hypothetical Stock B (HSB) plotted against returns from market portfolio.

Figure 8-2. A graphic example of Beta: two stocks.

those of the general market, they are only one-fourth as volatile as returns from Hypothetical Stock A with its Beta of 2.0.

Although a Beta can be calculated for any stock, in some cases it "explains" very little about a stock's relative volatility. To illustrate, in Figure 8-3 the returns for Hypothetical Stock C (HSC) are plotted relative to the returns from the general market.

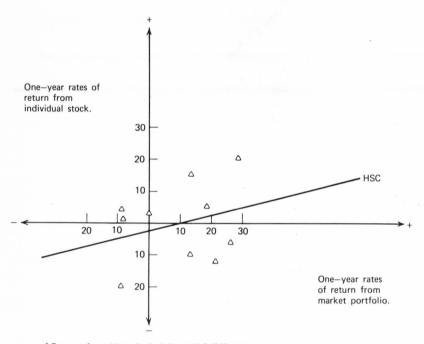

△ Returns from Hypothetical Stock C (HSC) plotted against returns from market portfolio.

Figure 8-3.   A graphic example of Beta that "explains" little.

In this case the relationship between the two sets of returns is not very consistent. In one year the return from HSC was +15 percent while the return from the market portfolio was +13 percent. In another year the return from HSC was −10 percent while the return from the market portfolio was +13 percent. As portrayed in Figure 8-3, there is no evident pattern to the scattered points. Nevertheless a "line of best fit" can be mathematically plotted for HSC, and the slope (Beta) of this line calculated. Thus Beta for HSC is 0.24. Despite its apparent accuracy to two decimal places, such a Beta is a much less reliable "on-average estimator" than that of 2.0 for HSA and 0.5 for HSB. This visual awareness that the Beta for HSC leaves unexplained much of the relationship between returns from HSC and the general market can be also shown mathematically.[3]

Not only does Beta fail to explain much about some stocks, but the same stock can have different Betas! For example, during a recent time period four different investment research services reported the Beta of General Motors stock as follows:[4]

	Reported Beta of GM
Service 1	.71
Service 2	.90
Service 3	1.08
Service 4	1.23

How can the same stock have at least four different Betas, so that the largest Beta (1.23) is almost twice the smallest Beta (.71)? Is GM stock 1.23 or only .71 times as volatile as the general market?

Betas for individual stocks depend largely on how Beta is calculated. In particular, calculation of Beta requires specification of:

1. The *total time period* during which returns from a stock are compared with market returns (e.g., in Figures 8-1 to 8-3, the comparisons cover a total time period of 10 years).

2. The *subperiods* during which the stock returns and market returns are calculated (e.g., in Figures 8-1 to 8-3, the returns being compared are one-year returns).

For the same stock, different past total time periods can be specified: for example, the past five years, the past 10 years, or the past 15 years. Similarly for the same stock, different subperiods for which past returns are calculated can be specified: for instance monthly, quarterly, semiannually, or annually. Since various time periods thus can be specified and none is inherently best, Betas calculated for the same stock can vary depending on the choice of time periods. Betas can also vary depending on whether total returns or price changes are being com-

---

[3] The R^2 for the line of best fit is relatively low, indicating that the line fails to explain most of the relationship between the two series of returns.

[4] As reported by Don Peterson in a letter to the editor published in the *Financial Analysts Journal*, May–June 1972, pp. 104–105.

Table 8-1. Betas of Selected Stocks

Illustrative Stock	Recent Three-Year Period Subperiods			Recent One-Year Period Subperiods		
	Quarterly	Monthly	Weekly	Quarterly	Monthly	Weekly
American Telephone & Telegraph	.86	.88	.63	a	.45	.14
General Motors	.81	1.00	.96	a	1.10	1.13
Northwest Airlines	1.94	2.16	1.94	a	4.20	2.12

aNot reported because calculations rest on only four subperiods.

Note: To simplify calculations, Betas reported in this table are based on comparative price changes (not total returns) between each illustrative stock and the Standard & Poor's Index of 425 Industrial Stocks. As shown in the text, other measures of a "market portfolio" can be used.

pared and according to which market portfolio (or index) a stock is being compared.

To demonstrate how different Betas can refer to the same stock, Table 8-1 has been developed to show recent Betas for shares of:

American Telephone & Telegraph (AT&T)

General Motors (GM)

Northwest Airlines (NWA)

As shown in the table, Betas for the same stock vary depending on the specified time periods. Despite these differing Betas for each stock, there is a general pattern that the Beta of NWA is higher than that of GM, which is higher than that of AT&T. Using Beta as a measure of risk, for these past time periods, the stock of NWA was riskier than a market portfolio and also riskier than the shares of GM and AT&T. Extending such past numerical relationships into the future must be done with caution, however, because of evidence that Betas of many individual stocks are unstable over time.

How Betas differ for the same stock is further demonstrated in a published Letter to the Editor of the *Financial Analysts Journal.*[5] The letter writer highlights the wide divergence in Betas provided by four different investment research services for the 30 stocks in the Dow Jones Industrials Average. To summarize his report, the following list presents the Betas for every fifth stock in his total list of 30 stocks:

	Service$_1$	Service$_2$	Service$_3$	Service$_4$
Allied Chemical	1.47	1.07	1.26	1.04
Anaconda	1.16	.85	1.04	.96
General Electric	1.36	.71	1.17	1.05
International Nickel	1.24	.72	.88	.67
Sears Roebuck	1.07	.76	1.03	.89
Union Carbide	1.28	.91	1.05	.94

Inspection of these Betas shows, for example, that Service$_1$ reports a Beta for General Electric stock that is almost twice the Beta reported by Service$_2$. Similarly is the stock of International Nickel more volatile than the general market as reported by Service$_1$ or about two-thirds as volatile as the general market as reported by Service$_4$? Be-

[5] *Ibid.*

cause of such divergence, the letter writer urges security analysts to be cautious using Betas to characterize an individual stock. Now introduced to Beta, individual investors also understand why they should Beware of Beta—especially for single stocks. The use of Betas for portfolios of stocks will be examined next.

chapter 9
Risk of Owning a Portfolio of Stocks

Investors benefit from adopting a portfolio viewpoint. Their perspective then broadens from analyzing a stock in isolation to assessing its potential place in a portfolio of stocks.

A portfolio viewpoint is featured in the following types of prevalent investment statements:

To reduce risk an investor should develop a portfolio diversified among stocks of high-quality companies.

Beta measures enable modern investors to manage more effectively the risk levels of their portfolios.

Investors should realize that to obtain higher returns they must accept greater risk; or, more concisely, high risks lead to high returns.

Portfolio management has recently been a center of theoretical and practical developments. Advanced books and articles about portfolio theory are now available. Although some complexities of portfolio theory are unresolved, individual investors gain additional understanding by examining combinations of single stocks into portfolios of stocks.

Reducing Risk by Diversification

Owning shares in different companies involves less risk than holding the stock of only one company. In other words, investors can be more confident about future returns from a portfolio of stocks than they can be about future returns from any one of the stocks in the portfolio.

To illustrate this principle, predict the total returns from the common shares of each of the following companies one, five, and 10 years from now:

Aluminum Company of America

Anaconda

Chrysler

Eastman Kodak

General Electric

Goodyear

Proctor & Gamble

Standard Oil of California

Texaco

United Aircraft

Predictions of total returns from each of these common stocks involve estimates of future dividends and prices. In a dynamic economy, diverse—often unpredictable—factors can dramatically affect future outcomes for any *one* of these companies. For example, there can be increased national and international competition, changes in the legal and regulatory environment affecting certain industries, and shifts in consumer tastes. Thus uncertainty surrounds the expected total return from any one of these common stocks.

Confidence about future total returns is greater, however, if an investor diversifies by holding all 10 of the above common stocks, with no one of the stocks constituting a predominant part of the portfolio. While recognizing the uncertainty of future returns from any one of the stocks, the investor knows that some of the 10 stocks will eventually provide relatively high returns and some will provide relatively low returns in future holding periods. Because these diverse returns from the individual stocks will somewhat offset one another, the investor can be more confident about the total return from this 10-stock portfolio than he can be about the future returns from any one of the 10 component stocks.

Shares of small new companies in highly competitive technological industries involve substantial risk. Any one of these companies may be the proverbial "future IBM," but an investor realistically cannot predict such an outcome with much confidence. Shares of such companies combine the potential for high positive returns with the possibility of returns of −100 percent if the company is subsequently declared bankrupt. Thus future returns from any one such company are very uncertain, more so than future returns from any one mature industrial company, such as those represented in the Dow Jones Industrials Average. Because of their broad range of possible future returns, with a realistic possibility of complete loss, each of these stocks of small new companies can be classified as *speculative.*

An investor can diversify among many speculative stocks. Some are likely to provide substantial future returns while others will provide negative returns. These extreme outcomes become "averaged out" in the total portfolio return. Thus, by diversification, the investor can be confident that he will not lose all his initial investment, as can happen to a speculator who places all his funds into one stock. In the same way, however, he reduces his opportunity for the exceptionally high returns that will occur if he is sufficiently astute (lucky?) to concentrate his investment funds in the one stock that subsequently becomes a Wall Street success story.

Investors thus can be more confident of future returns from any diversified portfolio of stocks than they can be about the future return from any one common stock in the portfolio. However, diversified portfolios continue to have a second dimension of risk: *market risk.* This risk remains even after the risk of individual common stocks is substantially reduced by diversification.[1]

An investor holding a portfolio diversified among 10 of the 30 stocks comprising the Dow Jones Industrials Average (DJIA) can be confident that his future portfolio returns will approximate that of a portfolio comprising all 30 DJIA stocks. A 10-stock portfolio of DJIA stocks is the following:

Aluminum Company of America

Anaconda

Chrysler

Eastman Kodak

General Electric

Goodyear

Proctor & Gamble

Standard Oil of California

Texaco

United Aircraft

[1] Early specification of this concept at an advanced level was by William F. Sharpe, "Capital Asset Prices: A Theory of Market Equilibrium under Conditions of Risk," *The Journal of Finance,* September 1964, pp. 425–442.

If the market, as measured by the DJIA, is substantially higher five years from now, then the value of this 10-stock portfolio also will be substantially higher. Conversely if the market is substantially lower, then the value of the 10-stock portfolio also will be substantially lower. There are few, if any, stocks that do not decline in price in a general market slump. Similarly, most stocks will participate in a broadly based market advance. Even an investor holding a mutual fund diversified among 100 to 200 different common stocks will find that his future portfolio returns are closely associated with future market returns. Diversification among common stocks does not enable investors to avoid this risk of future market fluctuations.

No matter among how many different common stocks an investor diversifies his portfolio, he cannot remove the market risk. (At the logical extreme, even a portfolio diversified among all stocks listed on the New York Stock Exchange remains subject to market fluctuations.) By thus increasing the number of different stocks in the portfolio, however, he increases his confidence of approaching the market return in subsequent time periods. Yet, on the same basis, it then becomes difficult, if not impossible, to "beat the market." For all practical purposes, returns from a portfolio diversified among 100 to 200 different common stocks can only be similar to future market returns. Returns from broadly diversified portfolios will fluctuate with the general market, with little chance of the portfolio returns being substantially greater or less than market returns. In contrast, returns from portfolios concentrated in only several different stocks have the potential to fluctuate more widely around future market returns.

Among how many different stocks should investors diversify their portfolios? Some writers indicate that portfolios diversified among 10 to 20 different stocks involve substantially less risk than portfolios of only 1 or 2 stocks.[2] Although substantial diversification benefits can be achieved by increasing portfolio size from 1 or 2 stocks to 10 to 20 stocks, adding more stocks further increases investor confidence in achieving market returns over various time periods. The cost of thus achieving benefits of broad diversification is relatively small for individual investors who diversify indirectly by purchasing shares of diversified investment companies (Chapters 24 and 25).

Diversification is concerned not only with the number of different stocks in a portfolio. In thus focusing on different stocks, there is an implicit assumption that such stocks are of companies in different in-

[2] Analysis of the relationship between the number of different stocks in a portfolio and the level of portfolio dispersion is presented by John L. Evans and Stephen H. Archer, "Diversification and the Reduction of Dispersion: An Empirical Analysis," *The Journal of Finance*, December 1968, pp. 761–767. See also Per B. Mokkelbost, "Unsystematic Risk Over Time," *Journal of Financial and Quantitative Analysis*, March 1971, pp. 785–796.

dustries that are not closely interdependent. To illustrate, owning 10 different chemical stocks cannot provide the same diversification benefits as holding 10 stocks in diverse industries, such as aluminum, banking, chemicals, and retailing. All chemical companies are subject in varying degrees to factors affecting their industry, such as international and national competition, environmental issues, and changes in consumer spending patterns. Diversification among shares representing various industries reduces the chance that portfolio returns are heavily influenced by future events primarily affecting one industry or closely related industries.

In contrast to simply diversifying among many different stocks representing diverse industries, it is possible to achieve more efficient diversification. Investors can identify efficiently diversified portfolios by predicting for various stocks the expected returns, distributions around these expected returns, and how these expected values for individual stocks are interrelated.[3] Enough has already been said in this book, however, about the hazards of predictions. While it may be possible to identify efficient portfolios, most individual investors are unlikely to find the quest to be very practical.

What has been learned about reducing risk by diversification? Reconsider the first statement introducing this chapter:

"To reduce risk an investor should develop a portfolio diversified among stocks of high-quality companies."

Such a strategy indeed involves less risk than that of holding one or two individual common stocks. An investor adopting such a strategy of broad diversification can be confident that his future portfolio returns will closely approximate market returns, such as for NYSE stocks in general. However, such a strategy cannot reduce the *market risk* that remains even after broad diversification. Furthermore the benefits and limitations of diversification are not limited to stocks of high-quality companies; they are also applicable to strategies involving speculative stocks.

Managing Portfolio Risk

Portfolio risk remains after an investor effectively reduces the impact of individual stock risk by diversification. How can investors measure and manage portfolio risk?

[3] A major work on portfolio diversification is by Harry M. Markowitz, *Portfolio Selection: Efficient Diversification of Investments,* Monograph 16 (Cowles Foundation for Research in Economics at Yale University: 1959).

Beta can be used to measure a portfolio's risk. Just as a series of past returns from a *single stock* can be related to those of a market portfolio by a line of best fit, so can a series of past returns from a *portfolio of stocks* be related to a market portfolio. The Beta of the stock portfolio is the slope of the line of best fit. It shows how volatile the portfolio's returns have been relative to the volatility of general market returns. For example, a portfolio with a Beta of 1.15 is more volatile, on average, than the market portfolio (Beta of 1.00), while a portfolio with a Beta of .90 is less volatile than the market portfolio.

Betas of portfolios of stocks generally are more stable indicators of relative volatility than are Betas of individual stocks. Because of diversification, the volatility of portfolio returns more closely approximates the volatility of general market returns over time. For example, a portfolio broadly diversified among 100 to 200 different NYSE stocks is likely to have a Beta near 1.0 because its portfolio composition closely approaches that of the NYSE market portfolio to which it is being compared. Less diversified portfolios will have Betas scattered more widely around 1.0.[4]

Investors can try to use Beta to manage their portfolios. Aggressive risk management is advocated in the illustrative statement:

"Beta measures enable modern investors to manage more effectively the risk levels of their portfolios."

An aggressive investor who expects general market returns to be positive will seek to combine various stocks into a portfolio expected to have a Beta in excess of 1.00. When he expects general market returns to be negative, he will seek to reduce the expected volatility (Beta) of the portfolio. A portfolio's Beta can be reduced, for example, by shifting the portfolio more toward low Beta stocks and cash.

Aggressive use of Beta to manage a portfolio is illustrated by an investor who expects general market returns to be about 20 percent next year. Therefore, he constructs a portfolio with a Beta, say, of 1.50. This portfolio, 1.5 times more volatile than the general market, is expected to return 30 percent (1.5 × 20%) in the coming year when the general market is expected to return 20 percent. What will happen, however, if next year's general market return is about −10 percent, instead of the expected +20 percent? The aggressive investor's portfolio with a Beta of 1.5 also will be more volatile on the downside. Its expected return then will be −15 percent, or 1.5 times the general market return of

---

[4] A more advanced, analytical discussion of these basic relationships is provided by Marshall E. Blume, "On the Assessment of Risk," *The Journal of Finance*, March 1971, pp. 1–10.

−10 percent. In a similar way, an investor who shifts his portfolio to a lower Beta for protection in an anticipated market decline will experience relatively low returns if the general market rises instead of falls as expected.

Using Beta aggressively to manage a portfolio is not easily done in practice. It requires a portfolio manager to *predict* major changes in the general market environment so that he can modify his portfolio's expected volatility, as measured by Beta. Evidence to date indicates that investment managers do not have uncanny abilities to predict future market turns. To illustrate, to answer the question of whether or not portfolio managers have the *ability* to anticipate major turns in the stock market, the performance record of 57 mutual funds was studied during the period from 1953 through 1962.[5] The authors state that their study shows "no statistical evidence that the investment managers of any of the 57 funds have successfully outguessed the market." They further conclude that probably the best assumption that investors can make is that "investment managers have no ability to outguess the market and should not try to." Such a conclusion demonstrates the practical problems of successfully using Beta *aggressively* to manage a portfolio's risk. What about *passively* using Beta to construct higher-risk portfolios that over time are expected to provide higher returns?

Seeking High Returns by Accepting High Risk

Ideally investors would like to obtain *high* returns with *low* risk. However, most are aware of a basic economic principle: "There's no such thing as a free lunch." Therefore, if offered a note or bond promising to pay 10 to 15 percent interest, realistic investors immediately question the risk involved. They infer that future receipts of interest and principal from this asset are less certain than from riskless assets, such as government bonds and time deposits at federally insured financial institutions. Similarly, since future returns from common stocks are uncertain, astute investors are particularly skeptical of assertions about any stock having high returns with little risk. Few, if any, such opportunities can exist in a competitive market.

Since practical investors are aware that high returns are unlikely to be associated with low risk, an alternative approach is to obtain high returns by accepting high risk. Such a strategy is summarized in the illustrative statement:

[5] Jack L. Treynor and Kay K. Mazuy, "Can Mutual Funds Outguess the Market?" *Harvard Business Review*, July–August 1966, pp. 131–136.

"Investors should realize that to obtain higher returns, they must accept greater risk; or, more concisely, high risks lead to high returns."

What is the evidence typically supporting such a view?

Case examples and hindsight often are used to illustrate the high-risk high-return (HR-HR) strategy. The strategy sometimes is supported by pointing out:

No one will become rich from future share price appreciation of major corporations such as American Telephone or General Motors. While these are wonderful companies, to multiply one's capital it is necessary to seek out, for example, shares of emerging growth companies having the potential to be future industrial giants. Such shares, while admittedly more risky, offer greater opportunity.

Another HR-HR proponent also can point out that someone who bought shares of Control Data Corporation (CDC) when they first were publicly traded must have known that the shares were more risky than those of mature companies, such as those represented in the Dow Jones Industrials Average. However, if the investor continued to hold his original CDC shares and those subsequently received from stock splits and dividends, then his investment has appreciated more than if he had purchased the same dollar amount of shares of a mature company. Conclusion: by accepting higher risk this investor achieved higher returns. Perceptive investors now recognize that such selected examples prove next to nothing. What have been the outcomes over time of the other risky investments made by this investor and by many other investors? Why *should* one *expect* to receive higher long-term returns from investing in high-risk stocks in contrast to lower-risk stocks? Realism requires logical support and appropriate evidence before accepting the HR-HR strategy.

HR-HR strategies can be effectively evaluated only for portfolios of stocks over time, not just for single stocks. Some high-risk stocks will become valueless, and others will provide exceptionally high positive returns. It is impossible to predict with confidence which stocks will fall into these extreme categories, or into intermediate categories. To reduce the uncertainty surrounding individual stocks, an investor can diversify broadly among high-risk stocks so that his portfolio returns will closely approximate general returns from speculative stocks over time. These portfolio returns can be compared with those from portfolios diversified among lower-risk stocks (such as those of mature companies) of which few, if any, will become valueless; but also few will provide exceptionally high returns. The key point is that effective testing of the HR-HR strategy requires comparisons between portfolio returns over an extended period of time, not just selected examples of extreme outcomes.

From a portfolio viewpoint, modern theory suggests that, under specified conditions, higher returns should be associated with higher risk.[6] Why should any investor be willing to hold a portfolio of risky stocks, as measured by expected volatility, unless he *expects* that over time he will be rewarded by receiving higher portfolio returns? This viewpoint emphasizes that, in principle, higher *expected* returns should be associated with higher *expected* risk. It is more cautious in asserting that higher *realized* returns are associated with acceptance of higher risk.

In practice, should investors *expect* that long-term returns from portfolios of high-risk stocks will be higher than those from portfolios comprised of lower-risk stocks? Since individual stock risk can be essentially removed by diversification, returns from portfolios of high-risk stocks will consistently exceed returns from portfolios of lower-risk stocks only if the market risk over time is greater for the high-risk stocks. For example, returns from high-risk stocks as a group are likely to be more volatile over time than are those from lower-risk stocks. In this event investors may require higher returns to induce them to hold the stock portfolios that are comparatively more volatile. But this inducement cannot be very large in a competitive market; otherwise investors willing and able to hold portfolios for a long time will construct diversified portfolios of high-risk stocks, knowing that although their future returns will be more volatile they will be rewarded by higher returns in the longer run. Thus such competing investors, by their portfolio actions, assure that the HR-HR strategy is unlikely to provide substantially above-average returns over time.

Does recent evidence support the high-risk high-return view or the competitive-market view?

Recently a comprehensive study of various risk-return relationships of NYSE common stocks was published.[7] Acknowledging that Beta can be used to classify stocks into various risk classes, for convenience Sharpe and Cooper choose to use a measure of "market sensitivity" that they demonstrate is very similar to Beta both in principle and in practice. For the 37-year period from 1931 through 1967, the authors calculate the market sensitivity for common stocks listed on the NYSE.

[6] Jack Clark Francis and Stephen H. Archer, *Portfolio Analysis* (Prentice-Hall, Inc.: 1971) present an advanced discussion of portfolio theory.

[7] William F. Sharpe and Guy M. Cooper, "Risk-Return Classes of New York Stock Exchange Common Stocks, 1931–67," *Financial Analysts Journal*, March–April 1972, pp. 46–54 ff.

They report that "the number of securities for which market sensitivity was calculated ranged from 478 (in 1931) to 985 (in 1967)." For each year of the study, each stock was classified into one of 10 categories ranging from highest risk to lowest risk, as measured by market sensitivity. With this information the authors then tested the outcomes of various strategies of constructing portfolios of stocks in various risk classes.

In reporting their results, the authors observe that for average annual returns the general relationship is that portfolios of stocks in higher risk classes tend to provide a higher average return. However, for an "investor concerned *only* with the very long run (in this case, 36 years)" the outcome is much less clear. Portfolios of higher-risk stocks typically provide a higher average return, but with greater variability of portfolio returns over time. Because of the compounding process over time, "the net effect over the very long term is thus relatively unpredictable."[8] To illustrate, based on annualized returns from 1931 through 1967, the annual return from the highest risk strategy was 14.5 percent while that of the lowest-risk strategy was 9.9 percent. However, the highest return was 15.8 percent, but this was associated with an intermediate risk strategy. Furthermore returns from combining medium-risk stocks into portfolios, were in the range of 14.0 percent to 14.6 percent, results not very dissimilar from the 14.5 percent return from the highest-risk strategy.[9] In summary, the results of this study of NYSE common stocks demonstrate the need for caution in accepting statements that high returns are associated with high risk.[10]

Additional evidence indicates that higher *realized* returns are not necessarily associated with higher risk. A recent study examines portfolio returns from stocks on a regional over-the-counter (OTC) market from 1946 through 1967.[11] This market is comprised principally of shares of small new companies ineligible for listing on the New York

---

[8] *Ibid.*, p. 51.

[9] *Ibid.* Returns are from Figure IVc, p. 52, except the returns of 14.0 and 14.6 percent. These were derived from Figure IVc by taking the arithmetic average of the returns reported for the middle two risk classes (5 and 6) and middle four risk classes (4 to 7), respectively.

[10] Confirming this need for caution, an advanced study reports on a large sample of common stocks divided into six risk classes. Consistently the portfolios of stocks in the highest-risk category are associated with the lowest realized returns. As reported by Robert M. Soldofsky and Roger L. Miller, "Risk-Premium Curves for Different Classes of Long-Term Securities, 1950–66," *The Journal of Finance*, June 1969, pp. 429–445 (esp. Table 1, p. 436). A rather technical follow-up "Comment" and "Reply" to this article were published in *The Journal of Finance*, September 1972, pp. 933–943.

[11] Paul F. Jessup and Roger B. Upson, "Opportunities in Regional Markets," *Financial Analysts Journal*, March–April 1970, pp. 75–79.

Stock Exchange because of their small size and brief corporate histories. Of the 235 stocks that were traded in this market sometime during the time period 1946 through 1967, almost *20 percent* were valueless by the end of 1967. Among various criteria, such a proportion of valueless securities indicates that investing in stocks in this regional OTC market involves more risk than investing in NYSE stocks. Notably, however, portfolio returns from these regional OTC stocks seldom exceed those from portfolios of NYSE stocks. Strong support of these results from one regional OTC market is reported in a subsequent, more comprehensive study of returns from stocks quoted in various OTC markets.[12]

Results from several studies of returns from common stocks do not necessarily refute the HR-HR view. However, a major study of returns from various risk classes of corporate bonds also concludes that high-risk bonds do not provide higher realized returns than low-risk bonds.[13] Thus, while the HR-HR view is not conclusively disproved by various studies, its credibility is reduced, especially when its support involves selected examples of successful risky stocks or short-run records of several mutual funds holding portfolios of high-risk stocks during a major stock market advance. In conclusion, realistic investors, while reserving judgment, will remain skeptical of the view that high risks lead to high returns.

[12] Paul F. Jessup and Roger B. Upson, *Returns in Over-the-Counter Stock Markets*, (University of Minnesota Press: 1973).

[13] This study and others are reviewed in an article by Lemont K. Richardson, "Do High Risks Lead to High Returns?" *Financial Analysts Journal*, March–April 1970, pp. 88–92 ff.

REVIEW OF PART THREE

Question: How shall I evaluate common stocks?

Answer: The answer conventionally offered to individual investors is that they should learn as much as possible about any stock they own or are considering owning. This conventional answer encourages current or potential investors to become part-time analysts of stocks. It stresses the need for individual investors to learn basic techniques of stock analysis, such as how to read corporate financial reports, and how to use price-earnings ratios for evaluating stocks.

How does the conventional answer respond to serious part-time analysts who become aware of practical complexities of evaluating stocks? For example, their readings and personal investment experience soon alert serious part-time analysts to problems of earnings credibility in a changing accounting environment. The conventional answer to such growing awareness encourages serious investors to commit themselves *even more fully* to mastering the skills of stock analysis.

The conventional answer, however, fails on two major counts. First, it neglects to specify the costs involved in trying to be a part-time analyst. For many individuals the costs include not only cash outlays but also a potentially large commitment of personal time and effort. Second, the conventional answer basically accepts the market-opportunity view (Chapters 2 and 3). It assumes that commitment to part-time stock analysis is likely to prove rewarding to serious, diligent investors.

Going beyond the conventional answer, Part Three provides answers to two basic, related questions:

How can an investor begin to evaluate common stocks?
Should an investor strive to become a part-time stock analyst?

An investor can begin to evaluate common stocks by learning basic techniques of security analysis. Knowledge of a company's past and current operations is the usual basis for projecting its future prospects. Stock analysis therefore rests on skills in analyzing corporate financial reports. Often an analyst must dig deeply into a company's financial reports to assess whether and how reported results are related to the choice of accounting procedures. The analyst may decide to adjust reported information to make it more useful for his past comparisons and future projections. A part-time analyst can commit himself to acquiring these basic analytical skills used by full-time analysts.

To select among the many available stocks, an investor needs a valuation procedure judged useful for distinguishing between undervalued and overvalued stocks. Price-earnings ratios are popularly cited for use in assessing a stock's relative value. Popular use of P-E ratios is suspect. P-E ratios are easily misleading if their components—such as *which* EPS figure—are not carefully specified. Also they logically fail to provide a basis for evaluating common stocks. In contrast, the P_v model for discounting future streams of dividends is logically impeccable. The P_v model can be simplified for easier use, but then the user is locked into the simplifying assumptions. This dilemma can be avoided by working with the general P_v model on a computer. Most individual investors, however, do not have ready access to extensive computer facilities. Despite practical problems of specific applications, the P_v model provides an appropriate conceptual framework for rationally assessing a stock's price relative to the discounted stream of expected benefits from the stock. Part-time analysts can commit themselves to learning more about the theory and practice of stock valuation.

Risk analysis is another basic aspect of stock evaluation. Unfortunately the term "risk" is used in diverse ways by investors and investment commentators. Not only is the term potentially misleading in practice, but there is no general agreement about risk in principle. Thus confronted by unresolved issues, stock analysts cannot dismiss the need to assess a stock's risk dimensions. They must remain open to new methods that attempt rigorously to specify and measure risk. Beta has become popularized as such a risk measure, with less specific attention to its potential pitfalls. Modern portfolio theory builds on assumptions and theorems about risk and provides new insights into various dimensions of risk. Part-time analysts thus can commit themselves to learning much more about how risk analysis can be used to evaluate not only individual stocks but also potential combinations of stocks into portfolios.

Once introduced to basic techniques for evaluating common stocks, serious part-time analysts soon realize that diligent analysis is a demanding part-time occupation. In-depth evaluation of a stock cannot rely on short-cut methods applied to summary information available to the general investing public. In-depth evaluation requires a part-time analyst to devote almost a full-time effort. For perspective, professional analysts devoting full time to stock valuation are not usually expected to remain well informed about stocks of more than 30 to 50 different companies. Therefore a devoted part-time analyst is likely to be able to evaluate even a smaller number of stocks for his potential purchase or sale.

Individual investors can begin to evaluate common stocks by learning basic analytical techniques. As they appreciate the complexities of detailed analysis, they can commit themselves to additional refinements and applications of basic techniques. However, unless commitment to part-time analysis is itself a goal, an individual investor should ask himself a related question: *Should* I strive to be part-time analyst?

Committing individual resources to evaluating common stocks is generally warranted only if expected benefits can be reasonably expected to exceed the costs of being a serious part-time analyst.

An abundance of investment opportunities that will adequately reward part-time analysis is unlikely to exist in a competitive market. Competition among many skillful investors reduces the probability that exceptional investment opportunities can be consistently identified (Chapters 2 and 3). Many of these competing skillful participants are committed full-time to the profession of investment management. Before committing themselves to part-time analysis, individuals should put their commitment in the perspective of a competitive market.

Also before committing themselves to part-time evaluation of single stocks, individual investors should adopt a portfolio perspective. Emphasis on part-time stock analysis potentially detracts from focus on the benefits of portfolio diversification. Diversification facilitates reduction of the impact of the risk of individual stocks. Furthermore, as will be shown in Part Six, there is a strong case for many individuals to focus on evaluating *portfolios of stocks* instead of striving to be part-time analysts of *individual stocks*.

* * *

Basic concepts of stock valuation and modern portfolio theory are compressed into the four chapters of Part Three, which challenges conventional justification for part-time stock analysis. To become committed to part-time analysis is a personal decision. Toward this end, additional reading from the following recent books is encouraged.

I. Basically introductory books:

Bolten, Steven E., *Security Analysis and Portfolio Management: An Analytical Approach to Investments* (Holt, Rinehart and Winston, Inc.: 1972).

Francis, Jack Clark, *Investments: Analysis and Management* (McGraw-Hill Book Company: 1972).

Graham, Benjamin, David L. Dodd, and Sidney Cottle, *Security Analysis: Principles and Technique*, 4th ed. (McGraw-Hill Book Company: 1962). While not as recent as the other books in this list, this volume is a comprehensive classic that remains useful to serious security analysts.

Latané, Henry A., and Donald L. Tuttle, *Security Analysis and Portfolio Management* (The Ronald Press Company: 1970). This volume is more mathematical than the others in section I.

Williamson, J. Peter, *Investments: New Analytic Techniques* (Praeger Publishers: 1970).

II. These books focus more on modern portfolio theory, usually involving more mathematical notation:

Francis, Jack Clark, and Stephen H. Archer, *Portfolio Analysis* (Prentice-Hall, Inc.: 1971).

Levy, Haim, and Marshall Sarnat, *Investment and Portfolio Analysis* (John Wiley & Sons, Inc.: 1972).

Markowitz, Harry M., *Portfolio Selection: Efficient Diversification of Investments*, Monograph 16 (Cowles Foundation for Research in Economics at Yale University: 1959). This classic book is generally agreed to be the basis for modern portfolio theory.

Renwick, Fred B., *Introduction to Investments and Finance: Theory and Analysis* (The Macmillan Company: 1971).

Sharpe, William F., *Portfolio Theory and Capital Markets* (McGraw-Hill Book Company: 1970).

Smith, Keith V., *Portfolio Management: Theoretical and Empirical Studies of Portfolio Decision-Making* (Holt, Rinehart and Winston, Inc.: 1971).

PART FOUR
EVALUATING SOME BASIC INVESTMENT STRATEGIES

chapter 10
Growth Stocks

Proponents of a growth-stock strategy often summarize their case as follows:

Investors who want to increase their capital in future decades should buy growth stocks. Such stocks are especially suitable for younger investors who plan to build an estate over time and do not require much current dividend income. Substantial capital gains and growth in dividends are the likely rewards to investors who construct portfolios of good growth stocks.

Conventional investments books typically build on such a growth-stock doctrine. They present examples of historically notable growth stocks and suggest methods to help individuals identify and select growth stocks.

Because the growth-stock doctrine is widely accepted, a dissenting viewpoint is easily dismissed as heresy or foolishness. Open-minded investors, however, welcome challenges to conventional doctrine. They want to know the validity of a growth-stock strategy, in principle and in practice.

Identifying Growth Companies

What is a "growth company"? The answer depends almost entirely on the criteria various investment writers use to identify "growth companies." All focus on a company's having an above-average rate of growth in its earnings per share (EPS) over time. Furthermore they insist that the EPS growth reflect corporate progress, not just a company's creativity in modifying its reporting practices. Beyond this basic requirement of a credible, above-average, growth rate in EPS, many analysts and investors specify various additional criteria for identifying growth companies.

The magnitude of a company's *superiority* in EPS growth can be used to distinguish "growth" from "nongrowth" companies. In a growing economy, most companies are expected to show EPS growth. What is newsworthy are companies with substantially above-average growth. To illustrate, the average EPS growth rate of the 425 companies whose shares comprise the Standard and Poor's Industrial Index can serve as a comparative standard. To qualify as a growth company, analysts agree that a firm's EPS growth must be superior to such a standard; but they differ on the magnitude of this superiority. For example, if the average EPS growth is four to six percent per year, then some analysts will classify a firm as a growth company only if its EPS growth is, say, greater than eight percent. Others may insist on 10 or 12 percent as minimum standards. In addition, they may identify as "supergrowth" companies those having an EPS growth rate greater than 15 or 20 percent.

Consistency of superior EPS growth also is usually necessary for identifying growth companies. Such consistency can have several dimensions. First, an initial minimum duration, such as three or five years, of superior EPS growth can be required. Second, for firms once identified as growth companies, a maximum interruption of their records can be specified. To illustrate, companies can retain their growth classification if their annual growth rates only occasionally drop, for example, to the average rate. Some analysts go even further in their identification of growth companies by focusing on rates of change in EPS growth on a seasonally adjusted quarter-to-quarter basis. In summary, because their standards of superiority and consistency of EPS growth rates vary, investment analysts often differ in their identification of growth companies.

Investors and analysts do not analyze *past* EPS growth rates as an exercise in past history. They seek to identify *future* growth companies, therefore they use generally available past information as a guide. In focusing on past growth rates of companies such as Avon Products, IBM, and Xerox, most analysts and investors use such information as guides to possible future growth rates which, after all, is the key practical issue.

To answer whether past growth companies are likely to continue growing in the future, many analysts and investors evaluate additional factors, as illustrated by the following summary checklist of questions:

Is the company in a growth industry (or in growth industries)?

Is the company a principal factor in its industry?

To maintain and improve its competitive position, does the company commit major resources, for example, to research and development and to marketing?

Is management innovative, so that the company can sustain or increase its growth rate in a competitive economy?

Although intended as guides to a company's future growth rate in EPS, answers to such questions basically are derived from generally available past and current corporate information. Also, while many competing financial analysts differ in the importance they assign to various aspects of past information, they devote their careers to developing and distributing their evaluations of the future prospects of various growth companies.

Valuing Growth Companies

Growth stocks are not necessarily the same as growth companies.[1] This important distinction is overlooked by many investors.

Growth companies are identified by specific *corporate* attributes, such as rate of growth of EPS, industry position, and commitment to research and development. As shown, past information about such factors often is used as a guide to identifying above-average future corporate growth, especially of EPS.

Companies that provide above-average future growth in EPS eventually will be able to pay out increasing dividends to their shareholders. By currently accepting a lower level of current dividends from a company having unusually profitable investment opportunities, today's investor is hoping that eventually this strategy will yield substantially higher dividends on his stock. Furthermore, if his judgment is correct, then the market price of the stock is likely to be subsequently higher, reflecting the actual growth in the company's earnings and dividends. In this way, investment in a growth company can result in substantial capital gains, a component of total investor returns. Thus investor returns from such a stock over time should be substantially above aver-

[1] Peter L. Bernstein, "Growth Companies vs. Growth Stocks," *Harvard Business Review*, September–October 1956, pp. 87–98. Although Mr. Bernstein clearly calls attention to this important distinction, the views expressed in his article differ somewhat from those developed in this section.

age, qualifying the stock as a "growth stock." While such a strategy sounds fine in theory, how practical is it over time in a world of uncertainty and in a competitive market?

Competing analysts and investors know the distinguished records of growth (both in EPS and share prices) of companies such as American Hospital Supply, Avon Products, IBM, Polaroid, and Xerox. Furthermore they are continually evaluating future growth prospects of these and other companies. Their evaluations are based on generally available information about a company, its competitors, industry conditions, and the general economy. Furthermore no one security analyst who interviews top management is likely to have unique access to new information about a company. Large publicly owned companies are required to make prompt, public announcements of major new developments. While there is a continual process of reexamining possible future corporate prospects, especially in response to new information, at any one time a stock's price reflects competing evaluations of the company's EPS prospects relative to those of other investment opportunities. Thus, for example, today's stock prices of IBM and Xerox summarize, on the margin, investor expectations about future prospects of these companies and their shares. Also, if investors generally are more confident about the future prospects of these firms compared with some small new companies in competitive technological industries, then this relatively greater confidence also is reflected in the current stock prices. In a competitive market, current prices are a best estimate of what a stock is currently worth to many competing investors.

If an investor today plans to invest in a stock having a distinguished record of past growth (EPS and share price) and bright prospects of future growth, then he should explicitly recognize that many other investors are similarly aware of this stock. To illustrate, examination of its current P-E ratio is likely to show that the stock is selling around 30 times last year's reported EPS, whereas shares of some large mature companies are currently selling around 15 times their last year's EPS. If these various figures are credible and not abnormal, then the price of the stock selling at the relatively high P-E ratio almost certainly reflects investor expectations about future EPS growth. In other words, other investors also see this as a growth company, and the competitively determined market price already is discounting the company's future corporate prospects as evaluated by many competing investors.

There are four principal investment outcomes for an investor who proceeds to invest in a popular growth stock, selling, for example, at 30 times its recent EPS. All four are related to the occurrence of future events that lead to revised evaluations of corporate prospects. (To illustrate, while next year's EPS of IBM are today uncertain, when the figure becomes available it will provide new information for investors to use in reexamining, at that point in time, their future expectations about the company and its shares. This dynamic process contributes to revision of market prices over time.) These four principal outcomes, representing a broad distribution of possible outcomes, are for a reasonable time horizon, say one to three years.

Outcome One: expected future growth in EPS fails to occur. In a dynamic competitive economy, there are many unpredictable factors outside the control even of very capable corporate managers. Abrupt shifts in consumer taste, major new competition, revised government policies, and unforeseen production difficulties are some of the future events that can suddenly disrupt any company's record of EPS growth. Instead of growing, profits then can decline. Unless many investors see such events as merely transitory, the stock's price will fall, reflecting revised expectations of many investors about the company's future growth. Outcome one exemplifies a former growth company that no longer is identified or valued as a growth company by investors.

Outcome Two: EPS grows in the future; but not as rapidly as generally expected. Many events, as outlined above, also can contribute to slowing down a company's superior growth rate of EPS. The company, while not showing a decline in its EPS, no longer maintains the past record that qualified it as a growth company. Investors aware of this new information will reexamine their expectations about this company; and, associated with this revision process, the stock price most likely will fall. In the example, investors will be unwilling to continue paying a price for a stock that results in a current P-E ratio of 30 if the company's new results no longer qualify it as a growth company.

Outcome Three: EPS continues to grow in the future about the same as in the past. For example, the company continues to report credible annual increases of about 12 percent in its EPS; to increase periodically its cash dividend; and to commit substantial funds to developing new products and markets. This new information confirms the views of investors who see this firm as a growth company; and the stock's price is likely to reflect these sustained expectations. Thus, in the example the stock's price is likely to increase so that it continues to be around 30 times the newly reported, higher, EPS. While the stock price is likely to increase for this third possible outcome, the increase need not be a major upward movement. As described, the growth company's results are basically an extension of its past record that was known to many investors and reflected in its previous share prices. The subsequent growth, although realized, already has been somewhat discounted in the stock's previous prices.

Outcome Four: the company's EPS growth rate suddenly accelerates because of events that were generally unpredictable. For example, a major research breakthrough results in a patentable product, for which potential demand is substantial. While such an unanticipated acceleration can possibly occur, it is unlikely to happen for most large growth companies continually monitored by many analysts and investors. (For example, although possible, how probable is it that IBM or Xerox suddenly can accelerate its distinguished record of corporate growth?) Nevertheless, if a "growth" company suddenly becomes generally reclassified as a "supergrowth" company by many analysts and investors, then its price can jump sharply. Revised expectations can result in a higher price, so that the illustrative growth stock selling for 30 times recent EPS can shortly be selling at a higher price that results in a P-E ratio of, say, 50 times recent earnings. Substantial capital gains and, hence, high total investment returns thus will result from outcome four.

Four principal investment outcomes are thus possible from today's investment in the stock of a growth company. The future return from this investment is uncertain, since it is linked to which of the outcomes in fact occurs. Investing in the stock of any growth company thus is risky, although usually less risky in a large diversified growth company than in a small new one-product company in a highly competitive industry.

Predicting Returns from Growth-Stock Portfolios

To reduce the risk of investing in any one growth company, an investor can diversify among shares of different growth companies. (For brevity, this now will be called a *growth-stock portfolio*.) Among the stocks in his portfolio, some will be of companies whose growth suddenly ends and, at the other extreme, others will be of firms that unpredictably become "supergrowth" companies. What total returns should an investor expect over time from a portfolio diversified among shares of growth companies?

The *growth-stock* view indicates that returns from diversified growth-stock portfolios will provide long-term investors with higher total returns than will broadly diversified portfolios of common stocks. After all, investing in stocks of growth companies within growth industries would seem to be a promising long-run investment strategy. However, according to the *competitive-market* view, since many investors are competing for shares of growth companies, competitively determined market prices will discount much of a company's expected growth. Not that the market is always correct in its expectations for individual stocks; but market estimates, reflected in price, generally are as good, or better, than those of any one investor or analyst. For this reason growth-stock portfolios are unlikely to provide consistently or substantially higher returns than broadly diversified portfolios of common stocks.

Does evidence support the growth-stock view or the competitive-market view?

Ten growth stocks were recommended in a popular investments book published in 1956.[2] The recommended stocks included Aluminum Company of America, Corning Glass Works, Dow Chemical and, of course, IBM. An investor, wanting to reduce individual stock risk by diversification, is likely to have spread his initial investment (at year-end 1956) among all 10 of the stocks. What were his investment results? Were his subsequent portfolio returns substantially higher than those available from broadly diversified portfolios of common stocks, as measured, for example, by the annual rates of return from the Standard & Poor's Index of 425 industrial stocks? Through year-end 1970 the annual rate of return from the growth-stock portfolio was about eight percent, while that from the S & P Index also was about eight percent. Thus any difference is minor.

Fifteen "AAA rated" growth stocks were cited in an article about growth stocks in 1960.[3] The list included distinguished corporate names such as Aluminum Company of America, Eastman Kodak, Minneapolis-Honeywell, Minnesota Mining and Manufacturing and, of course, IBM. An investor seeking diversification is likely to have spread his initial investment (at year-end 1960) among all 15 stocks. How do the rates of return from this 15-stock growth portfolio compare with those from the S & P 425 stocks? The annualized rate of return from the growth-stock portfolio was about six percent through 1970, in contrast to eight percent for the 425 stocks. While many of the 15 growth companies grew on the average over the 1960s, this growth had been largely discounted in previous market prices.

Two tests do not conclusively disprove the growth-stock view. Its proponents can claim that the subsequent time periods were inadequate; the illustrative portfolios would have been revised to substitute "more-promising" stocks for those that were "performing poorly;" or other initial portfolios of growth stocks (e.g., those of smaller, "less-monitored" companies) would have provided higher returns. Also they can cite examples of some investors who reportedly have been relatively successful by following the growth-stock strategy in some

[2] Carl Roth and John T. McKenzie, *Standard & Poor's Selecting Stocks To Buy for Profit.* (Henry Holt and Company: 1956), p. 8.

[3] John F. Bohmfalk, Jr., "The Growth Stock Philosophy," *Financial Analysts Journal*, November–December 1960, pp. 113–123.

past time periods. Additional evidence is clearly welcome. Unfortunately many brokerage firms and advisory services apparently fail to retain their *past* lists of recommended growth stocks.

While one welcomes further evidence, the logical point of reference remains: in a competitive market, why *should* an investor expect consistently and substantially above-average returns from a growth-stock strategy?[4] To illustrate, toward year-end 1972, shares of the following companies were among the largest holdings of the four largest mutual funds having "growth" as a principal investment objective:

Avon Products
International Business Machines
McDonald's
Polaroid

Unless competing investors fail to discount appropriately the possible future growth of such large, well-monitored companies, following a growth-stock strategy is unlikely to provide future returns above general-market returns. Investors who prefer to apply a growth-stock strategy to less-known, "emerging growth companies" will profit from the next chapter, New Issues.

[4] A case for growth stocks recently was presented by Walter R. Good, "Valuation of Quality-Growth Stocks," *Financial Analysts Journal*, September–October 1972, pp. 47–54 ff.

chapter 11
New Issues

The potential payoff from buying new issues of common stock often is suggested by the following types of observations.

New issues enable investors to participate in emerging growth companies from the beginning. For example, shares of Kentucky Fried Chicken were first publicly offered at $15 in 1966. In about five years, through stock splits, each original share grew to $7\frac{1}{2}$ shares; these were worth about $20 each, representing a total capital appreciation of about 900 percent over the new-issue price.

Stock of Educational Computer Corp. was first offered to the public in 1968 at $7.25 per share. In about four months the stock was selling for the equivalent of $260.

Stock in Communications Satellite was offered to the public in 1964 at $20 per share. Later the same day the stock's price was about $26.

Alert to selected hindsight, sensible investors require more comprehensive examination of investor experience in new issues. Therefore this chapter provides answers to the following questions:

Why *should* investors expect above-average returns from investing in new issues of common stock?

What is the evidence concerning investment returns from purchasing new issues over time?

Answers to these questions enable investors realistically to assess their opportunities in new issues.

Participating in Emerging Growth Companies from the Beginning

What can give greater financial and personal satisfaction to investors than today purchasing shares in a company that will generate a future record similar to those of Avon Products, IBM, or Xerox in recent years? Because many security analysts and investors closely monitor stocks that today are well known for their past growth records, the market prices of such stocks reflect past information and current expectations. In a competitive market, this discounting process reduces opportunities for above-average returns from shares of popular growth companies. However, current popularity was not always the case. All stocks were comparatively obscure new issues at one time. Therefore why not search among new issues for emerging growth companies? Timely purchases of only several highly successful new issues can provide high returns. How feasible is such a strategy?

From a market viewpoint, "new issues" of common stock refer to shares being publicly offered for the first time. This viewpoint, used in this book, contrasts with the corporate viewpoint whereby a publicly owned company at times sells new (additional) stock. For example, many major electrical utilities and banks periodically sell additional shares to their existing public shareholders or to the general public. However, since a market already exists for the stock, the new (additional) stock is offered at a price closely associated with the market price of the outstanding shares, again illustrating how market price is the focal point of a stock's value.

New stock issues cover a broad range, from those of *established companies* to those of *new ventures*. Established companies have corporate histories that include information about a company's products or services, markets, and past revenues and profits. To illustrate, during the past 20 years shares of the following companies were first publicly offered: Campbell Soup; Ford; Merrill Lynch, Pierce, Fenner & Smith; and Upjohn. At the time of their public offerings, these companies already were well known; and there was extensive past operating information that could be made available to potential investors. In contrast, new ventures have little or no past history. They often involve new products or new concepts. A prominent illustration of a new venture is Communications Satellite Corporation (Comsat). It had no operating history when its shares were first offered to the public in 1964. The proceeds from its sale of stock were used to develop, for the first time, a communications system centered around space satellites. Most new ventures have less prominence and less initial financial support than did Comsat, and they represent generally the expectations of new teams of corporate managers and their initial financial sponsors.

By purchasing stock in a new venture, an investor is possibly buying into an emerging growth company near its beginning. Other investors, however, typically can buy stock at even lower prices. New ventures generally are created by organizers, promoters and sometimes, investment banking firms that will subsequently sell the stock to the public. In return for their contributions of some property, skills, or creative ideas, organizers often are able to buy—or obtain options to buy—shares at dollar costs below the public offering price. Similarly, diverse investment banking firms compete for the opportunity to sell new issues of common stock. These firms are directly compensated by underwriting or sales fees and, at times, indirectly by receiving securities enabling them to participate in the subsequent profits, if any, of the new venture. To generate new issues for public sale, some investment banking firms have established venture-capital affiliates that provide "seed money" to promising small ventures. Those ventures compiling an initial record of operating success then can have public offerings of their shares, but in such cases the public investors are not participating from the beginning. In summary, since new ventures are created by profit-oriented organizers, promoters, or sellers, why should the buying public believe that it is being offered unusually attractive profit opportunities?

A new issue can be a *primary* or *secondary* offering or a combination of the two. A primary offering is when the cash proceeds from the public sale of stock go entirely to the company for corporate purposes. The initial offering of Comsat was a primary offering. A secondary offering is when the cash proceeds go to selling stockholders of what previously had been a closely held company. The initial offering of Ford was made by the Ford Foundation that reinvested much of its sale proceeds in other securities in order to diversify its investment portfolio. Diversification is but one of many reasons why shareholders in a closely held company choose to sell shares. Both in primary and secondary offerings the companies and the selling stockholders basically are selling shares to meet their objectives, not to provide unusually attractive opportunities to the general public.

To protect investors, offerings of new stock issues generally are subject to legal and regulatory restrictions. A proposed offering to residents in several states typically must be registered with the Securities and Exchange Commission (SEC). A prospectus containing extensive information about the company must be filed with the SEC. For an established company the prospectus will contain detailed information about the company's past operations and some general statements about its future prospects. For a new venture, relatively greater emphasis will be on the company's organizers and general plans. Accuracy of information reported in a prospectus is reviewed by the staff of the SEC. Note, however, that the SEC does not try to protect the investing public by judging the relative merits of a new issue but, rather, by insisting on full and fair disclosure. By law, sellers of a new issue must provide a copy of the prospectus to potential purchasers who, by using this information to assess possible returns and risk, are expected to protect themselves through informed decisions. As additional protection, investors can seek legal recourse against the organizers and sellers of a new issue if the information contained in the prospectus subsequently is shown to be erroneous.

Exemption from SEC regulation is possible for new stock issues to be sold only within a state. However the various states have diverse laws and regulations governing such intrastate new issues. Some states have laws requiring the securities commissioner to try to protect state residents by prohibiting the sale of securities of doubtful potential. These so-called *blue-sky laws*, intended to prevent promoters from selling novice investors "a piece of blue sky," thus involve greater discretionary power for state officials than in other states that, similar to the SEC, basically require only full and fair disclosure. Therefore a potential investor in intrastate new issues will want to learn the type of protection provided by the laws and regulations of his state.

When do companies go public with new issues? Periods of generally increasing stock prices provide an opportune environment for new issues. During such periods, closely held companies are encouraged to have a public offering in order to establish a market price for their shares. Furthermore, established companies that have recently compiled impressive growth records can go public with their demonstrated performance as a selling point. (Not many companies are likely to have new issues if their preceding operating performance has been comparatively poor.) Similarly, when stock prices are generally high, investors typically are more receptive to public offerings by new ventures. In the past decade there was a proliferation of offerings by new companies proposing to enter popular areas such as bowling alleys, computer hardware and software, electronics, and franchising. Some of these new ventures subsequently proved successful as companies and as investments. However, many failed to develop and are forgotten except by investors who have basically written them off.

The phenomenon of disappearing new issues is illustrated by a SEC study that attempted to trace the results of 504 companies that had new issues from 1952 to 1962.[1] The SEC staff, with its resources, could not find a trace of 12 percent of the companies. Furthermore 43 percent of the companies had been dissolved, liquidated, or placed in re-

---

[1] Cited in *The Wall Street Journal*, August 7, 1968, p. 1.

ceivership; and 26 percent, although still in business, had reported losses in their most recent financial reports. Such outcomes are easily forgotten or neglected in popular stock market communications. More conveniently cited are examples of the new issues that subsequently proved successful.

Benefitting from Underpricing of New Issues

It is certainly news when a new stock issue offered early one day sells later the same day at a much higher price. Such rapid price appreciation is illustrated by some past new issues.[2]

> Shares of Friendly Ice Cream Corp. were offered to the public at $28 each early one afternoon in 1968. Within hours they were quoted at around $50, and they closed the day at around $45.

> A new issue of Holobeam. Inc, was offered to the public at $12.50 in 1968. In the same day the price subsequently climbed to about $30.00 a share.

Investors buying such issues at the offering price can achieve rapid price gains. Repeating this process over time will be an unusually attractive investment strategy, offering high annualized returns. Before committing much money, practical investors will question the feasibility of obtaining such high returns in a competitive market.

The general wisdom is that sellers of a new issue have incentives to set an offering price somewhat below the price that will just clear the market. For example, if a syndicate of investment banking firms decides that a new issue is likely to have a competitively determined market price of about $12 per share, it may choose to set the initial offering price at $10, expecting the stock's price to increase quickly to about $12 in the "after-market" established for the new stock. Intentional underpricing of a new issue has been justified by the following line of reasoning.

1. Investment banking firms cannot be very confident which price will just clear the market for a new issue. (This is especially the case for new ventures being sold principally as "a concept" with highly uncertain future outcomes.) Because of this *uncertainty*, it is preferable to try to underprice an issue instead of setting a higher price at which the issue may not sell well.

[2] Cited in *The Wall Street Journal*, August 7, 1968, pp. 1, 14.

2. Investment bankers benefit from participating in new issues that sell out quickly and then increase in price in the after-market. Their marketing skills are favorably publicized; their clients who bought shares at the offering price are pleased; and, if underwriting the sale, their chances of an unprofitable offering are substantially reduced.

3. The company in which the shares are sold also can benefit by an initial offering in which the shares are somewhat underpriced. A successful offering, with the shares increasing in price in the after-market, should please the initial public shareholders and also help broaden recognition of the company's stock. This successful image may be remembered by present and potential shareholders if and when the company later decides to sell additional stock.

4. Various shareholder groups benefit from a bias toward underpricing of new issues. Shareholders who buy at the initial offering price are rewarded by the rapid adjustment of the price to a competitively determined market price. Furthermore the organizers or original shareholders of a closely held company also benefit because they are likely to retain a substantial percentage of the company's stock after the initial public offering. To illustrate, the principal shareholders of a closely held firm may sell 0.5 million shares in a secondary offering and retain 4.5 million shares. If the stock is sold out to public investors at $10 and goes quickly to $12, the value of the substantial holdings of the principal shareholders now can be related to a competitively determined market price. Also the initial success may contribute to investor receptivity to subsequent secondary offerings of the company's stock at higher prices.

Some of these conventional reasons rest on the questionable assumption that investors have long memories and allegiances.

Although there can be a bias toward the underpricing of new issues, there cannot be *substantial* or *consistent* underpricing in a market in which many investment banking firms are competing to sell new issues. While there is no direct competitive bidding for new stock issues, investment banking firms are constrained by market forces in their negotiations for new issues. They must try to serve the various parties to a new issue: themselves, various shareholders, and the company having its shares sold. An investment banking firm that tries to underprice new issues by a substantial amount may create a satisfied clientele of new-issue buyers who profit from the substantial price increases. However, on the other side, the companies or major shareholders who sold the stock are likely to question why they did not receive higher prices.

Minor underpricing can be acceptable to them, but not substantial underpricing.

Because only minor underpricing is a feasible goal, new issues cannot be consistently underpriced. While an investment banking firm may try to underprice its new issues by a small amount, such as five percent, major uncertainties surround the stocks' after-market prices. Therefore, of the new issues intended to increase about five percent in price in the aftermarket, some will increase, say, by 20 to 30 percent and some will decline so that the market price is below the initial offering price. Thus, although *some* new issues turn out to have been substantially underpriced, there cannot be substantial or consistent underpricing of new issues in general.

Look for Yourself

Each week *Barron's* has a list of the subsequent market prices of selected new issues. Inspection of several of these tabulations will show that while some have substantially higher prices, many others trade near their initial offering prices, and some have market prices below their offering prices.

"Hot" new issues are those in which the market prices are likely to increase sharply and quickly above initial offering prices. While most new issues cannot have such substantial short-run price appreciation, what are the probable returns to investors who learn about and participate in hot new issues?

Learning about hot new issues is relatively easy because of the subscription process used for selling new issues. An interstate new issue usually is offered by a syndicate of investment banking firms temporarily combining their marketing skills. Officials of the firms evaluate the issue to try to agree on a suitable offering price. The proposed offering then is registered with the SEC, which reviews the preliminary prospectus. If approved, the syndicate sets a final offering price that is publicized among the firms' salesmen who will then inform their clients whose investment goals are judged to be met by the new issue. Interested clients then must indicate how many shares they want to buy at the offering price. Since a new issue offering generally involves a specified total number of shares, if many clients, for whatever their reasons, begin requesting shares, their demand will begin to exceed the supply of available stock. In such a case, the new issue is said to be "hot." Furthermore, since the offering price also is set, the price is likely to be higher in the competitive after-market. Other investors hearing about a potentially hot issue also will express their desire to participate, thus adding to the total demand. When there is excess demand for a new issue at its offering price, it is said to be *oversubscribed*.

Although investors can usually learn about hot new issues, they find it impossible to participate fully in many such issues. When issues are oversubscribed at a set price, the demand can be met only through an *allocation* process. Since hot issues are potentially profitable for investors initially receiving shares, investment banking firms basically are distributing potential profits to selected clients. Such a distribution can be done using diverse allocation procedures.

Investment banking firms are likely to allocate hot new issues only among existing clients or potentially profitable new clients. Since most investors have accounts with only one firm, they are likely to participate, at most, only in the occasional hot issues of that firm. They are unlikely to receive allocations in the hot issues of other firms. This procedure insures that investors cannot possibly participate in all hot issues they learn about.

Even among a firm's clients, at least three different allocation procedures can be used. First, the shares can be allocated on a pro-rata basis. For example, if clients subscribe to 400,000 shares and a firm has only 200,000 shares to allocate, then each subscriber will receive one-half his original subscription. Second, the shares can be allocated on a first-come first-served basis whereby the earliest subscribers receive their full requests and later subscribers get none. Third, allocations can be used to reward clients who are most profitable to the firm and its salesmen. To illustrate, two clients each subscribe to 200 shares of a hot issue. One client owns only a small total amount of stock and infrequently buys or sells. He does not generate much brokerage revenue for the investment banking firm and the salesman. The second client is a wealthy investor with an active account that contributes substantial revenue to the firm and the salesman. Given only 200 shares to allocate between the two subscribers, and other things equal, how are the shares likely to be allocated? Since investment banking firms and their salesmen presumably focus on long-run profits, their allocation of most hot issues is likely to reflect their profit goals.

Measuring Returns from New Issues

The rationing process for hot new issues again demonstrates that "there is no such thing as a free lunch." Hot issues are difficult to obtain because each investment banking firm has only some for its clients, and among these clients the allocation "rewards" realistically can be viewed as partial rebates to clients who contribute substantially to the firm's revenues. This rationing process must be explicitly recognized because examples and studies of new issues frequently assume that investors can buy various new issues at their offering prices. To illustrate, one study reports on returns from 53 new issues offered from December 1963 to June 1965.[3] Of these 53 issues, at least 30 were oversubscribed, yet much of the analysis of possible investor returns assumes purchase of all the issues at their offering price.

In the practical world of investments, it is invalid to assume that any investor can purchase equal dollar amounts of various new issues. He will receive, at best, only limited allocations of hot issues. (To illustrate, the offering of Comsat reportedly involved a maximum allocation of 10 shares to many of the individual investors wanting to subscribe.) In contrast, an investor is likely to obtain nearly his full request for issues that are not oversubscribed. Therefore any realistic measures of investor returns from new issues must explicitly recognize such unequal distribution of various new issues. Also since allocation of hot new issues basically involves a partial rebate, realistic return measures also require explicit recognition of the "price" investors pay to receive allocations of hot issues.

Investors can buy new issues in the after-market; but, except for occasional price stabilization permitted to underwriting syndicates, this is a competitive market. Investors who believe they can successfully identify stocks of emerging growth companies in their early stages must recognize that other skillful investors also are trying to do so and also are willing to buy stocks at prices reflecting such expectations. Thus there is little reason, if any, to expect consistently and substantially above-average returns from buying such stocks in the competitive after-market.

[3] Frank K. Reilly and Kenneth Hatfield, "Investor Experience with New Stock Issues," *Financial Analysts Journal*, September–October 1969, pp. 73–80. In one sentence the authors state that most investors "are not able to subscribe to new issues at the original offering. . . ." (p. 78).

chapter 12
Special-Situation
Stocks

Opportunities in special-situation (S-S) stocks are popularized by many investments books. Such books cite episodes of large companies that passed through periods of major operating problems and then dramatically recovered. Typically the examples also portray how the operating recovery was accompanied by a burst in the company's share price, providing large profits to investors who had predicted the successful turn of company fortune.

Proponents of special-situation (S-S) stocks also cite another advantage of such an investment strategy. Because their expected performance depends on "special circumstances," some S-S stocks can provide high returns even in periods when stocks in general provide low or negative returns. Similarly some S-S stocks will provide exceptionally high returns in periods when stocks generally provide high returns. In principle, therefore, attention to S-S stocks enables investors to construct portfolios somewhat independent of general movements in stock prices.

Five stocks on the New York Stock Exchange had percentage price gains ranging from about 70 to 120 percent in 1970.[1] (During the same year the average share price was down slightly, as measured by the Standard & Poor's Index of 425 industrial stocks.) Most of the five stocks were not of well-known or emerging growth companies. Instead they were of companies in which investor interest apparently was sparked by special events. Overnite Transportation Company, for ex-

[1] Based on a computer study, by James Psaltos, covering 1251 securities and excluding any securities added to the NYSE after the beginning of 1970. Cited in *The Wall Street Journal*, January 7, 1971, p. 23.

ample, is a trucking firm that reported sharply higher EPS in 1970, apparently because of increased freight tonnage, rate increases granted during 1970, and effective cost controls. Furthermore, analysts and investors probably anticipated further progress for this company. Also among the five stocks were Coca-Cola Bottling Company of New York and General Cigar which, while long-established firms, were developing new products and markets.

Illustrating potential benefits from holding S-S stocks provides only partial information to practical investors interested in more than antedotes. More complete analysis also requires examination of the "costs" of identifying and holding S-S stocks.

Identifying Special-Situation Stocks

Each S-S stock is seen to reflect certain unique ("special") circumstances. For convenience, however, such stocks are of companies that can be classified into three principal categories:

1. Hidden-asset firms.
2. Turn-around candidates.
3. Beneficiaries of revised environments.

While such a framework provides general guidelines in identifying special situations, in practice some companies fall into more than one category. How these special situations can arise will now be illustrated, at times with examples of past outcomes. It is necessary, however, to go beyond past examples and examine the practicality of benefitting from S-S stocks.

Shares of *hidden-asset firms* can be special situations if the value of these assets is likely to be subsequently recognized by other investors. A first step, the search for "hidden assets" among various firms, requires skills in financial analysis, and patience. A company's financial reports, especially the footnotes, must be examined in detail. Important supplementary information is available from other sources, such as the various reports filed with the SEC and, in the case of regulated industries, with other government agencies.

A search for hidden assets must analyze diverse aspects of a firm's reported financial information. Some companies hold marketable securities that are carried at a cost well below current market prices. For example, among the marketable securities owned by Superior Oil Company at year-end 1971 were about four million shares of Texaco that were reported in its balance sheet at a cost of $64 million, but that had a market value of about $133 million. Southern Pacific Company recently carried over 88,000 shares of Standard Oil Company of California on its books at a total value of $92.[2] At the end of 1970 these shares had a total market value of about $5 million.

Various companies report their extensive land holdings at their historic acquisition cost. This is illustrated by various railroads, paper companies, and sugar companies owning extensive acreage in areas where land values have risen substantially because of new housing and recreational developments. Hidden assets may also be found among other components of corporate financial reports. Some companies do not consolidate their foreign assets directly into their balance sheets, while others have plant and equipment or patents that, although largely depreciated or amortized, have substantial market values.

In searching for hidden assets, analysts also must be alert to possible "hidden liabilities." Companies that are defendants in legal actions can face substantial financial penalties if they lose their cases. Assets such as capitalized costs for research and development or for acquisition of additional business may be overstated if expected benefits are not realized. The asset value of old plant and equipment, even though largely depreciated, can be misleading if outmoded facilities will meet new antipollution standards only by very large capital outlays. Searching for hidden assets and hidden liabilities thus requires in-depth analysis of the probable economic relevance of various items in accounting reports.

Turnaround candidates are companies likely to report sharp increases in earnings per share (EPS) because of more effective use of their assets. Since share prices are likely to respond to unexpected sharp increases in EPS and revised expectations of future dividends, stocks of successful turnaround candidates can provide high returns. Such financial results often occur after new management assumes control of a company. Therefore changes in top management can provide a clue to identifying turnaround candidates.

A notable turnaround is Chrysler Corporation during the early 1960s. At the beginning of 1961 its common stock sold at $38. In that year new management assumed control. Seeking to improve the company's financial performance, the new top management reduced costs and sold redundant assets. Furthermore it began committing substantial resources to improving the company's product line and its production and distribution systems.[3] Chrysler's successful turnaround is reflected

[2] *Moody's Transportation Manual* (Moody's Investors Service, Inc.: 1971), p. 229.

[3] Robert Sheehan, "The Price of Success at Chrysler," *Fortune*, November 1965, pp. 139–143 ff.

in the subsequent price appreciation of its stock. Within four years an illustrative investment in Chrysler stock at $38 provided a compound return of about 60 percent per year. Other established companies also have been successfully transformed, often by new strategies and/or new teams of top management. Prominent among these companies have been International Telephone and Telegraph and Kresge.

Beneficiaries of revised environments are companies likely to benefit from sudden changes in their industry and/or regulatory environment. If such benefits result in sharp increases in future EPS, then shares of such companies may provide above-average returns as the market price adjusts to reflect revised expectations. For example, many major railroads are asking for reduced government regulation of their industry. With reduced regulation, they claim they can be more competitive in their rate structures and more effective in closing what they judge to be unprofitable branch lines. If the industry does become less regulated and more effective in using its assets, this can result in higher future EPS and higher stock prices. Investors must recognize, however, that the nation's economy is a complex system of interrelated parts. Thus, if the railroads are likely to benefit from a revised regulatory environment, this can adversely affect their principal competitors: trucking companies and water carriers.

In an economy increasingly subject to government policies, it is necessary to assess probable directions and changes in such policies in order to identify companies likely to benefit from sudden revisions in laws and regulations. Similarly, probable government policies must be examined to identify companies susceptible to more restrictions, such as food companies (consumer and nutritional issues), automobile companies (safety and exhaust-emission standards), and firms having outmoded plant and equipment that fail to meet more restrictive antipollution levels.

In summary, S-S stocks can provide high returns, as illustrated by selected past outcomes. However, realistic investors must ask for answers to the following questions:

How special is any S-S stock?

How confident should an investor be about future returns from any S-S stock?

What are the *probable portfolio returns* over time from S-S stocks?

Answers to these questions follow directly from examining S-S stocks in the context of a competitive stock market.

Benefitting from Special-Situation Stocks

How "special" is any special-situation (S-S) stock? This question confronts an investor trying to *predict* future returns from a stock believed to represent a special situation.

Most individual investors will find that personally trying to identify S-S stocks is costly in terms of time, talent, and money. Skillful financial analysis of diverse information is necessary for identifying hidden-asset companies. Changes in top corporate management, reported regularly in financial newspapers, can be a clue to a possible turnaround candidate. Nevertheless, individual investors still must use financial analysis to assess the likelihood of a substantial turnaround. Similarly, the prediction of possible beneficiaries of revised environments requires that investors seek and evaluate information, for example, about possible major changes in government fiscal and regulatory policies.

Individual investors, instead of committing substantial personal resources to trying directly to identify S-S stocks, can indirectly learn about such stocks from investment advisory reports, financial journals, and brokers. Such sources transmit information about stocks judged to be special situations by financial analysts who devote substantial resources to seeking S-S stocks. However this competitive process of searching for S-S stocks by skillful analysts makes it unlikely that such stocks can, in fact, be very "special."

To illustrate, *how well hidden* are the "hidden assets" of most companies likely to be? Recent policies of the accounting profession, the SEC, and the stock exchanges foster more complete and timely corporate disclosure. Footnotes of corporate financial reports generally have become more extensive and more detailed. Many full-time financial analysts have access to corporate financial reports, which now are generally available on microfiche.

In this context of skillful competition for generally available information, reconsider the previous examples of hidden-asset firms. The value of Superior Oil's holding of marketable securities is generally known by many financial analysts, some of whom also develop estimates of the value of the company's oil reserves in order to provide estimates of the company's total asset value. Similarly, skillful analysts concerned with transportation stocks are unlikely to overlook the current value of Southern Pacific's holdings in Standard Oil of California. For companies with extensive land holdings, various analysts publicize the fact that land reported on a cost basis is likely to be worth more at today's land prices. Not all analysts agree in their appraisals of hidden-asset firms. Nevertheless, by providing competing investors with new insights and information, these analyses reduce the likelihood that "hidden assets" are, in fact, well hidden.

Competing financial analysts also monitor industries and companies that are turnaround candidates or possible beneficiaries of revised environments. They watch for major changes in top management of companies having undistinguished records of EPS. Such changes are broadly publicized in the investment community. To illustrate, control of a medium-size steel company with a past record of marginal profitability may pass to a new management team having a successful record in other steel companies. Various analysts, especially those monitoring steel stocks will be alerted by these new developments. They can then apply their skills of financial analysis to assessing probable future EPS if the new management can use the company's assets more effectively. In a similar way, analysts are continually monitoring industries and companies for possible environmental changes that can contribute to sharp revisions in estimates of future EPS.

As a general illustration, the *Financial Analysts Journal* periodically publishes articles examining the outlook for established industries undergoing major changes. In recent years these articles have examined industries such as railroads ("Railroad Prospects—Amber to Green")[4] and steel ("Is There a Renaissance in Steel?")[5] With the resource support of their firms, analysts can probe more deeply into possible legal, legislative, and regulatory developments than can most individual investors. Nevertheless these analysts also are competing with one another, so that no one of them is likely to be consistently more accurate than his skillful competitors.

Special situations are unlikely to be very "special" because many competing investors can learn directly or indirectly about them. The stock price of a company having "hidden assets" is likely to reflect general investor awareness of these assets, along with other generally available information used to develop expectations of the company's future earnings and dividends. For example, if analysts and investors foresee little likelihood of the hidden assets being effectively used by the company in the near future, then the market price of the stock will also reflect these expectations. In this event there is no reason to expect above-average returns from an investment in such a S-S stock.

Stock prices of possible beneficiaries from revised environments also reflect investor expectations. To illustrate, some states are likely to amend their laws to permit expansion of branch banking and bank holding companies. In this revised environment, several large banking

---

[4] Pierre R. Bretey, *Financial Analysts Journal*, November–December 1967, pp. 61–66.
[5] Richard I. McClow, *Financial Analysts Journal*, July–August 1969, pp. 80–84.

organizations will bid for smaller banks to absorb into their systems. While the exact timing of such revised legislation is uncertain, in a competitive capital market the share prices of the smaller banks are discounting some of the probable benefits from their being acquired.

When environmental changes are less predictable, revision of stock prices can be sudden and substantial. On August 15, 1971, President Nixon announced abrupt changes in government trade and fiscal policies. Among these proposed changes were repeal of the seven percent excise tax on automobiles, imposition of a 10 percent surcharge on imports (affecting imports of foreign automobiles), and revision of investment tax-credit policies. Many investors saw these moves as an abrupt revision of the economic environment for American automobile producers. On the next day (Monday), the stock of Ford and General Motors did not open for trading on the New York Stock Exchange. When the stocks opened the following day (Tuesday), their prices were above the preceding Friday's close as follows: Ford (+6%); and General Motors (+11%). Such rapid price adjustments to new information and revised expectations imply that investors, while not fully anticipating such a major change, can respond rapidly to important new events.

How confident should an investor be about future returns from any special-situation stock? Hindsight shows what might have been achieved by timely purchases of selected S-S stocks. However other stocks at times have been classified as special situations, but they subsequently failed to provide exceptional returns. For example, some investors must have seen a turnaround candidate in Curtis Publishing as it underwent a succession of changes in top managers striving to revive the firm's earning power by more effective use of the firm's assets. However in 1968 the company's common stock was delisted from the New York Stock Exchange, principally because of continuing operating losses.

The Penn Central Company, product of the 1968 merger between the New York Central Railroad and the Pennsylvania Railroad, had many characteristics of a special situation. Duplicate railroad assets could be sold or used more effectively, for example, in nonrailroad activities. The company's extensive land holdings, especially in Manhattan, and its investments in nonrailroad companies, for example, in land development, pipelines, and leasing, were viewed as hidden assets. New management teams were created, drawing on the pool of executives from the merging organizations. This revised leadership was expected to achieve substantial operating economies, especially if the railroad's regulatory authorities became more willing to permit discontinuance of passenger service judged unprofitable by the company. Shares of the

Penn Central Company, thus having many attributes of a special situation, increased in price after the merger, attaining a high of $86 in 1968. However from this peak the price underwent an extended, substantial decline to $11 just before the company's principal railroad affiliate announced its filing of a bankruptcy petition. This recent episode portrays how a stock, with many characteristics of a special situation, resulted in substantial losses for many institutional and individual investors.

Investors cannot be very confident about future returns from any one S-S stock. New management at times is unsuccessful in turning around a marginal company. In other cases, the benefits from hidden assets, turnarounds, or revised environments are not as great as had been expected. Furthermore the time value of money must be explicitly recognized in considering S-S stocks. It can take years before some S-S stocks suddenly have large increases in EPS and sharply higher share prices reflecting revised investor expectations. To illustrate, because of special circumstances, a stock currently paying no dividends goes from $20 to $30 in one year, for a rate of return of 50 percent. Compared to returns from other stocks in that year, this 50-percent return may have been exceptionally high. What about an investor who invested in the stock five years previously at $15 in the belief that the stock *then* qualified as a special situation? His annualized rate of return over the five-year holding period is 15 percent (assuming no dividends or capital changes), and this may be unexceptional compared to returns from alternative investment opportunities during the same time period. In conclusion, most investors who buy what they judge to be a S-S stock cannot confidently predict, or influence, future events affecting the company, its future EPS, or its future price.

In contrast, investors with substantial resources can at times act to exploit special situations they have identified. This is done by seeking control of a company having attributes of a special situation.

Proxy fights periodically arise as investors outside a company's current management seek to replace existing management. In bidding for the voting support (proxies) of other shareholders, the outside investors typically claim they will manage the company's assets more effectively so that the market then will be likely to place a higher value on the company's shares, thus benefitting all the firm's shareholders. A classic case was Louis Wolfson's bid to acquire control of Montgomery Ward, which had been steadily increasing its holdings of U.S. government securities to about $270 million, amounting to almost 40 percent of the retailer's total assets. Similarly, large investors, apparently perceiving a special situation, battled for control of the New York Central Railroad in the mid-1950s. In such proxy fights, even if outside investors fail to depose existing management, their direct challenge is likely to stimulate management to use corporate assets more effectively in order to forestall subsequent proxy fights.

Tender offers also enable large investors to seek effective control of companies having attributes of special situations. Tender offers basically involve a group of large investors, or another company, making a public offer to buy a company's stock at a premium over recent market prices. For example, to obtain control of a company currently selling for around $44 a share, a group of investors may announce an offer to purchase, say, up to 50 percent of the company's outstanding stock at $50 a share. Existing shareholders who find this premium sufficiently attractive will tender (offer) their shares to the bidding group, which thus achieves effective control of the company.[6] It then can move to use the assets of the company more effectively with the intention of increasing the market valuation of the company's shares.

To illustrate, in 1968 a financier, Kirk Kerkorian, made two tender offers for shares of M-G-M. The tender-offer prices exceeded the recent stock price of M-G-M. Thus obtaining control of this movie producer, the new management apparently is planning to increase the company's future profitability by more effective use, or disposal, of existing assets, that were estimated to be worth around $69 per share of M-G-M.[7] While some of these assets may be considered hidden, their publicity in financial reporting demonstrates the unlikelihood of hidden assets or turnaround candidates being very well hidden from the scrutiny of many competing analysts and investors with access to substantial resources.

The key issues therefore become *whether* and *when* managers representing new controlling investors can implement policies to improve operations that will be reflected in a higher market price per share. Even these large investors cannot afford to be too confident about future returns from their S-S investments. Some planned benefits may never occur, and others may occur only after substantial delays. Thus a talented group of investors with large resources may, at times, acquire control of a S-S company that over time fails to provide the investors with returns above general market returns.

Investors, lacking confidence about the outcome from any one S-S stock, can diversify among S-S stocks. The question then is: What are the *probable portfolio returns* from S-S stocks? The integrating framework of a competitive stock market implies that returns from port-

---

[6] Further details about tender-offer strategies are presented by Samuel L. Hayes, III, and Russell A. Taussig, "Tactics of Cash Takeover Bids," *Harvard Business Review*, March–April 1967, pp. 135–148.

[7] Irwin Ross, "Kirk Kerkorian Doesn't Want All the Meat off the Bone," *Fortune*, November 1969, pp. 144–148 ff.

folios of S-S stocks are unlikely to exceed, substantially and frequently, general market returns. Because of many competing analysts and investors, special situations are unlikely to be very "special." Their current market prices, on the average, are appropriately discounting probable future returns relative to those from alternative investment opportunities.

Recent studies, however, do not test this thesis that portfolios of S-S stocks fail to outperform the market. This lack of evidence probably is because of the difficulties of rigorously defining possible S-S stocks. (One investor's "special situation" is often viewed by another as a "speculation.") Therefore, although the possibility of above-average returns from S-S stocks is not disproved, practical investors ask themselves and others hard questions:

1. How can S-S stocks exist (except by hindsight) in a competitive market?
2. Even if they exist in some sense, should investors realistically expect above-average returns from portfolios of such stocks?
3. If not, what makes S-S stocks very "special" from the critical viewpoint of shareholder returns over time?

As demonstrated, these key questions provide a practical checklist for investors subsequently offered opportunities to buy S-S stocks.

chapter 13
Warrants

Investors typically are introduced to warrants from one of two principal viewpoints. One view basically dismisses warrants as highly speculative instruments having limited life, wide price fluctuations, and no stockholder rights. The contrary view asserts that these attributes of warrants provide exceptional opportunities to skillful investors. To buttress this second view, the following types of episodes typically are cited:

In 1942, warrants of Radio-Keith-Orpheum were quoted at around $0.06 each. Four years later their market quotation was $13. The total appreciation was about 21,500 percent, so that a $500 initial investment could have grown to somewhat over $100,000.

In early 1968 National General Corporation's common stock traded at $25 and its warrants around $14. Within six months the common stock more than doubled in price. Moreover, during the same time interval, the price of the warrants more than tripled.

Since perceptive investors are no longer content with provocative statements based on selected hindsight, it is necessary to examine more completely the investment opportunities in warrants.

Magnifying Investment Returns

Warrants are basically investment instruments enabling their owners to purchase a company's common stock at a specified price within a specified time period. To illustrate, early in 1973 a company issues warrants to purchase its common stock at $20 per share from July 1973 to December 1979. At any time during this period a warrant holder can

exercise the warrant by arranging to exchange it plus $20 in cash in re-
turn for one share of the company's common stock. The warrant holder
is protected against dilution. For example, if the common stock is split
two-for-one, he is entitled to exchange his warrant plus $20 cash for two
of these recently split common shares. During the time that he holds
the warrant, he receives no dividends and has no voting rights.

Investors, however, must be alert to variations in the general characteristics of warrants. Terms of some warrants stipulate that the amount
of cash necessary to exercise them will increase over time. For example, a warrant with a total 10-year exercise period may stipulate exercise prices of $20 during the first five years and $25 during the second
five years. Also, some warrants permit the exercise price to be paid by
exchanging some of the issuing company's bonds at face value, instead
of paying cash. Some warrants have infinite time periods ("perpetual
warrants"). Warrants also differ concerning the amount of protection
they provide holders against the issuing companies' increasing, directly
or indirectly, their outstanding common stock and thus potentially
diluting the warrants' role in the capital structure. Since warrants thus
can vary substantially in their individual terms, financial information
services usually alert investors to the need to check in detail the terms
and trading basis of any warrant.

The currently outstanding warrants of American Telephone & Telegraph illustrate the preceding outline of how warrants work. These
warrants, issued in 1970, enable holders to buy the company's common
stock at $52 a share until May 15, 1975. The exercise price, which must
be paid in cash, is protected against dilution. While these particular
warrants illustrate some general characteristics of warrants, investors
should obtain detailed information about the terms and trading basis
of any warrant.

Warrants generally arise in one of two ways: (1) in association with
a company's issuance of debt securities, and (2) in mergers. In evaluating its different sources of funds, a company may decide to sell bonds
instead of additional common stock. Furthermore the company can
evaluate the issuance of a package of securities that includes both
bonds and warrants. Such a package can be attractive to potential investors who basically prefer to hold bonds but who also want an opportunity to share in the firm's future prospects by exercising the warrants for common stock. In return for this profit opportunity, investors
generally accept a lower rate of interest on the bonds than they would
have required if there were no warrants. To illustrate, the AT&T warrants issued in 1970 were offered to shareholders as part of a package
containing $100 of a debenture (bond) and warrants to purchase two
shares of common stock.

In evaluating various securities to offer shareholders in a merger proposal, acquiring companies are likely to consider warrants as part of a package. Many currently outstanding warrants were thus issued by companies especially active in acquiring other firms during the late 1960s. Until recently such warrants, although they could result in an increase in a firm's outstanding common stock, were not included in a firm's number of outstanding common shares when reporting EPS. Recent accounting changes now recognize the potential increase in a company's common shares because of outstanding warrants and thus require reporting of fully diluted EPS (Chapter 6).

Summarizing the principal reasons why companies decide to issue warrants should make it evident that they are only one of many financing tools available to most companies. Warrants are used when in management's judgment they are likely to meet various corporate goals.[1] They are not intended as boons to potential buyers but rather as one way to obtain funds in a competitive capital market.

Once issued, warrants generally begin to be traded in the nation's security markets. Warrants that were initially offered as part of a package of securities usually become detachable so that the warrants and, say, the bonds begin to be traded as separate investment instruments. In this market process, competing analysts and investors become involved in evaluating the profit opportunities from various warrants and, by their investment decisions, in establishing competitive prices for warrants.

Why would investors want to buy warrants? A principal reason is because warrants provide a means of magnifying investment returns. However, although providing the potential for exceptionally high returns, negative returns also are magnified by investing in warrants.

To see how investment in a warrant can magnify possible returns, consider a hypothetical example. A warrant enables its holder to buy a share of the company's common stock at $35 until 1980. Today the stock, paying no dividends, is selling at $45 per share. Therefore the warrant has a current *base value* of $10 because at any lower price it is profitable for alert investors to buy the warrants and immediately exercise them at a profit.[2] (For example, if in the unlikely event that warrants are available at $5, then an investor can buy a warrant at $5 and exchange it plus $35 cash for a share of stock that can be sold at its market price of $45, providing a rapid profit of $5 per share.) Its

[1] For more information about warrants from a corporate viewpoint, see Samuel L. Hayes, III, and Henry B. Reiling, "Sophisticated Financing Tool: The Warrant," *Harvard Business Review*, January–February 1969, pp. 137–150.

[2] A more detailed examination of arbitraging and hedging procedures is presented in Chapter 17.

base value thus sets a practical lower limit on a warrant's market price at a given point in time.

To participate in the potential magnified returns from the illustrative warrant, competing investors currently are willing to pay a market price of around $15 so that the warrant is selling at a 50-percent *premium* over its base value. An investor who confidently expects the price of the stock to increase to $60 by, say, a year from now can buy the stock at $45 for a potential return of 33 percent (no dividends). However, consider what will happen if, instead, he buys a warrant at $15. When the stock price goes to $60, then the warrant will have a base value of $25 (the difference between $60 and the $35 required to exercise the warrant). Its market price will be at least $25 and probably greater as investors continue to pay some premium for this warrant. Thus the investor who purchases the warrant at $15 need not subsequently exercise it. He can sell it to other investors and achieve a capital gain of at least $10, which is 67 percent of the purchase price and *twice* the return of 33 percent from the direct purchase of the common stock. By investing the same initial dollar amount in the warrants as in the common stock, the capital gain, both in absolute and percentage terms, is twice as great. This is only one illustration of how warrants can magnify positive investment returns.

Warrants similarly magnify negative returns in comparison to direct investment in the underlying common stock. Consider further the warrant, selling for $15, enabling its holder to purchase a share of the company's common stock for $35 in cash. The stock currently sells for $45, so that investors are paying a premium for the warrant. As shown, an investor confident about the stock's price increasing to $60 will magnify his investment return by purchasing the warrant instead of the stock. What will occur if the investor's expectations prove to be incorrect as the stock's price drops to $30 by the end of a year's holding period? If the common stock is purchased at $45, the capital loss will be $15, which is 33 percent of the purchase price. If, instead, the warrant is purchased, its base value will be zero. (Why exercise a warrant to buy common stock at $35 if the common stock can be directly purchased in the market at $30?) Nevertheless, if the warrant's exercise period is for several more years, then it will have some positive price, say $5, at which investors will be willing to buy it because of the *possibility* that the common stock will subsequently be higher in price and the warrant will again have a positive base value. However, even at $5, this warrant price represents a capital loss of 67 percent on the initial purchase price of the warrant, showing how warrants also can magnify negative returns.

At the extreme, a 100-percent loss is possible from investing in a warrant that subsequently is without value on its expiration date. An example is a hypothetical warrant, expiring on December 31, 1972, that required $25 in cash in order to buy a share of stock that at the time sold for $15. Under these circumstances the warrant will have expired valueless. Its holders will have realized losses of 100 percent relative to any price they previously paid for the warrant.

How warrants can magnify investment returns also is demonstrated by comparing the price range of a warrant with that of the associated common stocks. To illustrate, in 1972 the highest market price for the AT&T warrants was $9\frac{1}{4}$, almost 70 percent above the lowest price of $5\frac{1}{4}$. In the same year the highest price for the company's common stock was $53\frac{1}{2}$, which was about 30 percent above the year's lowest price. Since price changes are a major component of investment returns, these differing price spreads further demonstrate how warrants can magnify investment returns in comparison with those from the associated common stock.

Assessing Returns from Warrants

An unexpired warrant provides an opportunity for high returns, but what is the likelihood of this outcome? Furthermore, by considering portfolios of warrants instead of just an individual warrant, why should investors expect consistently superior returns from investing in warrants?

Reconsider this chapter's introductory illustration of a Radio-Keith-Orpheum warrant that, by increasing in price from $0.06 to around $13 in four years, resulted in potential capital appreciation of 21,500 percent. Such an episode, while stimulating, is potentially misleading. The assumed purchase of the warrants for a total dollar amount of $500 may appear reasonable, but at $0.06 per warrant this implies a purchase of over 8000 warrants; and it is not evident that any investor could have bought 8000 warrants at that price. Furthermore, recognizing that this episode focuses on only one historically successful warrant, practical investors now are alerted to ask what are likely to be the investment returns from investing a similar amount, say $500, in many different warrants over time.

Although a warrant provides an opportunity for an exceptionally high return, this is only one of many possible outcomes. Because it magnifies both positive and negative returns, its range of possible outcomes is greater than for the associated common stock. Furthermore the possibility of a return of −100 percent is real because, with the exception of perpetual warrants, a warrant can expire and become valueless even though the company's common stock continues to have value. Warrants thus can be viewed as risky investment vehicles. In addition to these investment characteristics, historically many warrants arose from corporate reorganizations or were issued by companies whose financial condition limited their alternative sources of investment funds. For such reasons the New York Stock Exchange, for over 50 years, refused to list any warrants. This policy was revised in 1970 when AT&T, with its strong financial condition, decided to innovate by giving its common stockholders rights to subscribe to units of debentures and warrants. Since then the NYSE has permitted listing of warrants that meet specified criteria, so that at year-end 1971 there were 11 warrants listed on the NYSE.

Knowing the principal risk-return features of warrants, competing analysts and investors evaluate possible returns from warrants relative to those available from other investment vehicles. In such a market the price of a warrant reflects generally available information about a common stock for which a warrant can be exercised and also about the various terms of the warrant. Frequently warrants sell at premiums over their base value. Such premiums reflect expectations about future returns from the warrant and the associated common stock relative to other investment opportunities. In this perspective, for example, the AT&T warrant opened on the NYSE at about $9 at the beginning of 1973, when the common stock traded at about $53. Since the exercise price (52) of the warrant approximates this market price for the common stock, the warrant's market price of $9 must reflect investor expectations about how the warrant's future prices will be associated with possible future market prices of the common stock of AT&T.

While it is theoretically possible to have high returns from a warrant, in practice the competition among skillful investors makes such an outcome highly unpredictable and unlikely. What can be generally known or predicted is already discounted in a warrant's price. Sometimes, however, because of events that cannot be generally anticipated, a warrant may provide an exceptionally high return. However, other warrants may provide large negative returns because the price of the associated common stock is affected by unpredictable events. By diversifying among warrants, an investor can be more confident about the possible portfolio return than he can be about the returns from the individual warrants in the portfolio. Should, however, an investor expect substantially above-average returns over time from portfolios of warrants? In competitive markets such exceptional portfolio opportunities are unlikely to persist. Evidence consistent with this logical conclusion is presented in the next chapter, which examines investment opportunities in convertible securities.

chapter 14
Convertible Securities

Convertible securities are often cited as representing "the best of all investment worlds." This viewpoint is illustrated by some representative investment communications:

A convertible bond combines the comparative safety of a bond with the opportunity to participate in any substantial price appreciation of the common stock. What more can one want from an investment?

The convertible preferred stock of AT&T looks like a comparatively good buy. At the beginning of 1973 the preferred stock yielded almost 6.6 percent on its market price, while the common stock yielded 5.3 percent, based on the indicated dividend rate of $2.80. Thus the current dividend yield is higher from the preferred stock, and yet its holders, by just converting their shares, can participate in any major price appreciation of the common stock.

In December 1970 an issue of convertible debentures of Ramada Inns began trading at about 128 on the New York Stock Exchange. One year later the price reached 224. This 75 percent price appreciation along with an interest yield of over 6 percent provided a total return of about 80 percent, which is not bad for a bond.

Although such statements illustrate selected features of convertible securities, practical investors are skeptical of investment instruments that seem *too good*. Instead of examples of historically successful convertibles, they require more complete examination of convertible securities in the context of competitive securities markets. Knowing that other skillful analysts and investors understand the principal features of convertibles, realistic investors want evidence concerning investment returns from convertible securities over time.

Combining Low Risk with High Returns

A convertible debenture basically is a bond that provides its holder with the option to convert it into a specific number of the company's common shares. A debenture has a claim to a company's income and assets that stands ahead of the firm's stock.[1] Interest on a debenture is a contractual obligation that requires a company to make interest payments on specified dates or else face bankruptcy. Debentures typically are in units of $1000, which is the amount of principal that the issuing company agrees to pay the bondholder at the specified maturity date. This is a fixed liability that in the event of liquidation stands ahead of the residual rights of the company's stock. These contractual obligations concerning the company's payment of interest and principal on its bonds result in greater confidence about investment returns from the bonds, in contrast to returns from the company's stock.

In addition to its bond attributes, a convertible debenture gives its holder the right to convert the instrument into a specific number of the company's common shares. To illustrate, a debenture ($1000 unit) may be convertible into 20 shares of common stock, in which case the *conversion price* is said to be $50 per share ($1000/20 = $50). An investor owning the bond knows he can currently exchange it for 20 shares of the company's common stock.

Returns from a company's convertible preferred stock also are more certain than those from the company's common stock, although generally less certain than those from the company's bonds. Relative to its common stock, a company's preferred stock has prior claim to a specified amount of income and, in the event of liquidation, assets. In addition, it is convertible into a specified number of common shares. For example, the $4 cumulative convertible preferred stock of AT&T basically can be converted at the holder's option into 1.05 common shares.

As with warrants, however, investors must investigate carefully the specific terms of any convertible security. Some convertible securities provide for specified changes in the conversion terms over time. A debenture maturing in 1990, for example, may be convertible into 25 com-

---

[1]A debenture typically involves a general claim against a company's income and assets. In contrast, a bond often is secured by specific sources of income or specific assets, such as real estate. Such technical differences do not detract from the basic fact that these debt instruments all stand ahead of stock in a company's capital structure.

mon shares from 1970 to January 1, 1980, after which it can be converted into only 20 shares. Thus the conversion price in this example increases from $40 ($1000/25) to $50 ($1000/20). Similarly, convertible securities differ on their provisions to protect holders against dilution of conversion rights. In addition, most convertible securities, unlike warrants, can be redeemed (called) at the option of the issuing company. This redemption privilege is built into the terms of the convertible security. Redemption may be at one specified price or, more typically, at a specified price related to when and why the security is called. To illustrate, the AT&T convertible preferred stock is initially redeemable by the company at $51 through July 31, 1975, after which the redemption price declines in two steps to $50, plus dividends. Since characteristics of convertible securities can vary substantially, various financial services report in detail the contractual provisions of most convertible securities.

Convertible securities usually are issued by companies to acquire new funds or to exchange for securities of a firm being acquired by merger. (During the 1960s, in particular, many issues of convertible preferred stock were created for mergers.) From the corporate viewpoint issuance of convertible securities is one of many procedures for obtaining new funds in a competitive capital market. Other procedures and instruments include bank loans, sale-and-leaseback agreements, nonconvertible bonds, bonds with attached warrants, nonconvertible preferred stock, common stock, and other financing techniques. Thus, in deciding whether to sell convertible securities, a corporation's financial managers assess this procedure from the company's viewpoint. Their concern is with effectively meeting the terms of a competitive capital market, not with providing unusually attractive opportunities to investors.

Why are convertible securities often publicized as providing unusually attractive investment opportunities? Basically it is the "best-of-all-investment-worlds" viewpoint. Compared to its common stock, a company's convertible securities provide more certain returns with the opportunity to participate, through the conversion right, in any unusually high returns from the associated common stock.

The "best-of-all-investment-worlds" viewpoint can be effectively illustrated by a hypothetical example. A company has just sold an issue of convertible debentures that mature in 1990. The interest rate is 5 percent ($50 per year on each $1000 of principal). Each debenture is convertible, until redeemed, into 20 shares of common stock, so that the conversion price is $50. Furthermore each debenture is redeemable, at the company's option, at $1000; and the conversion right is effectively protected against dilution.

In now considering whether to buy this convertible debenture instead of the firm's common stock, investors will focus on its conversion right and bond attributes. The current market price of the associated common stock is $45 per share. An investor who believes the common stock will be selling at $60 a year from now can directly purchase the common stock for $45; if he is correct, his one-year return will be 33 percent, assuming no dividend. As an alternative, he can buy the convertible debenture at $1000. If the stock price increases to $60 a year from now, then, unless redeemed, this debenture's market price will be at least that of its *conversion value* of $1200, which is the number of shares into which the debenture can be converted times the current market price per share. In fact the debenture is likely to have a market price somewhat above the conversion value.[2] Thus, if the stock price goes to $60, then the minimum one-year return from this bond will be 25 percent (20% capital appreciation plus the interest return of 5%). In this event, the investor's return of 25 percent will be somewhat less than if he directly purchases the common stock.

Now what if the stock's price a year from now is $30, instead of the expected $60? Direct investment in the common stock at $45 will thus result in a return of −33 percent. However, investment in the convertible bond at $1000 is unlikely to result in as large a negative return because its price will then be related more to its *straight value*, which is estimated from the market prices of nonconvertible bonds that are similar in such features as interest rates and estimated risk. If, for example, the bond's price, based principally on its straight value, is $900 at the end of the year, then investment in the convertible will provide a −5 percent return (−10% capital return plus 5% interest return). This return from the convertible bond will not be as adverse as the −33 percent return from direct investment in the common stock if the price declines to $30.

In summary, the conversion privilege enables a debenture holder to participate in high positive returns almost as fully as if he directly purchases the common stock, yet avoid possible negative returns as extreme as those possible from the firm's common stock. On this basis a company's convertible security combines low risk (i.e., greater confidence of returns) with the potential for high returns.

Low-risk attributes of convertible securities can be over-emphasized.

---

[2] Because the conversion right enables the debenture holder to exchange at his option the bond for 20 common shares, with the stock price at $60 any price much lower than $1200 for the bond will make it profitable for professional investors to buy the bond, say at $1150, immediately convert the bond, and sell the 20 shares for $1200 for a rapid, riskless profit. Therefore this conversion value basically sets a floor at any point in time.

Substantial uncertainty surrounds future returns from some convertible securities, even though they are nominally debentures or preferred stock. A company in marginal financial condition may have a convertible security outstanding that on the surface involves less uncertainty of returns than the company's common stock. In the event of major financial difficulties, however, the prior claims of the convertible can be without much substance. Returns can be almost as negative as those from the common stock; and, at the extreme, both the holders of the convertible security and the common stock can have returns of −100 percent. Returns from convertible securities of marginal firms thus can be more uncertain than returns from common stocks of companies such as AT&T, duPont, and General Motors.

The low risk of convertibles rests generally on their estimated straight values, which change over time. Two principal factors can affect a convertible security's straight value: (1) a general shift in the level of interest rates, and (2) revision of investor views of the security's risk category. During periods of rising interest rates, for example, the straight value will decline, thus providing less protection against possible negative returns. Such a pattern characterized the 1960s when, because of generally rising interest rates, straight values were more analogous to a declining escalator than to a floor. A straight value also can change in response to investor reassessment of the security's risk classification. For example, if a company begins to report major earnings deficits, then investors are likely to become less confident about future returns from the company's convertible security so that, other things being equal, their assessment of its straight value will decline.

In summary, at one level convertible securities can be said to combine low risk with high returns. Examination of the "low-risk" attribute, however, demonstrates that convertible securities, although they have prior claims in a company's capital structure, are not necessarily low-risk instruments, especially when compared to some other possible investments. Furthermore their protective features (straight values) change in response to general changes in interest rates and to investor reassessment of the security's risk classification. Now alerted to the "low-risk" attribute of convertibles, investors can examine the credibility of "high returns" from convertibles.

Investors typically "pay a price" to participate in the publicized opportunities of convertible securities. They accept a lower current return from interest or preferred dividends than is currently available from a similar nonconvertible security. Furthermore they pay a market price that exceeds the security's conversion value.

Investors usually are willing to pay a premium to purchase a company's convertible security instead of its common stock. Not only do premiums vary among convertible securities, they vary for the same convertible security over time. In particular, when a convertible security sells above its redemption price, the premium over its conversion value generally diminishes as the conversion value of the debenture increases. There are two principal factors that explain this relationship: (1) possible early redemption of the convertible, and (2) the widened gap between the convertible's market price and its straight value.

Investors will pay at least the conversion value for a convertible security because, even if the company decides to redeem the instrument, they know they can realize the conversion value by exercising the right to convert. At the same time the market price of the convertible is unlikely to be much above the conversion value, because investors also know that the conversion value is the maximum amount they are likely to get if the convertible is called.

When a convertible is trading principally on the basis of its conversion value, there can be a substantial gap between its market price and its straight value at that point in time. Investors realize, however, that if the price of the common stock drops sharply, then the price of the convertible also can fall sharply toward its straight value. Therefore they will not be willing to pay as large a premium as they will when the debenture's conversion value is only somewhat above its straight value. Since the premium for a convertible security diminishes as the instrument sells increasingly above its redemption price and above its straight value, this implies that its potentially large positive returns *cannot* be as large as those from direct investment in the associated common stock.[3]

Measuring Returns from Convertible Securities

Investors in convertible securities usually pay a competitively determined premium for the opportunity to reduce risk. Thus they "pay a price" to hold the best-of-all-investment-worlds instrument.

What is the evidence concerning investor returns from convertible securities, and how do such returns compare with those available from diversified portfolios of common stocks? A recent study measures "the average rates of return an investor would have realized, before income

---

[3] This conclusion is based on nonleveraged positions in each security. For a more complete analysis of the relationships involved in valuing a convertible security, see Eugene F. Brigham, "An Analysis of Convertible Debentures: Theory and Some Empirical Evidence," *The Journal of Finance*, March 1966, pp. 35–54.

taxes, from straight commitments in the convertible debentures listed on the New York Stock Exchange during the 1956–68 period."[4] Basing his analysis on a sample of 77 convertible debentures selected at two-year intervals, the author measures rates of return for holding periods of various length. Furthermore, wherever possible, he compares these returns from convertibles with the rates of return from common stocks listed on the NYSE, as reported in the studies by Fisher and Lorie (Chapter 5). Among his results is that, for the time period of the study, returns from the convertible debentures were substantially lower than those from diversified portfolios of NYSE stocks. The author also concludes:

"While the convertibles studied were more resistant to price decline than their matching stocks during periods of decline in the stock market—the heralded advantage of convertibles as an investment medium —investors who picked commitments *at random* would have fared better in the general population of NYSE stocks, even after making allowance for the disutility stemming from the greater risk."[5]

In addition the author concludes that the study's results support the thesis "that convertibles are a bad bargain in a rising stock market."

Another recent study measures annual yields (returns) from samples of convertible debentures from 1957 through 1969 and from samples of convertible preferred stock from 1960 through 1969.[6] The author concludes that "the performance record of convertible securities indicates that most owners of such securities generally have experienced a combination of low yields and high risk." Furthermore, "if past performance is any guide when compared with straight bonds and preferred stocks, the yields [from convertible securities] may be about the same but the risk greater. When compared with common stock directly, the yields on convertible securities have been less, and the risk has been almost as great."[7]

In conclusion, the viewpoint that convertible securities represent the "best of all investment worlds" is not supported by two recent studies. These results indicate that benefits of convertibles are widely publicized, leading investors to pay premiums that discount—perhaps too

[4] Charles E. Vinson, "Rates of Return on Convertibles: Recent Investor Experience," *Financial Analysts Journal*, July-August 1970, pp. 110–114.

[5] *Ibid.*, p. 114. The author recognizes that his results are probably somewhat affected by the absence of Federal Reserve margin requirements for convertible debentures until spring 1968.

[6] Robert M. Soldofsky, "Yield-Risk Performance of Convertible Securities," *Financial Analysts Journal*, March-April, 1971, pp. 61–65, 79.

[7] *Ibid.*, p. 79.

much—possible benefits from convertible securities. Thoughtful investors thus are again alerted that investment strategies involving frequently and substantially above-average returns are unlikely to exist in competitive securities markets. Furthermore, when they next read or hear how convertible securities can combine low risk with high returns, practical investors will question what logic and evidence is offered to support this best-of-all-investment-worlds viewpoint.

chapter 15
Leveraging

Leveraging is a strategy that magnifies investment returns. Investors can leverage indirectly by buying stocks of leveraged companies. In addition they can leverage directly by borrowing funds to purchase an individual stock or a portfolio of stocks. Direct leveraging is usually done through a margin account.

High-return opportunities from leveraging are presented in these illustrative statements.

This grocery chain currently has a profit margin of $1\frac{1}{2}$ percent, meaning that its net profit is $1\frac{1}{2}$ cents per dollar of sales. By increasing its margin only slightly to 2 percent, the company's earnings per share will increase around 30 to 50 percent. In this event, the stock's price should rapidly climb.

Last year's EPS was depressed for this steel company because of its below-average steel production and also because so much of its income had to be used to pay interest and preferred dividends. Since the demand for steel is likely to increase next year, this company's EPS can be expected to increase very sharply. Thus, in our judgment, this steel stock provides unusually attractive potential for capital gains.

We are not optimistic about the general market. Nevertheless, based on our in-depth financial analysis and interviews with top management, we believe the price of this stock is likely to increase 30 percent within six months. By buying it on margin, you can almost double this possible capital gain.

As with warrants, however, the quest for exceptionally high returns from leveraging also involves higher risk.

Identifying Leveraged Stocks

A "highly leveraged" stock is that of a company for which substantial changes in EPS can result from comparatively small changes in corporate operating revenue. Leverage can be reduced to a set of mathematical relationships enabling analysts to identify a spectrum ranging from highly leveraged stocks to stocks with little or no leverage. Most investors, however, must understand the basics of what leverage is and how it works. Therefore, it is convenient to subclassify corporate leverage into two principal components: (1) operating leverage, and (2) capital-structure (financial) leverage.

Operating leverage focuses on the responsiveness of a firm's operating profits to changes in the firm's operating revenue. This profit sensitivity is related to the firm's structure of total operating expenses. The principal components of these expenses are cost of materials, salaries and wages, depreciation, rental obligations, and taxes. When some of these components are comparatively fixed, a company can increase its production and revenues without a similar increase in total operating expenses. This can occur, for example, when a company begins to use excess capacity in its plant and equipment. Under such conditions the company's operating profits (the difference between operating revenues and operating expenses) will increase sharply. Much of the increased revenue is said to be carried through to profits. Conversely, operating profits can decline sharply in periods when the company's production and revenues fall while its operating expenses cannot be as rapidly reduced.

The concept of operating leverage sometimes describes situations where a company's management works to reduce various components of its total operating expense. Such cost reductions will result in higher operating profits even if the firm does not increase its operating revenues. Thus, for example, investors may read about companies' reporting substantially higher operating profits after new management began extensive cost cutting and cost control measures.

Knowing how operating leverage generally works, investors must be alert to inappropriate attempts to extend this financial concept. Reconsider, for example, this chapter's first illustrative statement:

"This grocery chain currently has a profit margin of $1\frac{1}{2}$ percent, meaning that its net profit is $1\frac{1}{2}$ cents per dollar of sales. By increasing its margin only slightly to 2 percent, the company's earnings per share will increase around 30 to 50 percent. In this event, the stock's price should rapidly climb."

The focus is not on how operating profits will respond to changes in operating revenues, but rather on what *may* happen *if* management can change the company's expense structure. There is a possibility of high returns if only the company can increase its profit margin by $\frac{1}{2}$ cent for each dollar of sales. While seemingly small in absolute terms and also small relative to a dollar of sales, such a $\frac{1}{2}$-cent change is a 33 percent increase in the profit margin, as it goes from $1\frac{1}{2}$ to 2 cents. While seemingly simple in principle, particularly if the company's present margin is below the industry average, in practice such an increase can only take place in an economy where various chain and independent stores generally compete intensely for consumers' grocery dollars. Therefore the grocery chain is unlikely to be able to increase abruptly its profit margin in the short run; and even in the longer run economic competition will make it difficult for management to increase the firm's profit margin by 33 percent. Economic realism thus must temper conjecture about how a firm's EPS can increase sharply in response to only small changes in profit margins. Investors must focus on how likely are projected changes in profit margins and how confident can one afford to be about such future events. Furthermore other investors and analysts, skilled in financial analysis, are monitoring past and possible future changes in the operating patterns of many companies.

Capital-structure (financial) leverage is the association between a company's EPS and the distribution of its operating earnings among its sources of capital, particularly its bondholders and stockholders. A company with substantial debt and preferred stocks usually has greater capital-structure leverage than another company having only common stock in its capital structure. If both companies have similar fluctuating patterns of operating earnings, then the firm with the capital-structure leverage will report more volatile EPS over time. The reason is that interest obligations and preferred dividends must be paid before calculating the EPS for the common stockholders. Once these prior claims are met, any increase in operating profit, after taxes, is reported as higher EPS. Highly leveraged companies thus have the potential to report sharp increases in EPS, but they also have the prospect of complete collapse if, under adverse economic conditions, a firm is unable to service its liabilities. The bankruptcy of the Penn Central Railroad is a notable recent illustration of the hazards confronting companies with high capital-structure leverage.

Large amounts of debt in a company's capital structure do not necessarily forecast disaster. Companies or industries for which operating earnings are comparatively stable over a long period of time usually can assume greater proportions of debt in their capital structure than can firms that experience wide fluctuations in operating earnings. Utilities, for example, typically have more stable operating earnings than do capital goods manufacturers; therefore utilities usually have more debt and preferred stock in their capital structures. Such situations indicate some of the complexities in analyzing capital-structure leverage.

Compound leverage, which combines operating leverage and capital-structure leverage, can result in explosive changes in EPS. To illustrate, a company can have both high operating leverage and high capital-structure leverage. During prosperous economic periods the company's output and sales revenues are likely to increase sharply; and much of the increased revenues can be carried through to sharply higher operating earnings. Furthermore, since the prior claims of bondholders and preferred stockholders are basically fixed, these higher operating earnings will be carried through to sharply higher EPS. In such a way compound leverage can result in an explosive increase in EPS, as illustrated by this chapter's introductory statement about a highly leveraged company:

Last year's EPS was depressed for this steel company because of its below-average steel production and also because so much of its income had to be used to pay interest and preferred dividends. Since the demand for steel is likely to increase next year, this company's EPS can be expected to increase very sharply. Thus, in our judgment, this steel stock provides unusually attractive potential for capital gains.

However, by focusing only on the possibility of substantial capital gains, this statement neglects to cite how compound leverage also can magnify possible declines in EPS.

Why should investors expect above-average returns from investments in highly leveraged stocks? An investor may invest through skill or chance, in a highly leveraged stock that subsequently provides exceptionally high returns. Consistent success in selecting such high-return stocks is dubious, however, in view of the uncertainty about future EPS of a highly leveraged stock and also about how the stock's price will be related to future EPS.

Because of prediction problems for individual highly leveraged stocks, an investor can combine several into a portfolio. Because of their structure of operating costs and debt-oriented capital structure, however, highly leveraged companies are particularly sensitive to general economic conditions. In prosperous economic periods such companies will report sharp increases in EPS; conversely, when the general economy slackens, their decreases in EPS will be magnified. Diversification is thus unlikely to be very effective among shares of highly leveraged companies for which EPS is not only associated with—but magnified by—general economic conditions. This contrasts, for example, with the benefits of diversifying among, say, growth stocks or new issues of companies whose financial performance is less directly linked to the general economy. Furthermore, as demonstrated in the next section, investors can go beyond stocks of highly leveraged companies and broaden their leveraging opportunities by creating their own leverage for almost all stocks.

Using Margin Accounts

Additional stock market opportunities are available to investors who borrow funds to finance stock purchases. By creating liabilities (borrowings) in his personal capital structure, an investor directly leverages his investment returns in a way similar to a corporation's using debt to leverage its returns. The investor thus can magnify his investment returns from any stock, rather than being limited to leveraging indirectly by purchasing highly leveraged stocks.

An investor should directly leverage his stock purchases only when confident that his expected total returns will exceed his borrowing costs, of which interest is the principal component. To illustrate, an investor may expect a 20 percent total return from his stock portfolio in the coming year. Therefore he decides to borrow funds at, say, eight percent with the intention of investing them for expected returns of 20 percent. Uncertainties, however, surround the actual outcome from such a leveraging strategy. Although the expected portfolio return is 20 percent, any such prediction of a future holding-period return from a stock portfolio is a best (guess) estimate. If the realized return turns out to be less than his borrowing cost, then the investor will have a negative net return, and he continues to be liable for the full repayment of his debt. Therefore an investor using direct leverage must analyze the potential for returns above those from unleveraged portfolios of similar stocks and relate this opportunity to the potentially negative net returns and fixed liabilities that he is accepting. As with EPS results for highly leveraged companies, capital-structure leverage for individuals generally results in magnified performance measures (rates of return) over time.

Direct leveraging is usually undertaken by purchasing stocks on margin, whereby investors borrow money to finance their purchase or holding of securities. To facilitate use of margin, the nation's stock market structure enables investors to open margin accounts that basically involve automatic borrowing privileges. Somewhat analogous to a charge account, a margin account enables an investor to buy stocks on credit, although only within carefully specified limits.

Power to regulate stock market credit has been given to the Board of Governors of the Federal Reserve System. Congress reportedly gave this regulatory power to the Federal Reserve System so that it would prevent the use of borrowed funds for excessive stock market speculation, as was prevalent before the stock market debacle of 1929. Under its powers the Federal Reserve System sets *initial margin requirements*, which specify the minimum down payment an investor must make when he buys stock on margin. To illustrate, if the margin requirement is 70 percent, then an investor planning to buy stock on margin must pay with $70 of his own cash for every $30 he borrows. In this way, for example, he can purchase $10,000 worth of a stock with $7000 of his own money and by borrowing $3000 through his brokerage account.[1]

Margin regulation by the Federal Reserve System is pervasive in coverage. All stocks listed on the nation's registered stock exchanges are subject to margin regulation. In addition about 500 stocks not listed on registered exchanges are subject to margin requirements, and the Federal Reserve System periodically revises its list of over-the-counter stocks thus subject to margin. Other investment instruments, such as convertible debentures, also come under the margin regulations, although the margin required for convertible debentures has been generally less than that required for stocks. These margin requirements must be observed by most institutions that lend funds with securities as collateral, such as brokerage firms and banks.

Over time the Federal Reserve System announces changes in its margin requirements. During the 1960s, for example, margin requirements for common stocks have ranged from 50 to 90 percent. At the extreme, the Federal Reserve System can set the margin at 100 percent, which means that new stock purchases must be paid for entirely in cash. Revisions of initial margin requirements affect only subsequent purchases of securities. If the margin requirement for stocks is raised, for example, from 60 to 80 percent, an investor is not required to reduce his outstanding borrowings; instead he will have to pay 80 percent cash and borrow no more than 20 percent of any new stock purchases.

The New York Stock Exchange also establishes margin rules for its member firms. In contrast to the initial margin requirements of the Federal Reserve System, the NYSE focuses on *maintenance margin*, which is concerned with the debt-equity relationships in investor margin accounts over time.

How and why maintenance margin is required can be demonstrated

---

[1] Technically, as an alternative to committing additional cash, an investor can use the unmargined portion of stocks he already owns, if any, to support some additional purchases on margin.

by example. Expecting to leverage his positive returns, an investor buys several stocks on margin. The stocks, purchased at the same time, have a total market value of $10,000; and these are all the stocks owned by the investor. Initial margin requirements at the time are 50 percent, so the investor pays for the purchase with $5000 in cash and with $5000 borrowed from his brokerage firm. Thus the investment is initially financed by 50 percent owner's equity and by 50 percent debt. To provide collateral for the loan the investor is required to leave his stocks on deposit with the brokerage firm.

What happens if, instead of increasing in value as expected by the investor, the margined stocks begin to decline in value? If, for example, they decline to $8000, then the investor's debt of $5000 is about 62 percent of the stocks' market value and his remaining equity of $3000 is about 37 percent of the value. If the portfolio's market value continues to decline to $6500, then the debt ratio becomes 77 percent and the investor's equity of $1500 is only 23 percent. At about this point the investor is likely to receive a margin call, requesting that he deposit more money in his account or repay part of his debt. These actions are to increase the owner's equity (margin) in his account back to at least 25 percent. The reason for requiring a minimum level of maintenance margin is to protect the brokerage firm against loss on its $5000 loan if the stocks continue to decline in price. If the investor is unable or unwilling to deposit additional cash or repay part of his debt, then, to protect its position, the brokerage firm will begin selling the investor's stocks, deposited as collateral, so that the sale proceeds can be used to reduce the loan and restore the owner's equity in his margin account to at least 25 percent. In this event the investor is forced to realize part of his stock market losses and is unable to continue holding all his stocks in the expectation that their prices will subsequently recover. Thus an investor, in assessing the profit opportunities from direct leveraging, must also consider the possibility of margin calls forcing him to realize capital losses if his stocks sell at substantially lower prices.

Requiring maintenance margin of at least 25 percent is a NYSE rule designed to protect its member firms. This is, however, a minimum requirement, a member brokerage firm can set a higher requirement as part of its own operating policies. Furthermore firms vary as to how much cash or securities an investor must have to open a margin account (the minimum requirement is $2000) and as to how they will value various stocks held as collateral in margin accounts. For example, if the market price of a particular stock drops to below, say, $5, then some firms may no longer consider these shares eligible as collateral. Such variations of margin rules among brokerage firms should alert the potential margin buyer to learn the rules before committing himself—not after he receives his first unexpected margin call. There is a similar need to understand clearly the ground rules when an investor proposes to finance stock purchases with funds borrowed from banks and other lending institutions.

A 100-percent margin is sometimes required for initial purchases of particular stocks listed on a stock exchange. In contrast to the Federal Reserve System's initial margin requirements, which are equally applicable to all stocks subject to margin, this 100-percent initial margin requirement for selected stocks is specified by the exchange on which the stock is listed. The list of selected stocks subject to a 100-percent margin generally is small and changes over time. Thus when considering a margin purchase, an investor must inquire whether any of his stock selections happen to be subject to a 100-percent margin, even when initial margin requirements for stocks in general are less than 100 percent.

Margin accounts open new opportunities to investors. By using borrowed funds an investor can directly leverage almost any stock. Instead of being limited to purchasing shares of highly leveraged companies, he can buy on margin the shares of companies that are not themselves highly leveraged. When holding-period returns from such margined stocks exceed the interest cost of the borrowed funds, then the investor increases his total investment return. Such a strategy was summarized at the beginning of this chapter by the following statement:

"We are not optimistic about the general market. Nevertheless, based on our in-depth financial analysis and interviews with top management, we believe the price of this stock is likely to increase 30 percent within six months. By buying it on margin, you can almost double this possible capital gain."

As illustrated, direct leverage thus provides an opportunity to increase investment returns.

Investors must assess the potential returns and hazards of using direct leverage. They will be buying stocks for which future holding-period returns necessarily are uncertain. At the same time they will be incurring fixed financial obligations. Interest must be regularly paid on the borrowed funds. (In recent years such interest paid by margin customers has contributed about 7 to 10 percent to the gross income of NYSE member firms.[2] Since these firms typically borrow funds from banks at lower rates than they lend them to their margin customers,

[2] *New York Stock Exchange Fact Book*, 1972, p. 64.

the difference contributes to brokerage-firm profits.) In addition to the interest costs, investors buying stocks on margin incur the hazard of receiving margin calls. Such calls—likely to occur at inopportune times—will require additional cash or securities and can result in the sale of margined stock.

In conclusion, use of direct leverage requires acceptance of interest and principal obligations of fixed debt and of meeting rules of maintaining adequate collateral under even adverse conditions. Furthermore, holding-period returns from leveraged portfolios are almost certain to vary more over time than will returns from similar non-leveraged portfolios. Investors thus should recognize how margin buying involves "costs" that can exceed its uncertain benefits in contributing to above-average holding-period returns over time.

chapter 16
Short Selling

Controversy surrounds short selling, especially by individual investors. Some commentators acknowledge that short selling involves risks, but they also show how the strategy opens new investment opportunities. Short selling enables investors to profit by selling stocks whose prices are expected to fall. While particularly appropriate in periods when stock prices in general are expected to fall, short sales also can be potentially profitable even in periods when most stock prices are expected to rise. A case for short selling is made in this illustrative statement:

> At its current price of $60, this stock has a multiple of 60 times this year's expected EPS and 50 times next year's expected EPS. In my judgment such a multiple is out of line relative to the firm's longer-run prospects, particularly in view of intensified domestic and foreign competition in the company's principal product area. Therefore I am now advising my clients to eliminate their holdings of this stock. Furthermore, more aggressive investors may want to sell the stock short in anticipation of the stock's price dropping about $20 within the year. Such an outcome can result in about a 33-percent holding-period return.

Opposing this position are commentators who dismiss short selling as a speculative strategy not suitable for most investors. They support their opposition to short selling by the following assertions:

> Short selling is too risky for most investors. The maximum gain is to double your investment, but the possible loss is infinite.

> Never sell America short. As its economy has expanded and pros-

pered over the years, so have stock prices generally increased. Therefore the odds are against the short seller.

Confronted by two such opposing positions, practical investors want to know more about risk-return opportunities from short selling. Is this strategy suitable for individual investors?

Why Sell Stocks Short?

In selling a stock short, individual investors should generally expect the holding-period return from the transaction to exceed those available from alternative investment opportunities. This motivation is illustrated by the initial illustrative statement asserting that if the stock's price falls from $60 to $40 as expected, this will result in a return of about 33 percent. This expected return may be as great, or exceed, the returns that are judged available at the time from other investment opportunities, such as purchase of selected common stocks, warrants, or convertible securities.

Short selling essentially reverses the usual investment strategy of buying a stock expecting its price to increase. This usual strategy is illustrated by an investor who, after careful analysis, decides to buy Stock A today at $30 in the expectation that its price will be $40 about a year from now. If the stock pays no dividend, the expected capital gain of $10 per share implies an expected return of 33 percent. The expected return is thus based on buying Stock A today in anticipation of selling it at a higher price a year from now.

Now what if the same investor also identifies another company about which, after careful analysis of the firm and its industry, he is convinced that future profits will fall sharply and that this profit decline is not being fully anticipated by the stock's current market price. Based on these beliefs the investor concludes that this stock's (Stock B) price, which now is $30, is likely to be around $10 in about a year. Since he thus expects a substantial price decline, he should not buy the stock and, if he owns any shares, these should be sold. Moreover, instead of then just avoiding the stock, his analysis of the stock price decline can be converted into a profit opportunity. He sells the stock, which he does not own, today at $30 in the expectation that within a year he can buy back the shares at around $10. The difference of $20 is his expected profit per share. Relative to his initial sale at $30 per share, this expected $20 profit provides about a 67 percent return if the stock pays no dividend. This expected return from selling Stock B short exceeds the expected return of 33 percent from purchasing and later selling Stock A. Under these conditions the investor can achieve a higher return by deciding to "sell high and buy low," which by merely reversing the sequence of his transactions, is similar to the much cited key to investment success, "buy low and sell high."

Short selling also is done by dealers and specialists who make markets for particular stocks. At times such a market maker is confronted by a routine buy order for which, at that point in time, he does not own the shares or immediately know of a potential seller. Since he does not have the shares in inventory, he is likely to sell short enough stock to fill promptly the customer's buy order. Subsequently the dealer will buy shares to offset those he sold. This market-making activity is a dynamic process of inventory management whereby short sales are an effective procedure enabling dealers and specialists to maintain orderly markets for various stocks. The extent of such short-selling activity is illustrated by the fact that about 57 percent of the short sales on the New York Stock Exchange in 1971 is reported to have been done by specialists in performing their market-making function in various stocks.[1] These specialists typically focus on the profitability of their continuous trading activity and are not very concerned with longer-run price expectations for stocks in which they make markets.

Individual investors can sell stock short only by using a margin account. Having identified a stock judged to be an attractive short-sale candidate, an investor calls his broker to set up the short sale. If the investor plans to sell short 100 shares of the stock, the purchaser, on the other side of the transaction, will expect to receive the 100 shares. Therefore, to make good delivery to the purchaser, it is necessary for the short seller to arrange through his broker to borrow the 100 shares that he wants to sell but does not own. The broker's firm usually can borrow shares from other customers having margin accounts or from other brokerage firms. At times, however, some stocks are not available for borrowing, in which case a short sale cannot be set up.

Margin requirements apply to short sales. For example, if initial margin requirements at the time of the short sale are 50 percent, then the short seller must deposit in his margin account cash or marginable securities having a dollar value of at least 50 percent of the sale price of the stock sold short. If 100 shares of the stock are sold short at $60 per share, then $3000 must be deposited in the margin account. This margin, in addition to the $6000 proceeds (less transaction costs) from the sale, serves as collateral to protect the brokerage firm and the investor whose shares were lent to the short seller.

[1] *New York Stock Exchange Fact Book*, 1972, p. 46.

Protection of the lenders is important because of a short seller's liability to replace the stock sold short even if its price subsequently should climb sharply.[2] In the case of the 100 shares sold short at $60 each, the short seller's goal may be eventually to buy 100 shares for $45, so that his total profit will be $1500, less transaction costs. Initially after the sale he can buy back 100 shares for around $6000. However what if the stock's price, instead of declining from $60 as expected, begins to increase? The short seller's liability to buy back the sold stock increases in dollar amount. If the stock price increases to $68, then the short seller's dollar liability approaches $6800. Against this liability the brokerage firm holds $9000 as collateral (the $6000 sale proceeds plus the $3000 initial margin). The dollar liability thus slightly exceeds 75 percent ($6800/$9000) of the total collateral. If the stock's price goes much higher, the short seller will be required to contribute additional margin in order to sustain his short-sale position. If he is unable to provide the additional required margin, then the brokerage firm will buy part or all of 100 shares of the stock sold short in order to replace the 100 shares borrowed for the short sale. Thus, if it were to buy back 100 shares at $7000, then the short seller's liability would terminate.[3] He will have $2000 left of his initial $3000 investment, having incurred a total loss of $1000, plus transaction costs, because he lost $10 on each of the 100 shares that went from $60 to $70.

Now recognizing how margin requirements generally apply to short sales, investors must remember (Chapter 15) that margin policies can vary among brokerage firms. Margin regulations of some member firms are stricter than the minimum requirement of the NYSE. Therefore, before becoming too active in using a margin account for leveraging or short selling, investors should learn the house rules of their brokerage firms.

Profits from short-sale transactions are all taxable as short-term capital gains. To illustrate, even if a stock is sold short today at $50 and replaced with shares bought nine months from now at $25, the profit of $25 per share is taxable as a short-term capital gain. Conversely, if another stock is bought today at $50 and sold nine months from now at $75, the profit of $25 per share is taxable under current laws and regulations as a long-term capital gain. Since the effective tax rate on long-term capital gains is usually lower than that on short-term capital

---

[2] The short seller is also liable to reimburse the lender of the shares for any cash dividends paid during the period the shares are borrowed. This dividend-reimbursement liability must be recognized as an additional cost of selling short.

[3] In practice the brokerage firm would probably buy only a sufficient number of shares to restore the short seller's equity to at least 30 percent.

gains, in this example most shareholders will achieve higher aftertax returns from the opportunity to buy and later sell for a $25 profit per share than they will by selling short for a $25 profit per share. This differential tax impact indicates why investment returns should also be examined on an aftertax basis and how investment decisions must be related to a complex and changing tax environment.

Risk of Selling Short

Short selling is not a complex procedure. By merely reversing the buy-sell sequence, short selling enables investors to seek profits from stocks whose prices they expect to fall. No longer need investors limit themselves to investing only in stocks whose prices they expect to rise. This broadened set of investment opportunities is available to all investors who decide to use margin accounts. However, despite the ease of short selling and the new opportunities it opens, investors often are reluctant to do so.

A major barrier to short selling is likely to be one of the conventional assertions given at the beginning of the chapter:

"Short selling is too risky for most investors. The maximum gain is to double your investment, but the possible loss is infinite."

While often made, such a statement does not stand up to realistic examination. It focuses only on two possible outcomes, each of which is extreme in the practical investment world.

The maximum gain of "doubling your money" can basically arise only if the price of the stock sold short should subsequently approach zero. For example, an investor can almost double his money if he sells short a stock at $25 and later buys it back for under $1. His per-share profit will be almost $25 which, relative to the initial sale price of $25, is "doubling your money."[4] However, although it is possible for a stock's price to approach zero, it is not likely. Such an extreme outcome generally arises only if the firm goes bankrupt, and bankruptcies are not frequent occurrences among companies whose shares, by being traded on principal stock exchanges, can be conveniently sold short.

Similarly the possibility of an infinite loss from a short sale is extremely small. At one level such a possible outcome is trite because it implies that the subsequent price of the stock approaches infinity, which is an extremely unlikely—if not impossible—occurrence. Fur-

---

[4] Technically he can more than double his money if he put up, as initial margin, only part of the short sale.

thermore, if the price of the stock sold short begins to climb, the investor is unlikely to lose even his full initial investment, let alone incur infinite losses. This follows directly from margin rules that require the short sale to be covered by buying back the stock before the short seller's equity is reduced much below 25 percent of the total collateral. (This process has been previously demonstrated in this chapter whereby a stock sold short at $60 is bought back at $70, in which case the short seller's total loss is only about 33% of his initial investment.) The short seller's loss can become larger only if he continues to contribute additional collateral to meet margin calls against his dollar liability on the poorly timed short sale. Even in this case, however, his resources are limited so that his short-sale liability will have to be covered before his losses even begin to approach infinity. In conclusion, conventional assertions about the riskiness of selling a stock short are unrealistic when they focus only on extreme outcomes that are improbable occurrences in the practical context of listing requirements, stock-price changes, and margin regulations.

Short selling against the box, which enables investors to defer tax liabilities, is basically a riskless short-selling procedure. In contrast to the usual short-sale procedure whereby an investor sells shares he does not own, short selling against the box involves the short sale of a stock already owned by the seller and held, for example, in his safe-deposit box. To illustrate, four years ago an investor bought 1000 shares of a stock at $10 per share. Today the stock has a market price of $40. Not only is the investor satisfied with his $30 capital gain per share, he is concerned that the future direction of the general market may be downward and that the price of his stock may then fall back toward $20. Therefore, to realize his total profit of about $30,000, he can now sell the 1000 shares at $40 per share. This year, however, he has substantial other income that he does not expect to receive next year. Therefore, because he then expects to be in a lower tax bracket, he prefers to realize the $30,000 capital gain next year.

Short selling against the box enables this investor to meet his dual goals of locking in his potential total profit of $30,000 and yet not realizing it for tax purposes until next year. He sells short 1000 shares of the stock at today's price of $40 while continuing to hold the 1000 shares he bought four years ago. Next year he can close out his short sale; and, no matter what happens to the price of the stock, he will realize a total profit of $30,000. For example, if the stock price falls to $30, he will make $10 per share on his short sale and lose $10 of the previous $30 capital gain. Thus, with the exception of transaction costs, his total gain of $10,000 from the short sale will just offset the total $10,000 decline in value of the shares he owns. In a similar way, if the stock price goes above $40, he will lose on his short sale just about any gains beyond the locked-in $30,000 on the shares he owns (his long position). Thus, whatever the price, next year the investor can realize his $30,000 gain by simultaneously closing out both his short and long positions. One way, of course, is just to deliver to the broker the 1000 shares he owns in order to close out the short sale previously established at $40 per share.[5] In summary, by selling short the shares he already owns in order to lock in a profit, there is no risk to the investor who sells short against the box.

Going beyond the short sale of a single stock, investors can sell short many different stocks. A "portfolio viewpoint" thus can provide additional insights into the risk of selling short.

Diversification of short sales among different stocks enables investors to achieve risk-reduction benefits similar to those achieved by diversifying among various stocks in which they hold long positions. As described in Chapter 9, diversification essentially involves an averaging process. The extreme returns in a diversified portfolio are somewhat offsetting. Similarly, by diversification, the uncertainty whether any one short sale will turn out to involve large negative returns is somewhat offset by holding other short positions, all of which will not display such extreme adverse outcomes.

Returns from diversified portfolios of short sales will approach the inverse of general market returns. In other words, if next year's general market return (as derived from a broadly based index) is −20 percent, then a broadly diversified portfolio of short sales is likely to provide a return of +20 percent. (The individual returns from the component short sales is distributed around this portfolio return, ranging, say, from −10 to +50%.) Similarly if the short sales turn out to be poorly timed so that the market return is +30 percent, then the diversified portfolio of short sales will provide a return of about −30 percent.

Evidence supports the viewpoint that short selling is not necessarily risky, especially when there is portfolio diversification of short sales. Two coauthors have reported their results from testing what would have been the percentage gain or loss realized from randomly selling short stocks from a sample of 573 stocks continuously listed on the NYSE from 1945 through 1965.[6] The time period of the experiment is 1961 through 1965, a period of generally rising stock prices. In each month during the total time period, new short positions are established

---

[5] Although short selling against the box thus is an effective tax deferral procedure, it cannot be used to extend short-term capital gains into long-term capital gains.

[6] Richard W. McEnally and Edward A. Dyl, "The Risk of Selling Short," *Financial Analysts Journal*, November-December 1969, pp. 73–76.

for each stock. These positions are held open for time intervals of one, three, and six months; after each interval the short positions are covered by buying back shares to replace those sold short. Because of the many stocks and time intervals covered, the authors report their study to be based on over 30,000 hypothetical transactions. As measures the authors use percentage gains or losses (not annualized total returns) adjusted for the dividend cost to the short-seller but not for transaction costs and differential tax treatment.

Results of this experiment by McEnally and Dyl demonstrate that short selling is not inherently risky. They report that on the average "investors would have realized a 1.35 percent loss from randomly selling short for one month over this period, a 3.65 percent loss for three months, and a 6.53 percent loss for six months."[7] (Losses are to be expected because the experiment is during a period of generally rising stock prices.) Percentage gains and losses from the individual short sales are found to be symmetrically clustered around the average losses. In other words, for the average loss of 1.35 percent for one-month intervals, most of the individual short sales provide gains or losses ranging from 10 percent to −10 percent, and the chances are about equal for realizing a similar-size gain or loss on an individual short sale. As the length of the time interval increases from one month to three and six months, the individual gains or losses are less clustered around the average, but the distributions continue to be relatively symmetrical. Extreme losses from individual short sales are found to be very infrequent for the strategies and time intervals tested. Recognizing certain limitations of their study, the authors conclude that they have "clearly found no evidence that short selling is actually the highly risky proposition that it is thought to be."[8]

Investment results from selling short are generally associated with the length of time that short positions are left uncovered. As demonstrated in the study by McEnally and Dyl, the odds are not necessarily against short sellers who cover their short positions after comparatively brief time intervals. But what is likely to happen as short positions are left open for longer time periods? Chances of larger losses increase. This conclusion follows from results of studies by Fisher and Lorie (Chapter 5), wherein it is found that portfolios of NYSE stocks generally provide positive returns as holding periods increase beyond one year. These positive returns from buying and later selling imply negative returns from selling short and later buying. Thus these results generally support the assertion given earlier:

[7] *Ibid.*, p. 75.
[8] *Ibid.*, p. 76.

"Never sell America short. As its economy has expanded and prospered over the years, so have stock prices generally increased. Therefore the odds are against the short seller."

The speaker's conclusion, however, is based on short-sale positions left open for long periods of time. It cannot realistically be generalized to short positions left open for comparatively brief time periods. (In fact much short selling is done by specialists who, in their continuous processes of inventory management, rapidly cover their short positions.)

In conclusion, short selling, in principle, enables investors to profit from stocks they expect to fall in price. In practice, however, tough-minded investors must assess their confidence in being frequently able to identify in competitive markets stocks whose prices will subsequently fall sharply. Isolated examples of historically successful short sales are insufficient evidence. The key issue is portfolio performance over time.

Short selling is not unusually risky. Under some conditions, such as short sales against the box, there is virtually no risk—but neither is there any opportunity for gain except as part of a total tax strategy. On a portfolio basis, short selling need not be very risky, but neither is it likely to result in unusually high returns over time. Short sales open additional risk-return opportunities when used in investment strategies based on hedging. How to hedge and returns and risks of hedging are examined next.

chapter 17
Hedging

Individual investors usually have not been alerted to hedging strategies. Traditionally hedging is viewed as a specialized area of stock market activities. From this perspective, hedging strategies are most appropriate for professional investors having convenient access to timely information, analytical skills, and large pools of capital. These in-depth resources are usually available to those who specialize in hedging and arbitrage activities for major investment firms.

Hedging concepts and practices now receive wider publicity, largely because of the proliferation of hedge funds in the late 1960s. By their willingness to discuss their underlying philosophy and techniques of running hedged portfolios, managers of these new pools of capital dispel some of the traditional mystique surrounding hedging operations. In addition new information about the performance of these hedge funds is becoming more available to investors.

Basically hedging involves combining diverse investment instruments into long and short positions. Appropriate combinations enable an investor virtually to "lock in" profits no matter which way stock prices generally move. Diversity of hedging opportunities is suggested by these illustrative statements.

Westinghouse Electric recently announced an offer to acquire Longines-Wittenauer Watch. For each share of Longines-Wittenauer, currently selling for around $25, Westinghouse proposes to exchange .45 share of its common stock that is currently selling at about $65.

A way to profit from this proposed merger is to establish a merger-hedge. You buy 100 shares of Longines-Wittenauer for around $2500 and, at the same time, sell short 45 shares of Westinghouse for around $2925. The total difference of $425 is your gross profit.

When the merger is completed, in exchange for your 100 shares of Longines-Wittenauer, you will receive 45 shares of Westinghouse that can then be used to close out your short position. The beauty of this operation is that your profits basically are locked in, no matter what subsequently happens to general stock prices or to the prices of the two stocks.

By simultaneously establishing positions in different securities of the same company, it is possible both to participate in large gains and limit any possible loss.

A hedge fund enables investors to have their investment funds aggressively managed by professionals using diverse strategies in seeking above-average returns. Moreover the fund's overall risk can be reduced by holding some short positions in volatile stocks.

The hedging strategies supported by such statements will be examined in the context of securities markets where many astute investors compete to increase returns and to limit risk.

Merger-Hedges

Opportunities to construct merger-hedges arise after one company announces plans to acquire a second company through an exchange of securities. The acquiring firm usually offers some of its common stock (or instruments convertible into common stock) in exchange for the shares of the company to be acquired. To make its offer attractive, the acquiring company typically establishes an *exchange ratio* so that, when announced, the market value of the shares offered by the acquiring company exceeds the market value of the shares of the company to be acquired. For example, in announcing a proposed merger, American Cyanamid offered to exchange .96 share of its common stock for each share of Shulton. Shortly before the announcement the price per share of American Cyanamid was around $33\frac{1}{2}$, while that of Shulton was around \$25. Thus the .96 share of American Cyanamid had a market value of about \$32 (.96 × $33\frac{1}{2}$), which was \$7 greater than Shulton's market price of \$25. Such a difference in market values typically persists in the days following an initial merger announcement, although the exact amount of the difference will vary over time.

Profit opportunities from merger-hedges arise from such differences in relative prices. To illustrate, two weeks later the market price per share of American Cyanamid was about \$34 and that of Shulton was about \$29. An investor with a margin account could then have set up the following illustrative merger-hedge. Provided he can borrow shares of American Cyanamid through his brokerage firm, he sells short 96 shares at $34 each for a total short sale of $3264, less transaction costs. At the same time he purchases 100 shares of Shulton for about $2900, plus transaction costs. The difference of $364, less transaction costs, is his potential profit. This profit essentially is "locked in" no matter what subsequently happens to the prices of the two stocks. When and if the merger is consummated, he will receive 96 shares of American Cyanamid in exchange for his 100 shares of Shulton. He can use these shares to replace those he borrowed for the short sale. In this way the transaction is closed out with a total profit of $364, less transaction costs. If he uses about $6164 to finance both his long and short positions, then his percentage profit on the total investment is about six percent.[1] In this illustration the merger was soon consummated, so that the six-percent return was realized within four months.

Knowing how to construct a merger-hedge and how it can be potentially profitable, realistic investors begin to focus on the uncertainty of the return from a merger-hedge. Profit from a merger-hedge is "locked in" *as long as* the merger goes through at the announced terms. Hazards exist, however. Basically, (1) the proposed merger can be cancelled; (2) the merger terms can be revised to the detriment of the merger-hedge; and (3) the merger can be delayed so that, although the dollar profit is eventually achieved, the return from the merger-hedge is substantially less than those available from alternative investment opportunities. These possible outcomes imply that a "locked-in" return does not result from every merger-hedge.

What can happen to a merger-hedge after the companies announce their merger discussions have ended? In one case, the shares held long can quickly fall in price while the shares sold short quickly rise in price. In this event, an investor can incur losses on *both* his long and short positions as he proceeds to undo the merger-hedge by selling the long shares and buying back the shares previously sold short. Conversely, depending on subsequent market prices, he may profit from both his long and short positions in the process of undoing an aborted merger-hedge. Other outcomes also are possible. In summary, no specific profit is locked into a merger-hedge if the intended merger is not consummated.

---

[1] Similar principles apply in analyzing proposed mergers involving convertible securities and/or involving other exchange ratios. Return calculations depend on whether the investor finances his position entirely with cash or with some margin. As an alternative procedure the investor may choose to close out his short position by buying the shares in the market and simultaneously selling the shares he receives in the merger. This procedure does not change the before-tax profits as "locked in" at the time the merger-hedge was established.

Merger terms are at times revised after the initial announcement. To illustrate, one company initially announces plans to offer three of its common shares for each one of a second company. A merger-hedge then can be created if, for example, the three shares have a total market value of around $60 while each share of the company to be acquired has a market price of $50. This relationship implies a potential merger-hedge profit of $10 per share of the acquired company. Merger terms, however, are subject to revision so that, in the example, the final merger terms may be set at 2.8 shares for each share of the acquired company. In this event the investor will not receive a sufficient number of shares to cover his short position. Therefore, he will have to buy some shares in the market to close out his merger-hedge. Because this purchase involves additional costs, his planned profit from the merger-hedge will be reduced. Conversely, if the acquiring company's merger terms subsequently become more generous, the realized profit will be above that originally foreseen from the merger-hedge. Possible revision of merger terms thus also adds uncertainty to the potential profit from any merger-hedge.

Delays in achieving the final merger also contribute to uncertainty of the return from a merger-hedge. Even when a merger subsequently is consummated at the previously announced terms, the return from a merger-hedge will be affected by the length of time between the creation of the merger-hedge and the completion of the merger. To illustrate, two companies plan to merge on the basis of a one-for-one share exchange. Shares of the acquiring company are sold short at $50, and shares of the company to be acquired are purchased at $45. The potential profit is $5, the difference between $50 and $45. If the merger is consummated within three months, this $5 profit on a maximum investment of $95 can be attractive. The potential profit is over 5 percent within three months. (By leveraging, of course, the potential profit can be magnified.) But now what if the merger encounters a series of delays such that the same $5 profit is achieved only after one or two years? Extended over a longer time period, the holding-period return becomes less attractive in view of additional costs in maintaining the merger-hedge. An extended time period thus can result in the merger-hedge's net return becoming less than those available from alternative investment opportunities.

Delays can arise at many junctures before a final merger outcome. Small companies in nonregulated industries can encounter various delays, such as opposition by management teams or major shareholders in either firm. Also either company may choose to delay in order to explore alternative merger opportunities. In comparison, potential delays are compounded for mergers between large companies in regulated industries. In addition to potential managerial or shareholder delays, the merger may be subject to study and approval by diverse regulatory agencies. Opposition to the merger can be carried to various courts, for example, by competitors or consumer groups. In addition the Justice Department may choose to oppose the proposed merger on the basis of antitrust laws. Such diverse factors, each affecting *whether* and *when* a proposed merger will be consummated, often vividly arise in regulated industries such as railroads.

The potential return from any merger-hedge generally is uncertain. New insights arise, however, by examining a potential merger-hedge in the context of a competitive market. Sensible investors realize that others also seek profitable opportunities. Some competing investors specialize in identifying merger-hedges and assessing the probabilities of whether and when various mergers will be achieved. They can devote substantial resources to this competitive process of search and analysis. Various investment banking firms have specialized units devoted to analyzing the profit opportunities and uncertainties of various hedging activities. Their assessments become reflected in the relative market prices of shares of merger-hedge candidates.

To illustrate this competitive market process, consider two companies that previously announced plans to merge. They have encountered no major opposition by officials or shareholders of either company. Regulatory agencies and the courts have not become involved in the proposed merger, nor are they judged likely to do so. The merger is scheduled for completion within a month. Because of general confidence that the proposed merger soon will be achieved, the relative share prices of the two companies will move closely together, largely because of the activities of merger-hedge investors. The potential profit per share will not be very large because the outcome is comparatively certain.

In contrast, two railroads announce plans to merge; but opposition at once arises at many levels. Because of the uncertain outcome, the potential per-share profit from a merger-hedge may appear large. This large potential profit, reflecting the relative share prices of the two railroads, generally reveals, however, the market's uncertainty about whether and when the merger finally will be consummated. Over time as merger-hedge operators become more or less confident of the outcome, this will be reflected in the relative share prices of the two railroads. In conclusion, the possible profit from a merger-hedge must be assessed relative to its implied risk; and competitive market processes provide insights into the risk as perceived by various skillful investors.

Case examples, selected by hindsight, can be used to illustrate realized returns from both successful and unsuccessful merger-hedges.

Tough-minded investors, however, go beyond selected past examples. Aware of competitive markets, they question whether merger-hedges are likely to provide consistently and substantially above-average returns over time.

Evidence concerning returns from merger-hedges is provided in a comprehensive evaluation by John P. Shelton. The study focuses on major questions posed by merger-hedge opportunities:

> "1. Do enough of the mergers fall through that the losses associated with hedging and unhedging offset the gains on the completed mergers?
>
> 2. Do the mergers take so long to be consummated that the effective rate of return is unsatisfactory?"[2]

Shelton's study evaluates the outcomes from 41 possible merger-hedges identified during the five-year period from 1958 through 1962. Eight of the 41 were not completed, and only four were unprofitable. Shelton observes that "a loss, when it occurs, will typically be larger than the profit from a successful merger-hedge, being offset by the greater frequency of successes than failures."[3] Returns calculated from these merger-hedges are dependent on hypothesized investment strategies, such as the selection, size, and timing of the hedges and the extent of leveraging. Based on carefully specified assumptions (such as an investor's committing the cash necessary to margin both the long and short positions), Shelton concludes that the annual rate of return from the 41 merger-hedges was 11.2 percent.[4] During the same five-year period, the return from a diversified portfolio of NYSE common stock is likely to have been around 16 percent.[5] These results suggest that, even if they commit substantial resources searching for and analyzing merger-hedges, most investors are unlikely to achieve substantially above-average returns over time from such a strategy.

Hedging with Convertibles and Warrants

Profit opportunities can arise from price differences among securities of the same firm. Furthermore major losses can be avoided by simul-

---

[2] John P. Shelton, "An Evaluation of Merger-Hedges," *Financial Analysts Journal,* March–April 1965, p. 50.

[3] *Ibid.*

[4] Other assumed strategies can result in higher annual rates of return. For more detail, see the appendix "The Research Procedure," Shelton, p. 52.

[5] This figure is from Lawrence Fisher and James H. Lorie, "Rates of Return on Investments in Common Stock: The Year-by-Year Record, 1926–65," Table 2, Part A.

taneously establishing long and short positions among the firm's securities. These hedging opportunities usually occur when a firm has convertible securities or warrants outstanding.

Hedging opportunities typically arise when a company's convertible security (Chapter 14) sells near its straight value and also near its conversion value. In such a case, when an investor believes that the company's stock price will drop sharply, he can sell the stock short and yet hedge his position by purchasing an appropriate amount of the convertible security. If, as expected, the stock's price falls sharply, the investor will profit from his short position. During the same time the convertible's price also is likely to fall but, because of its "floor" as a straight issue, not as sharply as that of the associated common stock. The difference between the profit from the short sale and the smaller loss from owning the convertible security is the investor's potential profit from the hedging operation. Moreover the investor is hedged, if the stock price goes up, instead of down as expected. In this event he can convert the bond or preferred stock into common shares to be used to cover his short position. In contrast, by not hedging, a large loss is possible from an increase in the price of the stock sold short.

Now to show numerically such a hedging operation with an illustrative convertible security. A bond, convertible until maturity into 20 common shares, currently sells for around $1000. The conversion price per common share is thus $50. Currently the common stock sells for $45, so that the bond is selling at approximately a 10-percent premium over its conversion value of $900 (20 × $45). As a straight bond, without the conversion feature, the bond is estimated to have a value of $950. Such conditions provide a basis for a hedging operation.

After careful consideration an investor estimates that the price of the company's common stock is likely to fall quickly to around $30. Depending on his degree of confidence and his alternative opportunities, he may decide to sell the stock short for an estimated profit of $15 per share, or about 33 percent on the sale price of $45. However, he can use the convertible security to hedge his short position. For example, at the same time that he sells short 100 shares for $4500, he also purchases five of the convertible securities for $5000 (5 × $1000). If the price of the common stock declines to $30 as predicted, then the investor can buy back 100 shares at $3000 to cover his short position. His profit from the short position will be $1500 ($4500 − $3000). However, with the price of the common stock thus declining to $30, the convertible bond is then likely to trade basically at its straight-bond value of $950, assuming no major changes in the level of interest rates. The value of the five convertible bonds owned long thus will decline from $5000 to $4750, for a total loss of $250. This loss of about $250 on the long position subtracted from the profit of about $1500 on the short position leaves a total profit of $1250, less the various transaction costs.

What if the price of the common stock, instead of dropping to $30 as expected, climbs quickly to $55? Having hedged his position, the investor is able to avoid much total loss. Buying back 100 shares at $55 to cover the short position established at $45 will result in a loss of $1000. However, as shown in Chapter 14, each convertible will then be selling for at least its conversion value of $1100 (20 × $55), plus some premium, say around 10 percent, for a market value of about $1200. In this event the total value of the five convertible bonds will be $6000, for a total profit on the long position of $1000 ($6000 − $5000). Under these conditions, even with the price of the common stock rising, the total loss to the investor will be his various transaction costs. Furthermore, his maximum possible loss is $500, plus transaction costs, even if the premium on the convertible bond drops toward zero. This follows from the fact that he can convert each of the five bonds into 20 common shares, for a total of 100 shares that he can use to cover his short position. Direct conversion of the bonds thus sets the maximum loss at $500 (plus some transaction costs), which is the difference between the short sale at $4500 and the bond purchase of $5000.

A price must be paid for the protection of the hedge position. In the illustration, if the stock price drops from $45 to $30 as expected, the unhedged short seller's total profit is $1500 less transaction costs. In contrast the hedged short seller's total profit is $1250 less transaction costs. By protecting himself against the possibility of the stock's rising in price, the hedged investor forgoes some potential profit if the stock price falls as expected.

Warrants also can be used in hedging operations. A warrant essentially enables its holder to obtain a fixed amount of a company's common stock (such as one share) at a specified price for a specified time period (Chapter 13). As such, under appropriate conditions, a company's common stock can be sold short and its warrant bought long in order to construct a hedged position that will provide profits from an expected decline in the stock price while limiting the magnitude of loss if the stock price unexpectedly rises.

Hedging with a warrant can be demonstrated with an illustrative set of securities. A company has warrants enabling a holder of a warrant to buy one share of common stock for $50. The warrants expire 10 years from now. Today the common stock sells for $45. Since the stock's current price of $45 is below the warrant's exercise price of $50, no one would logically buy the warrant except to participate in the *possibility* that the price of the common stock will exceed $50 in the coming years. Because of the leveraging opportunity from such a warrant, it will now have a positive market price, say, of $10. Such market relationships between a firm's common stock and warrants can provide an opportunity for a hedged short sale.

An aggressive investor who expects that the price of the common stock soon will decline to around $30 is likely to consider selling the stock short. His decision will be based on his confidence that the expected return of about 33 percent from this short sale will exceed probable returns from alternative investment opportunities. He may choose moreover, to hedge a short sale of say 100 common shares by simultaneously purchasing 100 of the warrants at $10 each. If the price of the stock drops to $30 as expected, the profit from the short sale will be $1500 ($4500 − $3000). During the same interval the price of each warrant will fall. However it can fall no further than zero and, in fact, it will have some market price because of the possibility that the common stock will sell for more than $50 sometime before the warrant expires. Thus, if the warrant price falls to $5, the total loss from the 100 warrants is $500 ($1000 − $500) which, subtracted from the short-sale profit of $1500, still leaves a total profit of $1000 less various transaction costs, from the hedged short sale.[6]

What if the common shares sold short begin to increase sharply in price instead of falling to $30 as expected? The price, for example, rapidly advances to $55. If the short position then is closed out, the loss per share will be $10 for a total loss of $1000. However, with the common stock at $55, the market price of the warrant will be at least $5 (its intrinsic value) and probably it will sell at a premium so that its price will somewhat exceed $5. For example, the market price of the warrant may be $15 when the common stock is $55, so that the hedge operator then will have a profit of $5 per warrant, for a total profit of $500 from the 100 warrants. This profit will somewhat offset the loss of $1000 from the short sale of the common stock, so that the net loss from the hedged position will be $500 plus various transaction costs.[7] Without this hedge the short seller will lose around $1000 by covering his short sale at $55, and he will lose more if he waits and covers his short position at a price above $55. As with convertible-hedges, such a warrant-hedge usually involves some sacrifice of potential return to avoid the possibility of a large loss.

---

[6] Of course an investor having strong beliefs that the warrants will drop from $10 to $5 as the common stock drops from $45 to $30 will achieve a higher rate of return by directly shorting the warrants. However by thus seeking the higher possible return, he forgoes the protection of the hedge.

[7] At the extreme the dollar loss from this hedged position cannot exceed $1500 plus transaction costs. The operator can exercise his 100 warrants, for which he paid $1000, in order to buy 100 shares of common stock for $5000 to cover the 100 shares he sold short for $4500.

Hedging opportunities from convertibles and warrants require realistic evaluation. A comparatively large return from a hedging operation arises only when the stock sold short falls sharply in price. If the hedging operator can confidently predict such a decline in a competitive market, why hedge? If he cannot confidently predict such a decline, then he is committing funds to an operation having only some *possibility* of high returns. Meanwhile he forgoes alternative investment opportunities. Moreover an investor can use other procedures, such as stop orders (Chapter 21), to avoid a major loss while seeking a substantial investment profit.

Realistic investors are not satisfied with knowing how various hedging operations might work in theory, if all goes well. Neither are they convinced by selected past operations that proved profitable. Because various skillful operators compete to find and exploit hedging opportunities, realistic investors realize that hedging with convertibles and warrants is unlikely to provide consistently superior returns for most of the nation's investors.[8]

Hedge Funds: Potential and Performance

Hedge funds are intended to provide their participants with the opportunity to achieve consistently high returns with comparatively low risk. This, of course, is almost an ideal investment goal. The funds generally seek to achieve this goal by providing substantial incentive and flexibility to encourage their managers to seek and exploit diverse investment opportunities.

A private hedge fund is generally organized for only a limited number of investors. Although comparatively wealthy and knowledgeable about investments, these participants usually have other full-time occupations, therefore they prefer to have some of their investment funds professionally managed. As an incentive for the manager to succeed, the participants usually agree that his compensation will include a performance fee that will reward him with part of the fund's above-average returns. Private hedge funds, because they are not generally regulated by the Securities and Exchange Commission, have substantial flexibility to develop imaginative and generous performance (incentive) contracts.

How is the hedge fund manager, with his incentive to succeed, sup-

[8] Additional variations of hedging with convertibles and warrants are possible. Furthermore investors can purchase put and call contracts to use in hedging operations. Analysis of these additional opportunities is beyond the scope of this book. Nevertheless readers now are alerted to the need for realistically assessing such additional hedging opportunities in competitive markets.

posed to achieve his clients' goals of high returns with low risk? Basically he is allowed—and expected—to use various "sophisticated" investment strategies. Not limited to well-known common stocks listed on the nation's principal exchanges, he is expected to search out emerging growth stocks, "hot" new issues, and obscure special-situation stocks. Furthermore he can invest in what he judges to be attractive convertible securities or warrants. He can leverage the fund's portfolio in order to augment the fund's profit opportunities; he can aggressively sell stocks short to profit from expected declines in their prices. In summary, a hedge fund manager has substantial flexibility to exploit opportunities judged to have unusual potential for high returns.

While aggressively seeking high returns, a hedge fund is also supposed to limit its risk by hedging the portfolio against unexpected major market developments. Generally this is done by committing a proportion of the fund's assets to short sales in selected stocks. To illustrate, a fund's manager is basically confident that stock prices generally are in a strong uptrend. Therefore he commits a substantial proportion of the fund's assets to sophisticated strategies expected to achieve high returns from such a predicted market environment. He realizes, however, that, while the chances seem small, future events such as wars or international monetary crises may rapidly be followed by substantial declines of most stock prices. To protect the fund against such unexpected events, the manager maintains short positions in some selected stocks. If the market goes down unexpectedly, the gains from these short sales will somewhat offset the losses from the aggressive long position. The total portfolio return will then be less adverse than if it had been totally committed to an aggressive long position. Conversely, if the general market goes up as expected, then the losses on the short sales will be overshadowed by the substantial profits expected from the aggressive long position. Under these conditions, the total portfolio return will be somewhat less than that of a similar unhedged long position. However this sacrifice can be seen by hedge fund participants as a small price to pay for "insurance" against unexpected events that can have major adverse effects on their portfolio return. After all, they choose to participate in a *hedge* fund instead of just an unhedged, aggressively managed portfolio.

Potential rewards to managers and investors in hedge funds attracted many participants by 1968. A recent study for the Securities and Exchange Commission reports that "total hedge fund assets grew very quickly from $333 million at yearend 1966 for the 35 hedge funds organized in 1966 or earlier to $1.3 billion for 140 hedge funds at yearend 1968."[9]

[9] *Institutional Investor Study Report of the Securities and Exchange Commission,* Summary Volume, (U.S. Government Printing Office: 1971), p. 29.

Despite their sophisticated investment techniques, management flexibility, and supposedly added protection of hedging against major market declines, many of these funds performed poorly during 1969 and 1970. Reportedly, "by September 30, 1970, the total assets of the 28 hedge funds which were largest at December 31, 1968, were almost 70 percent less than at yearend 1968. . . ."[10] Furthermore at least five of the 28 were either dissolved or in the process of being liquidated.

Poor portfolio performance is unlikely to explain all of the substantial decline in aggregate assets of the hedge funds. Some assets were sold to meet capital withdrawals by participating investors, to reduce borrowings used to leverage the portfolios, and to facilitate liquidation of some of the funds. Recognizing such diverse factors contributing to the decline in total assets, *Fortune* estimates that the hedge funds declined, on an average, 29 percent during a time period when the general market decline was about 20 percent.[11] Furthermore *Fortune* states that "it is difficult to arrive at any set of assumptions that would show the large hedge funds as a group performing as well as the market." Although these results occurred during a major market decline, a principal rationale for hedge funds is that they will *hedge* against such market adversity.

In conclusion, portfolio hedging conceptually provides opportunities for higher returns while insuring against adverse market events. The recent two-year performance record of hedge funds indicates the difficulty of implementing the hedging concept *in practice*. Unless an investor is always willing to hedge a fixed percentage of his portfolio, he must decide *how much* of the total portfolio should be hedged at various points in time. Such timing decisions basically must rely on predictions of future market movements. In addition, he must decide *which* investment securities should be held long or short at various points in time. In making such timing and investment-selection decisions, the portfolio manager competes with many other investors having access to similar information about the economy and about individual securities. Managers of hedged portfolios thus must continuously make investment decisions whether and when to buy, sell, or hold securities being valued by a competitive market process. Therefore there is little reason to believe that portfolio hedging is a practical technique for "beating the market."

[10] *Ibid.*, p. 30.
[11] *Fortune*, May 1971, pp. 269–270.

REVIEW OF PART FOUR

Question: Which investment strategies shall I use?

Answer: The question cannot be answered without: (1) a practical understanding of principal investment strategies, and (2) a basis for choosing from among strategies.

Most popular investments books do not provide the information necessary to answer the question. Directed toward individuals anxious to learn about stocks, investment books and articles conventionally proceed from the assumption that opportunities are available to diligent, committed investors. These primers then broadly survey many different strategies or focus on more detailed descriptions of specific strategies.

Whatever their breadth, these investment primers rely on two principal methods to describe various strategies. They use (1) selected examples of how strategies worked in the past, and (2) examples of how they might work under various hypothetical conditions. Thus records of companies like IBM are cited to illustrate a growth-stock strategy. Examples of notable turnarounds illustrate the merits of a special-situation strategy. Short selling is shown to be potentially profitable if the stock price drops sharply but to result in potentially "infinite" losses if the stock price starts to skyrocket. Warrants are generally described as providing an opportunity for unusually large profits, coupled with the possibility of complete loss if they expire valueless. In such ways, traditional materials describe the *possibilities* of many strategies.

Unfortunately the traditional form of information is inadequate for investors to choose among strategies. They leave the investor with three principal options. First, he can choose some strategies arbitrarily and then assess their usefulness to him over time. Second, he can draw on most or all of the strategies, such as managing a margined portfolio that includes shares of growth companies, new issues, special situations, convertibles, and some short sales. Third, he can commit himself to learning more about various strategies before choosing from them. All three of these options require additional commitment by the investor.

Realistic surveys must go beyond examples to evaluate the long-term logic, practical implementation, and results of various strategies. With these objectives, Part Four introduces various strategies, using examples to illustrate certain points. It dissects the logic of identifying "growth stocks" as those of "growth companies" in a marketplace where many informed investors compete to participate in shares of companies believed to have above-average growth potential. Using a competitive market framework, Part Four demonstrates practical problems of implementing popularized strategies such as buying "hot" new issues, identifying special situations that are indeed "special," and effectively hedging a portfolio by varying the proportions of long and short positions. Drawing on results of recent studies, Part Four provides evidence about returns over time from such strategies as investing in convertible securities, short selling, and constructing merger-hedges.

Practical investors now can use a similar framework to evaluate investment strategies in addition to those reviewed in Part Four. They will focus on a proposed strategy's logic and practicality in the context of a competitive market. In addition, they will focus on assessing evidence concerning whether a strategy provides above-average returns over time.

A general conclusion emerges from Part Four. It is that logic and evidence strongly indicate that none of the surveyed strategies provides returns substantially and frequently above those provided by broadly diversified portfolios of common stocks. This is a useful conclusion. It is not a negative or know-nothing conclusion. First, it demonstrates the difficulty of finding unusually rewarding strategies in a competitive market. Realistic skepticism is appropriate. Second, the conclusion highlights whether most individuals should commit their resources to learning more and more about various investment strategies. Expected benefits from the quest are small or uncertain, while the cost of commitment can be comparatively high. Third, since few, if any, such strategies consistently outperform broadly diversified portfolios of common stocks, there is a strong case for examining how investors can participate in broadly diversified portfolios at comparatively low cost. The logic and practical implementation of a low-cost, broad diversification strategy is presented in Part Six .

* * *

Before accepting this general conclusion to Part Four, investors are encouraged to evaluate further investment strategies as presented in textbooks, articles, and the following types of books.

Armour, Lawrence A., editor, *How To Survive a Bear Market: The Way the Wall Street Pros Do It* (Dow Jones Books: 1970).
——, *Investing for Profit: How Professionals Make Money Grow* (Dow Jones & Company, Inc.: 1969).
——, *Profits on Wall Street: How the Professionals Make Money Grow* (Dow Jones & Company, Inc.: 1968).
Finley, Harold M., *The Logical Approach to Successful Investing* (Henry Regnery Company: 1971).
Hazard, John W., *Choosing Tomorrow's Growth Stocks Today* (Doubleday: 1968).

Knowlton, Winthrop, and John L. Furth, *Shaking the Money Tree: How to Find New Growth Opportunities in Common Stocks* (Harper & Row, Publishers, Inc.: 1972).

Loeb, Gerald M., *The Battle for Investment Survival* (Simon and Schuster: 1965).

————, *The Battle for Stock Market Profits* (Simon and Schuster: 1971).

Peisner, Robert N., *How to Select Rapid Growth Stocks: Six Practical Tools for Finding Stocks with a Potential for Rapid Growth* (E. P. Dutton & Co., Inc.: 1966).

Phelps, Thomas W., *100 to 1 in the Stock Market* (McGraw-Hill Book Company: 1972).

Rosenberg, Claude N., Jr., *The Common Sense Way to Stock Market Profits* (The New American Library: 1968).

————, *Stock Market Primer*, Revised Edition (The World Publishing Company: 1969).

Thomas, Conrad W., *Hedgemanship: How to Make Money in Bear Markets, Bull Markets, and Chicken Markets While Confounding Professional Money Managers and Attracting a Better Class of Women* (Dow Jones-Irwin, Inc.: 1970).

PART FIVE

DECIDING WHEN TO BUY OR SELL COMMON STOCKS

chapter 18
Timing of Investment Decisions

Conventional investments books and articles present a case for individuals to improve their timing of investment decisions. Usually neglecting the costs of trying to make timely decisions, the conventional case focuses on possible benefits. It cites how large rewards can follow from correct decisions about *when* to buy or sell selected stocks. Such demonstrated benefits usually are based on either of two principal conditions. One is *hindsight*, the other is *hypothetical foresight*.

Successful timing decisions about purchases and sales of individual stocks are frequently illustrated by hindsight. Such success is summarized in the illustrative statement:

> It does no good just to buy and hold stocks. Two friends of mine each bought 100 shares of the same stock at around $40 per share early in 1972. One held the same shares all year; and by year-end the market price was $50, for a capital gain of 25 percent. The other bought and sold the shares several times during 1972, thus taking advantage of the stock's price fluctuations. His capital appreciation on this series of transactions was 50 percent.

Both investors purchased the same stock at the same time, so their different results were due to the subsequent timing decisions. The second investor, by successfully exploiting changes in the stock's price during the year, apparently did twice as well as the first investor who bought and held. However, not only does this comparison involve hindsight, it also rests on a selected example. A realistic standard for evaluating such selected examples is demonstrated later in this chapter.

Hypothetical foresight is another basis for many illustrations of the benefits of investment timing. Foresight frequently appears in the general form: "If a certain event will occur, then a logical investment decision now can be made." Such foresight is evident in the following statement:

> If you expect stock prices generally to fall sharply in the coming months, then you should sell your stocks and hold cash; or, if more aggressive, you should use your sale proceeds to sell short a diversified portfolio of stocks.

The concluding investment recommendation follows logically from the statement's introductory condition. What is missing, however, is the basis for the expectation. Unless such a market decline can be predicted with reasonable confidence, then such a hypothetical event is a frail basis for recommending investment actions such as converting the stock portfolio to cash or to a diversified short position.

The consistency-of-success (CS) standard enables investors to judge the plausibility of claimed benefits from various investment-timing decisions. Instead of accepting past case examples or hypothetical future possibilities, the CS criterion focuses on total performance over time. This criterion involves three principal dimensions.

First, comparisons must be based on net returns after various (1) search-and-analysis costs (2) transaction costs and (3) taxes.

An investor who frequently buys and sells individual stocks must recognize his costs in obtaining and evaluating the information on which he bases his decisions. Such search-and-analysis costs include subscriptions to various investment advisory services—or journeys to libraries to read such information. In addition there are costs involved in closely monitoring a stock's price action: for example, by plotting daily graphs of prices, subscribing to computerized price-information services, or sitting in a brokerage office watching a stock market tape. These various costs involve cash expenses and commitment of time.

Transactions costs must be explicitly recognized in determining net investment returns. Transactions costs include not only the brokerage costs and transfer taxes on each purchase and sale, but also the record-keeping costs resulting from frequently trading stocks. Record keeping is important for tax purposes.

Taxes can be an important element in assessing various investment-timing decisions. Currently the nation's tax structure allows recognized long-term capital gains generally to be taxed at lower effective rates than gains realized from stocks held for less than six months. Therefore results from frequently trading or buying-and-holding similar stocks must be compared on the basis of net returns—after taxes.

Second, the CS standard goes beyond a concern with one stock and focuses on comparisons that include the various stocks in investment portfolios. For example, in the illustrative hindsight statement, the investor who bought and sold a stock several times during 1972 had, for this stock, twice the total capital appreciation of the other investor who bought and held the stock throughout the year. (As demonstrated, the CS standard insists that the more relevant basis for comparison is net returns.) This, however, is based on a selected sample of one. Did the investor who successfully traded the sample stock similarly achieve higher returns by trading other stocks in his portfolio? To illustrate, the trader may have incurred a net loss by frequently buying and selling a second stock at what turned out to be the wrong times as the stock price trended upward from $20 to $30. On this stock the investor who held it throughout the year achieved the higher return. If one moves beyond only two stocks, a key issue is whether the frequent trader achieved a higher annual return from his *portfolio* of stocks than did the investor who bought and held similar stocks.

Third, the CS standard requires comparison of net returns from different timing decisions over a series of years. Even if the illustrative investor who traded the selected stock similarly achieved higher net returns, on average, from his various investments in 1972, this may be a chance occurrence. Realistic investors will want more evidence. They will want to know whether he has been similarly able to time his purchases and sales in order to achieve consistently higher returns on his portfolio over many years.

Usefulness of the CS standard goes beyond assertions about the benefits from past timing decisions. It enables realistic investors to evaluate the practicality of various procedures recommended for improving the timing of investment decisions.

No shortage exists of procedures suggested as aids for improving investment-timing decisions. Technical analysis, charts, stop-loss orders, and dollar-cost averaging are among the suggested procedures.

Not satisfied with conventional descriptions of how such timing procedures have worked in the past, serious investors want answers to tougher questions:

1. How is the timing procedure supposed to work? In particular, what is its rationale, and is it sensible?
2. How well has it worked in the past? Results count! In evaluating past results, realistic investors apply the consistency-of-success standard.
3. Why should I expect it to work in the future? Importantly, if it

works very well, are not other investors also likely to use this timing aid and, thus, reduce its possible future benefits?

Answers to this checklist of practical questions are provided in the subsequent four chapters that analyze diverse aids to investment timing.

chapter 19
Technical Analysis

Soon after developing an interest in the stock market, most investors begin to read or hear about opportunities from technical analysis. Its proponents emphasize its usefulness for improving the timing of investment decisions. Frequently they build their case on the following types of statements.

The stock market has a logic of its own. Therefore, by focusing on key indicators of what is happening in the market, technical analysts can identify clues as to the market's general condition and future direction.

In our judgment, the advance-decline line is an important technical indicator. Often when the direction of this indicator diverges from that of popular stock market averages, this signals a major change in stock prices.

Instead of relying on any one technical indicator, we regularly review many and use this information to aid our judgment about the future direction of stock prices.

Inquisitive about opportunities from technical analysis, realistic investors will want answers to three logical questions:

1. How is technical analysis supposed to work?
2. How has it worked in the past?
3. How is it likely to work in the future?

Objectives of Technical Analysis

Proponents of technical analysis basically believe there are market-related indicators that can assist investors in predicting future directions of stock prices.

Emphasis is on *market-related* indicators, such as recent changes in stock prices, trading volume, and short-selling activity. In contrast, technical analysis does not directly focus on broad economic indicators such as recent changes in monetary measures, industrial production, or a nation's balance of payments. Disregard of general economic indicators by technical analysts is based on their belief that shrewd investors evaluate and use such economic information to make decisions to buy or sell stocks. Actions of these shrewd investors then are reflected in indicators that can be monitored to assess the impact of new economic information in the stock market.

Emphasis of technical analysis also is on predicting future directions of stock prices. Underlying technical analysis is the critical assumption that certain market-related indicators go beyond merely indicating past events (What has happened?) and in fact can aid in predicting future events (What is likely to happen?). Such a key assumption is intertwined with the assumption that trends often persist, so that information about past events provides insights into future events.

Based on their general views about why technical indicators can be useful for predicting future stock prices, technical analysts offer many different indicators. For too long, however, the rationale underlying specific technical indicators has been generally vague or inconsistent. Furthermore typical "evidence" of their usefulness has been hindsight examples of apparent success in certain time periods.

Realistic investors demand more than vague generalities and selected past examples. Before accepting a technical indicator as a practical aid to investment timing, they want to know its reliability. Preferably there is a logical rationale explaining *why* it is supposed to work. Furthermore the indicator will have been tested so that investors can be reasonably confident about its predictive power. Such testing should demonstrate whether an indicator meets the consistency-of-success standard.

Results of Technical Analysis

Many technical indicators have been suggested; but, until recently, few have been tested. Reviewing here the rationale and results of many suggested indicators is impossible. Therefore two popular indicators will be assessed in some detail, followed by the results of a recent survey of tests of other technical indicators.

An *advance-decline* (A-D) *line* is frequently cited as a major technical indicator. What is an A-D line? How is it supposed to work? How has it worked?

An A-D line shows the relationship between the numbers of advancing and declining stocks in a specific time period, such as a day. To illustrate, on January 5, 1973 the number of NYSE stocks that advanced was 745; and the number that declined was 687. Advancing stocks thus exceeded declining stocks by a difference of 58 (745 − 687). Furthermore this difference can be compared to those of previous days to identify any trend or change in trend. For example, in the preceding four days advances generally outnumbered declines, resulting in the following series of differences:

Thursday	− 154
Wednesday	+ 242
Tuesday	+ 843
Monday	Market closed

These differences focus only on *how many* issues advanced compared to the number that declined, not on *how much* was the average price advance relative to the average decline. Of what use is this numerical summarization of differences between numbers of NYSE stocks advancing and declining within a specific week? It focuses on past events (What has happened?).

Prediction is the key, and toward this end followers of advance-decline relationships frequently calculate an A-D line. This line assumes various forms. It can be a chart portraying over time the cumulative differences between the numbers of advancing and declining stocks. However other technicians calculate various-length moving averages of daily or weekly A-D figures in the belief that such adjusted numbers provide greater insights into trends or changes in trends. Such a moving average also can be plotted as an A-D line.

Clues to future directions of stock prices are sought by technical analysts searching A-D lines for possible trends or changes in trends. Such a view of the predictive quality of an A-D line is presented in the second illustrative statement:

"In our judgment, the advance-decline line is an important technical indicator. Often when the direction of this indicator diverges from that of popular stock market averages, this signals a major change in stock prices."

Why is an A-D line supposed to be predictive? A typical rationale is that toward the end of a sustained uptrend in general stock prices—a bull market—many speculative issues of smaller, less-known companies start to decline in price as shrewd investors begin to sell such stocks in anticipation of a market setback. In this event the number of stocks advancing relative to those declining will turn downward before a subsequent general decline in more widely known stocks such as those comprising the Dow Jones Industrials Average. On this basis an investor attuned to an A-D line should be alerted to reduce his stock holdings before a general market decline. Further description of the A-D line and demonstration of how it has worked in selected past periods are provided in articles such as "Advance-Decline Line: It Provides a Clue to the Underlying Strength or Weakness of the Market."[1]

Identifying major turning points in an A-D line is easier with hindsight than with foresight. It is not difficult to identify past episodes of major declines in stock market averages that were preceded by downturns in an A-D line. Unfortunately this provides an incomplete analysis. In particular, it neglects other times when an apparent downturn in an A-D line *was not* followed by a major decline in the stock market averages. As one looks toward the future, what today may seem to be an initial downturn from a recent peak in an A-D line may in fact turn out to be only a "wiggle," so that the line soon advances again toward a new, higher peak. False signals thus can arise from an A-D line. Therefore practical investors want a total examination of the reliability of an A-D line as predictive technical indicator.

Forecasting power of the A-D line is evaluated in a recent study testing the reliability of the A-D line to predict market movements during two time periods between April 1963 and October 1967. Direct focus is on the need to define peaks and troughs of the A-D line as they apparently occur—not just with hindsight. Based on various tests, the authors conclude that "the Advance-Decline Line is virtually worthless as a leading indicator of the stock market, at least during the time period studied."[2]

The *Confidence Index* is another frequently cited technical indicator. As reported weekly in *Barron's*, this index is a ratio of representative yields from high-grade bonds and mixed-grade (on average, "riskier") bonds. To illustrate, early in January 1973 the ratio was reported as

[1] George K. Freeman, "Advance-Decline Line: It Provides a Clue to the Underlying Strength or Weakness of the Market," *Barron's*, January 21, 1963, pp. 9, 15–16.

[2] Alan J. Zakon and James C. Pennypacker, "An Analysis of the Advance-Decline Line as a Stock Market Indicator," *Journal of Financial and Quantitative Analysis*, September 1968, p. 299.

92.8.[3] This figure represents an average yield of 7.22 percent from 10 high-grade bonds divided by an average yield of 7.78 from 40 mixed-grade bonds. Such a number merely summarizes past relationships between bond yields. Therefore why do technical analysts frequently include this indicator in developing their assessments of future directions of stock prices?

A typical rationale for the predictive value of the Confidence Index focuses on a distinction between shrewd investors and unsophisticated investors. Shrewd investors are better able to obtain and assess various economic information. They then use their insights to predict future directions of the nation's economy. When they lack confidence in the economic future, they shift some of their funds from lower-grade ("riskier") bonds to high-grade bonds involving less risk. Other things equal, such shifts imply higher prices, and reduced yields for high-grade bonds and lower prices, and increased yields, for lower-grade bonds. Such changes affect the two components of the Confidence Index, resulting in a decline in the index. Followers of the Confidence Index, by thus watching its trend over time, can potentially detect whether shrewd investors are becoming less confident about future economic conditions. By similar reasoning, when the Confidence Index trends upward this can be interpreted to mean that shrewd investors are demonstrating greater economic confidence by shifting part of their holdings from high-grade to lower-grade bonds. Before accepting this rationale, realistic investors want to know more about the logical basis and demonstrated usefulness of the Confidence Index.

"A Vote of No-Confidence in the Confidence Index" is the title of an article challenging the practicality of the Confidence Index as a stock market predictor. The challenge is based on two principal issues:

"The underlying theory of why the Confidence Index should be a good stock market barometer is ill-conceived in several respects;

whether the theory is right or wrong, in actual practice during the full postwar period the Confidence Index has had a rather poor record as a stock market prophet."[4]

The rationale for the Confidence Index rests on several key assumptions: first, the existence of a group of "shrewd investors" capable of uncannily correct forecasts of future economic conditions; second, a consistent behavioral pattern of such investors shifting between high-

[3] *Barron's*, January 8, 1973, p. 67. This series is at times revised, for example, by substitution of different bonds in the two categories.

[4] Edward D. Zinbarg, "A Vote of No-Confidence in the Confidence Index," *The Institutional Investor*, March 1967, p. 37.

grade and lower-grade bonds; and, third, a consistent linkage mechanism between such economic forecasts, bond market behavior, and subsequent stock market prices. All these assumptions are debatable.

Weaknesses in the rationale of the Confidence Index can be overlooked in practice, however, if it is reasonably consistent in predicting future stock prices. After reviewing the postwar record of the Confidence Index to forecast major stock market turns, the author states:

"The conclusion is evident. The Confidence Index has not exhibited the characteristics of a good leading indicator of the stock market during the past twenty years. More often than not it was coincident or lagging."[5]

Thus the no-confidence vote is based on a critical review of both rationale and evidence. Another no-confidence vote is cast by another team of analysts also after testing the predictive power of the Confidence Index. Concluding their analysis, they state, "These findings suggest that the Confidence Index is not a leading stock market indicator and may in fact be a lagging indicator."[6]

Other popular technical indicators similarly have been tested in recent years. Many of these tests are summarized and reviewed in a recent survey of technical analysis. Among the indicators reviewed are: relationships between stock prices and trading volume; short interest in various stocks; stock transactions involving less than 100 shares (odd lots); and advance-decline statistics. Summarizing his review of studies testing such technical indicators, the author concludes:

"The findings of the studies in this area, while somewhat contradictory, indicate that; (1) there is a relationship between present or past movements in volume and present or future movements in price; (2) short interest has no discernible relationship to price; (3) odd-lot sales may provide some clues to expected price movements; and (4) advances and declines in securities may have enough relationship to price to be of some usefulness."[7]

Such evidence, while not conclusive, does not provide strong support for uncritical acceptance of these popular technical indicators.

Technical analysts will likely assert that such testing of individual

---

[5] *Ibid.*, p. 64.

[6] Cornelius F. Walsh and Gail Simonton, "The Confidence Index as a Stock Market Indicator," *Journal of Bank Research*, Summer 1971, p. 44.

[7] George E. Pinches, "The Random Walk Hypothesis and Technical Analysis," *Financial Analysts Journal*, March–April 1970, p. 109.

technical indicators is inadequate. In their view such tests fail to capture many subtleties of interpreting technical indicators. Also, since not all possible indicators have been tested, technical analysis cannot be generally refuted. In assessing this view, investors must consider what evidence they require before deciding to accept or reject the practicality of technical analysis.

Technical analysts observe that use of technical indicators reflects an "art of interpretation" that is incapable of being distilled into precise relationships for scientific testing. Such tests fail to capture all the subtleties of any one indicator, the interpretation of which can shift over time. Furthermore no technical analyst relies only on one indicator. Instead he uses a fluid set of different indicators to develop estimates of future stock prices. This viewpoint is outlined by the third illustrative statement:

"Instead of relying on any one technical indicator, we regularly review many and use this information to aid our judgment about the future direction of stock prices."

The complex decision-making process outlined by this statement cannot be effectively tested by applying the consistency-of-success standard to individual technical indicators.

A paradox results from asking investors to view technical analysis as a complex interpretive art. Technical analysis, if it does not follow a set of principles or general rules, is indeed incapable of being directly tested. However, it is also then incapable of being communicated to investors wanting to learn how to use technical analysis. They are being asked to accept the practicality of a vague stock market technique that is incapable of being rigorously described and communicated.

Furthermore practicality of the "art of technical analysis" is capable of *indirect* testing. Even if technical analysis is individualized and highly unstructured, its results over time can be evaluated. At least some technical analysts, using their interpretive skills, should be capable of compiling impressive records of successful stock market predictions. These predictions should be translated into a record of successful stock market transactions that will objectively demonstrate the usefulness of technical analysis for "beating the market." Unfortunately little, if any, evidence is thus available to support the practical benefits from technical analysis. Open-minded investors welcome such evidence. Until they receive it, they will be skeptical of the practical benefits of the subtle art of technical analysis.

How should investors respond to the assertion that technical analysis cannot be generally refuted because all possible technical indicators have not yet been tested? In addition to reviewing available evidence, realistic investors consider what counterevidence is likely to arise from a stock market comprised of many skillful competitors.

Recent tests of frequently cited technical indicators cast major doubt on their practicality as consistent predictors of future stock prices. Future tests of other popular indicators are likely to lead to a similar conclusion. This follows from the framework (Chapters 2 and 3) that competing investors, by their actions, will remove any net benefits from widely-known stock-market information, including technical indicators.

It is possible that some useful indicator—or combination of indicators—exists that is not widely publicized. However, if it compiles a reasonably consistent record of successful predictions, then it will become publicized, so that over time its net benefits will be removed by the actions of competing investors. Also, by committing substantial resources, an investor may succeed in identifying a new indicator or new combination of indicators. Yet practical investors, recognizing that through time many others are committed to a similar goal, will question whether rewards from such possible success are likely to exceed the commitment of substantial time and money to search for such indicators.

In conclusion, realistic investors cannot be satisfied with incomplete illustrations of how technical indicators are supposed to work or selected examples of how they have worked in certain past periods. They insist on learning why such indicators are *generally* supposed to work and how they have *generally* worked. Technical analysis basically has not been shown to meet these practical, generalized standards. Furthermore, in a competitive market technical indicators that are widely publicized are unlikely to provide net benefits to their users; and obscure useful indicators, while possible, are unlikely to persist. Therefore the burden of proof now falls on technical analysts to demonstrate objectively how their art can consistently aid the timing of invesment decisions.

chapter 20
Charting

Controversy surrounds use of charts to identify stock market opportunities. Chartists claim their charts can assist investors in making
decisions not only about *which* stocks to buy, sell, or hold, but also
when to act. Skeptics challenge chartists to prove their case. These
opposing viewpoints are outlined by the following illustrative statements:

> In searching for stocks to buy, I like to review my various charts
> to identify stocks forming breakout patterns.

> Charting is bunk!

> Charting is just one of many tools we use in our investment
> analysis. We keep charts on stocks in which we are interested in
> order to get a feel for each stock and to understand what chartists
> may see in the stock's pattern. Thus, while we do not rely on them,
> we do use charts—along with other information—in making invest-
> ment decisions, especially with regard to timing.

Unwilling to accept or reject charting without more information, practical investors want to know how charting is supposed to work in
theory and how it works in practice.

Chart Construction

Chartists typically distinguish between two principal types of charts: a
bar chart and a *point-and-figure chart*. Each is designed to contain
graphical information judged relevant for investment decisions.

Bar charts are easily constructed. Generally they summarize daily price information about individual stocks. The range of a stock's daily prices is represented by vertical line on a bar chart. The line's highest point represents the stock's highest price of the day, and the lowest point represents the day's lowest price. Intersecting this vertical high-low line is a small line to denote the stock's closing (last) price of the day.

To illustrate how to update a bar chart, consider these three prices:

Today's highest price	52
Today's lowest price	$48\frac{7}{8}$
Today's closing price	$51\frac{1}{2}$

Today's price information now can be plotted on Illustrative Bar Chart (I).

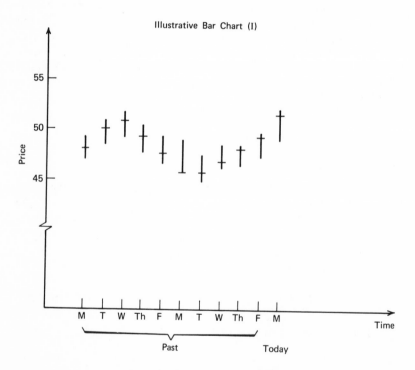

New price information thus is plotted regularly—such as daily or weekly—on bar charts, a procedure that will be seen to differ from that of point-and-figure charts.

Not limited to portraying prices of individual stocks, bar charts also can summarize price information about groups of stocks. Appearing regularly in *The Wall Street Journal* are bar charts of three Dow Jones stock averages: Industrials, Transportation, and Utilities.

Volume information also can be portrayed on a bar chart. For stocks listed on stock exchanges, the total number of shares traded on the floor of the exchange is reported daily.[1] To illustrate, today's trading volume for the illustrative stock is reported as 22,400 shares. Volume information thus can be added to the illustrative bar chart.

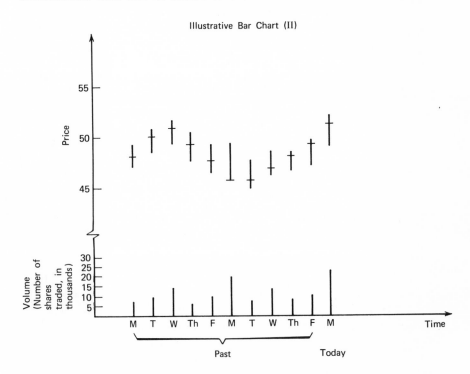

Illustrative Bar Chart (II)

Bar charts portraying price and volume information for individual stocks are published regularly by various financial services. Similarly, as published in *The Wall Street Journal*, bar charts of the various Dow Jones Averages are supplemented with a chart summarizing total trading volume on the New York Stock Exchange.

Point-and-figure (P-F) charts at first seem mysterious in their construction. What is the basis for the following columns of +'s and O's?

[1] Increasing numbers of shares of stocks listed on the New York Stock Exchange have been traded away from the Exchange in recent years. Therefore a stock's daily volume on the Exchange's floor does not necessarily represent all the day's transactions in the stock. Improved information about over-the-counter transactions now is becoming available.

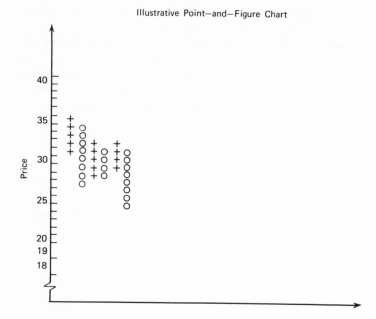

Illustrative Point–and–Figure Chart

Because chartists follow differing procedures in creating P-F charts, only the principal procedures for constructing representative P-F charts can now be summarized.

P-F charts are designed to portray only those major stock price changes judged to represent a continuation of a past trend or else a major trend reversal. Therefore, before beginning to plot a P-F chart, at least two principal criteria must be specified: (1) What amounts to a "major price change"?; and (2) How extensive must be a change in a price trend before it is classified as a "trend reversal"?

In specifying what is a "major price change," nearly all P-F chartists cite the importance of relative price change. They observe, for example, that a 50-cent price change on a $25 stock is a similar *relative* change (2%) to a one-dollar price change on a $50 stock. Therefore they plot only relative price changes, say two percent, for all stocks; or else they decide to plot smaller price changes of low-priced stocks and only larger price changes of high-priced stocks. For example, a chartist may decide to plot any price change totaling more than 50 cents for stocks selling below $20, but only price changes totaling more than one dollar for stocks selling above $20.

P-F chartists also must specify how to recognize a "trend reversal." To illustrate, consider a stock price that has trended consistently upward from $40 to $50, but in recent days has declined from $50 to $48. Has the "uptrend" from $40 to $50 now been sufficiently reversed to warrant reclassification as a "downtrend," or should such reclassification be deferred to see whether the stock's price continues to decline, say to $47 (a three-point drop from $50) or to $46 (a four-point drop from $50)? Therefore P-F charts can be constructed only after specification of what counts as a "trend reversal," such as, two, three, or four points or a stipulated percentage reversal.

Construction of the initially mysterious P-F chart now can be explained.

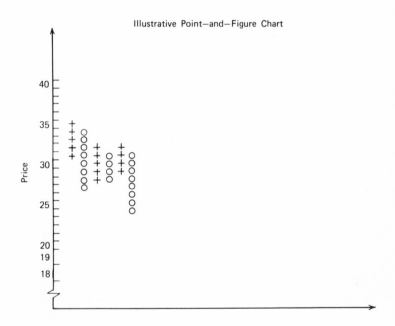

Illustrative Point—and—Figure Chart

In this illustrative chart of Modnar Fictitious Corporation prices are shown on the vertical axis. To adjust somewhat for relative price changes, the price scale is in one-dollar units above $20 and 50-cent units below $20. It is a four-point reversal chart.

The plotting of Modnar's price history on this chart began when the stock's price was $30. Subsequently the price rose steadily to $35, without this uptrend ever being reversed by four points ($4) or more. This uptrend is depicted by the initial column of +'s. Subsequently, however, the price declined from the peak of $35 to a price of $31. This four-point reversal is depicted by the top four O's in the second column. As long as the price trended downward, every time the price declined an additional point ($1), another circle was added to extend this column of O's downward. Thus the price is seen to have continued its downtrend to $27 before a four-point reversal signaled a new uptrend (+'s) to $32 (third column), before another four-point reversal signaled the new downtrend (O's) depicted by the fourth column. A P-F chart thus portrays a continuing process of trend, trend reversal, opposite trend, etc.

Portrayal of a stock's price history on P-F charts depends on specifications of "major price moves" and "trend reversals." For example, the same series of actual prices will look different when plotted as a P-F chart depicting 50-cent price changes and three-point reversals than when plotted as a P-F chart depicting one-dollar price changes and five-point reversals. Also, although +'s and O's are used in the illustrative charts, P-F charts differ in their symbols of uptrends and downtrends. Therefore investors must consider how P-F charts are constructed before they begin to interpret them.

Unlike bar charts, there is no explicit time dimension in a P-F chart, the horizontal scale of which need not represent equal-length time periods. Although construction of P-F charts requires regular monitoring of stocks, plotting is only updated when major price changes and trend reversals occur. Thus the price history of a volatile stock may require many alternating columns of +'s and O's while, on the same scale, several years of price history of a less volatile stock may be compressed into only several columns of +'s and O's. Also, unlike bar charts, P-F charts do not usually include volume information.

In summary, construction of bar charts and P-F charts is not complex, once the plotting procedures are specified. Both principal types of charts summarize in their own way a stock's price history and, in some cases, additional information such as past trading volume. Now introduced to chart construction, realistic investors are not interested in spending extensive time interpreting *past* information as graphically summarized in a chart. They focus on the key question: Of what practical use are charts in predicting future stock prices?

Chart Interpretation

Proponents of charting recognize that charts conveniently summarize past information, but they believe also that careful interpretation of charts provides clues to future directions of stock prices. What rationale and evidence underlie their confidence in charting as a predictive technique?

Chartists assert generally that dynamic supply-demand relationships are summarized in a stock's price. No investor can hope to monitor the many rapidly changing factors that contribute to such supply-demand relationships. Therefore he can better spend his time focusing on a chart, the changing patterns of which provide a capsule summary of shifting investor interest in a stock. Furthermore, such aggregate investor interest is believed continually to reflect new information and revised expectations. Monitoring a chart thus should alert an investor that a stock's price may be responding to important new developments, all of which he could not hope to monitor directly.

A related rationale for charting is that, by monitoring developing price patterns, chartists can gain clues into what the "smart investors" are doing. This viewpoint assumes that there are some astute, well-capitalized, and well-informed, investors who usually make wise investment decisions. In contrast, there are assumed to be many "naive investors" who often behave irrationally. The interplay of these forces is allegedly captured in chart patterns. By monitoring such patterns, chartists should be alerted to whether a stock is passing from the "strong hands" of smart investors to the "weak hands" of many naive investors, or vice versa.

To relate the rationale of charting to a specific illustration, consider the following chart pattern.

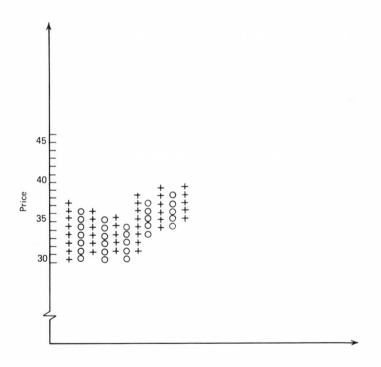

Many chartists interpret such a pattern as indicating the stock to have strong buying support ("demand") at $30, and that if it now "breaks out" above $40, then its price is likely to continue upward. Such an interpretation assumes that some astute investors, based on extensive information and analysis of the firm, apparently believe the stock is "a buy" at around $30. Therefore they are aggressive buyers when the price dips to about this level. In addition, the stock's high price has been moving progressively upward. Thus, there is apparently no substantial "supply" of stock available at some set price, such as $35. Therefore, if the stock's price soon goes above $40, there is no apparent major "resistance" to its continuing to advance upward. This description illustrates a breakout pattern, as cited in the first illustrative statement.

"In searching for stocks to buy, I like to review my various charts to identify stocks forming breakout patterns."

Also, it demonstrates how patterns of stock prices can be interpreted to show a stock's possible "support area" (where there is apparent buying demand) or "resistance area" (where there is an apparent supply of stock from sellers); and how such interpretations are linked to assumptions about supply-demand relationships and about behavioral patterns of "astute" and "naive" investors.

Although interpretation of a particular chart may seem quite sensible, the rationale of charting is open to major objections. Use of the words "supply" and "demand" give charting an initial aura of economic respectability. Usually, however, the words are hollow. Seldom, if ever, is there any attempt to specify rigorously how charts can identify or portray the shifting schedules of supply and demand for a stock. Moreover, the rationale of charting basically assumes a two-way split: (1) astute investors who are consistently successful, and (2) naive investors who are frequently unsuccessful. Such a two-way split of investors and their behavioral patterns is too simplistic a view of a competitive marketplace. Objecting to the rationale for charting, some critics summarize their view with a form of the second illustrative statement, "Charting is bunk!"

Despite major weaknesses in the rationale of charting, investors will not lightly dismiss a technique that can be shown to have practical usefulness for improving investment decisions. How does charting work in practice?

"Evidence" of charting's usefulness in predicting future stock prices too often rests on selected hindsight examples. Various investments books provide examples of charts that seem to demonstrate predictive qualities. Selected illustrative charts look like this:

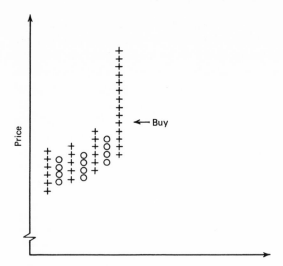

or like this:

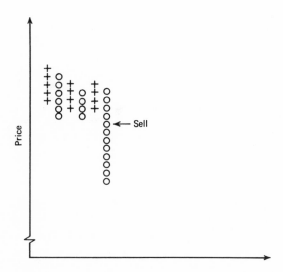

Unfortunately selected examples of seemingly predictive charts prove next to nothing. They merely illustrate several major fallacies of incomplete analysis.

By searching through many charts, some can be found that at first glance seem to demonstrate the merits of charting. Perceptive investors, demanding a general view, want to know how many other charts also provided similar "buy" or "sell" signals—only to be followed by an opposite or inconclusive outcome. In other words, what will happen to the following chart in the coming days:

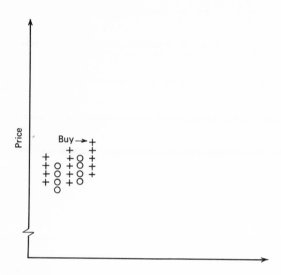

Will it look like this?

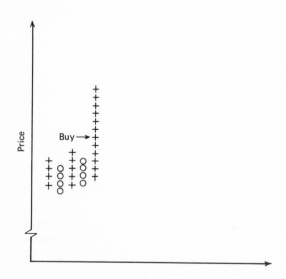

Or like this?

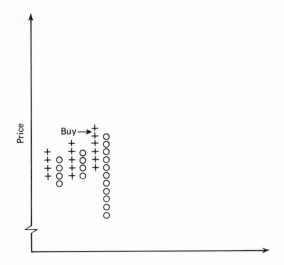

Or, most likely, somewhat like this?

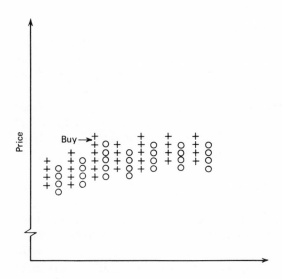

Although this exercise portrays only several possible future patterns, it demonstrates how today's "buy signal" may well turn out to be a "false signal" that is erroneous or irrelevant. Therefore, in evaluating charting, practical investors are not impressed with hindsight examples; they insist on knowing whether charting is generally predictive of future stock prices.

Apparent profit opportunities from some hindsight charts can be illusory. Reconsider the following chart:

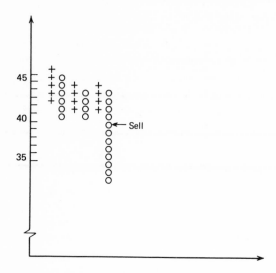

The implication is that an alert chartist, seeing violation of a "support area" of around $40, would have quickly sold his shares, thus avoiding major loss, or sold short some borrowed shares, thus profiting from the stock's continued decline to $32. However, there may not be adequate time for such decisions. For example, the stock price could have dropped from $41 to $34 within one day. In retrospect the chart seems to depict a clear "sell signal" at $39, but in practice most chartists could not have acted on a signal that only appeared when the chart was updated at the end of the day or week.

Charting has been apparently seen as incapable or unworthy of rigorous testing. Recently, however, the predictive significance of some charting patterns has been analyzed. After specifying 32 different price patterns that might signal "breakouts," the author tests the predictive merits of such patterns for 548 NYSE securities during a time span of five years (July 3, 1964 to July 4, 1969).[2] A total of 9383 "breakouts" are found to meet the author's specified criteria. Summarizing his results, the author states, *"after taking trading costs into account, none of the thirty-two patterns showed any evidence of profitable forecasting ability in either (bullish or bearish) direction."*[3] Citing other aspects of

[2] Robert A. Levy, "The Predictive Significance of Five-Point Chart Patterns," *The Journal of Business*, July 1971, pp. 316–323.

[3] *Ibid.*, p. 318.

charting still to be tested, such as inclusion of trading volume, the author acknowledges that his results do not conclusively prove charting to be useless. Nevertheless, practical investors can include this preliminary evidence in their assessment of the practicality of charting while awaiting possible counterevidence from proponents of charting.

Claiming that chart interpretation is an art, proponents of charting will be likely to claim that their techniques cannot be realistically tested. Acknowledging that charts can provide ambiguous "buy" or "sell" signals, chartists assert that only by studying the intricacies of developing price patterns can a devoted chartist acquire "a feeling" of whether a stock's price will go up, down, or sideways. However, although somehow derived from interpreting the stock's past price patterns, the basis for this feeling cannot be directly explained. Moreover, other chartists, looking at the same pattern, may develop different views about the future direction of the stock's price. Therefore, if different chartists develop conflicting predictions from the same charts and if none can effectively explain or communicate the bases for his predictions, then sensible investors must question whether mysticism might not as well be a basis for predicting future stock prices from past patterns.

Disclaiming total reliance on charts, some investors claim to use charts as *one of many* aids to their investment decisions. This viewpoint is outlined by the third illustrative statement:

"Charting is just one of many tools we use in our investment analysis. We keep charts on stocks in which we are interested in order to get a feel for each stock and to understand what chartists may see in the stock's pattern. Thus, while we do not rely on them, we do use charts— along with other information—in making investment decisions, especially with regard to timing."

Thus many chartists claim to combine fundamental and technical analysis in their search for stock market opportunities.

To illustrate this combined fundamental-technical (F-T) approach, consider an investor who identifies several stocks he judges fundamentally to be undervalued "special situations." He realizes, however, that other investors may not immediately, if ever, similarly recognize these stocks to be undervalued. Therefore, instead of committing funds to these several stocks now, he chooses to monitor them on charts. The assumption is that, as other astute investors also recognize the fundamental attractiveness of these stocks, their buying activity will become noticeable in the chart patterns. An investor who uses a combination F-T approach in this way admits that he is unlikely then to buy what he judges to be an undervalued stock at its bottom;

thus he must forgo "a few points of possible profit." In his judgment, however, the small missed opportunity can be a low price to pay to avoid tying up funds for long periods of time while he waits for other investors to "bid up" the prices of the stocks he selected by using fundamental analysis.

Although the possible success of such a combined F-T approach sounds fine in principle, in practice it rests largely on the assumption that directions of future prices can be predicted from patterns of past prices. Furthermore the practical results of this approach are difficult to test directly, especially when its proponents assert that many different factors enter into their final investment decisions. Indirect evidence about the usefulness of this approach can be expected to appear, however, in the performance records of investors claiming to follow it. Does the combination F-T approach enable them to "beat the market"? Sensible investors welcome such practical evidence to support the long-term success of the combined fundamental-technical approach to investment selection and timing.

Investors can now form their conclusions about the merits of charting. They understand how to construct charts and the rationale of how charts are supposed to assist investment decisions. Alert to fallacies of selected examples purporting to demonstrate by hindsight the merits of charting, they focus on logic and evidence supporting the practical value of charting, such as further direct testing of charts against the consistency-of-success standard or indirect evidence of some investors whose charting skills have enabled them, consistently and substantially, to "beat the market."

Valuing their limited time, realistic investors can conclude by relating charting to the view of competitive markets (Chapters 2 and 3). Many services provide charts to subscribers. If such information has substantial economic value, logically the charting firms would be expected directly to use it to manage investment portfolios, rather than generally distributing it to many subscribers. Instead these graphical summaries of past price patterns are made generally available to many investors competing to remove any possible net profits from this information. Yet if possible net benefits are thus removed, how can many different services continue to offer their charts to investors? Their very existence seems to imply the usefulness of charts for predicting future directions of stock prices. Consider, however, that over time many investors search for new ways to "beat the market." In their quest they are likely to subscribe to some charting services. Therefore a key issue is (1) whether the same investors basically continue to subscribe to the same charting services over time, thus implying that they receive net benefits from the charts, or (2) whether there is substantial turnover among subscribers as they continue to respond to introductory offers in their search for new charting services that they hope will be unusually valuable? Until presented with stronger evidence supporting charting, tough-minded investors remain skeptical and look toward other procedures to improve their timing of investment decisions.

Experiment

The illustrative four-point reversal chart for Modnar Fictitious Corporation was created by flipping a coin 100 times and recording the series of heads and tails. In such a series of 100 tosses, there will be occasional sequences ("trends") of several heads or several tails followed by a sequence of opposite outcomes ("trend reversals"). In this experiment, each head was counted as +$1, and each tail as −$1. Starting arbitrarily at $30, this random process generated subsequent price changes that could then be plotted as an illustrative P-F chart.

You can conduct similar experiments and develop your own patterns.

Although the generation of chart patterns by random processes does not disprove the value of charts, it does raise doubts.

chapter 21
Stop Orders

Investors who base timing decisions on technical analysis or charting will probably be disappointed over time. Neither logic nor evidence supports the view that such techniques result in predictions enabling an investor to "beat the market." Therefore, instead of trying to predict when is a good time to buy or sell a stock, investors can automate their timing decisions through a simple procedure—the stop order. As summarized in the following illustrative statements, this procedure often is cited as a means of protecting profits while avoiding major losses.

> A first principle for successful investing is to cut your losses and let your profits run. Stop orders provide an excellent device for easily putting this principle into practice.

> Five months ago I bought 100 shares of stock at $20 per share. Yesterday the stock closed at $35. To protect most of my "paper profit" of $15 per share, I have placed a stop order to sell at $32. Therefore, if the stock's price drops to that level, my shares will be automatically sold, ensuring that I realize a profit of about $12 per share.

Always willing to consider new opportunities, practical investors want to know how to use stop orders, in principle and in practice.

Cutting Losses and Letting Profits Run: In Principle

"Cut your losses and let your profits run." Such a summary key to investment timing is typically transmitted to new investors. Before and after buying a stock, an investor is advised to study it closely. If the price begins to fall, instead of rising as expected, he should admit his mistake and promptly sell the stock at a small loss before the situation further deteriorates and leads to a larger loss. By thus cutting losses, an investor not only avoids the possibility of a major loss, he also avoids tying up funds in a stock that fails to meet his profit objectives.

While advised to follow the principle of cutting losses, the investor is also counseled simultaneously not to take profits too quickly. Soon after he buys various selected stocks, some are likely to increase in price, thus providing potential profits. Quickly selling these stocks in order to realize rapid profits is not recommended by those who advocate letting profits run. They point out that these initial profits can be magnified many times if the stocks continue to rise in price. Furthermore only several such stocks are needed to provide substantial profits that can potentially *more than offset* a larger number of small losses incurred from the policy of cutting losses.

The "cut-losses, let-profits-run" strategy rests on several important, but usually unstated, assumptions. First, it assumes that trends persist, so that stocks that decline in price generally continue declining and stocks that increase in price generally continue increasing. Only on this assumption does it make sense to "cut losses and let profits run." Second, it assumes that the odds of selecting some potential losers and gainers are not so unequal that a large number of small losses more than offsets a small number of large gains. Third, it assumes that letting profits run will result in reasonably large percentage profits on an annualized basis. For example, not many investors will be satisfied letting their profits continue to run in a stock that appreciates in price only about two or three percent per year. Realistic investors welcome evidence supporting the general validity of each of these three assumptions underlying the cut-losses, let-profits-run strategy. Meanwhile, rather than totally reject the strategy, they are willing to proceed to examine its practicality.

In practice, cutting losses requires an investor not only to acknowledge that he can make mistakes in his initial decisions but also to decide *when* a mistake is sufficiently evident to act and accept a loss. This self-discipline is not readily accepted by investors who are reluctant to admit initial mistakes. Such investors are likely to delay action, hoping that an apparent mistake eventually will "turn out all right," thus justifying their initial decision. "Letting profits run" is also easier to say than to do. Aware that substantial paper profits can quickly disappear as a stock's price drops rapidly, investors are confronted with the practical problem of deciding *when* to let a paper profit continue running—with the possibility of its disappearing—instead of converting the paper profit into realized profit. In summary, investors who directly practice the cut-losses, let-profits-run strategy necessarily become involved in a continuing series of timing decisions.

Proponents of the cut-losses, let-profits-run strategy indicate that direct involvement in timing decisions can be avoided by using stop orders. This view is summarized as follows:

"A first principle for successful investing is to cut your losses and let your profits run. Stop orders provide an excellent device for easily putting this principle into practice."

How can the use of stop orders thus implement the strategy of cutting losses and letting profits run?

Using Stop Orders: In Practice

A stop order, which basically is used only for listed stocks, can be contrasted with two principal types of procedures for buying or selling stocks listed on registered exchanges.

When an investor decides to buy or sell a stock, he usually telephones his broker to obtain a recent price quotation for the security. Then, if this reported price is acceptable, he will proceed to place a *market order*. To illustrate, having decided to invest in General Motors, an investor telephones his broker, checks the price of the most recent transaction, and then places an order for, say, 100 shares "at the market." The order will be promptly transmitted by the broker to the floor of the New York Stock Exchange where it will be rapidly executed, and a report of the purchase will be communicated back to the broker and his customer. This entire process occurs quickly. Note that in placing an order at the market, the customer does not specify a price. He is aware, however, that the NYSE strives to maintain an orderly, continuous market in its listed shares; and therefore the customer is confident that the price he pays is similar to the prices reported for transactions immediately before and after his purchase, especially for actively traded shares. A market order to sell 100 shares is similarly executed, with the seller expecting to receive a price close to those for transactions immediately preceding his sale.

An alternative procedure is for the investor to place a *limit order* with his broker, in which case the customer places an order to buy, for example, 100 shares, but only at or below a specified price. At the time the limit order is placed, the specified price most likely will be below the current market price. Such a limit order is transmitted to the floor of the NYSE, where it is recorded by the specialist making a market in the specific stock. This limit order will be executed only if the market price drops to or below the specified price before the order is cancelled. By thus choosing to place a limit order instead of a market order, the investor may be able to buy 100 shares at a price below the market price at the time of the order. However, if the price does not decline to the limit price, then the order will not be executed, so that the investor will forgo profit opportunities if the stock price advances sharply. Limit orders similarly can be placed when selling a stock, in which case the customer specifies a minimum price, above the current market, at which he is willing to sell a specified number of shares. Limit orders can be placed for any listed stock, but generally they are more relevant for volatile stocks subject to comparatively wide price fluctuations within short periods of time.

A *stop order* now can be summarized as a conditional market order. In essence it says, "I place a conditional order for a specified number of shares of a stock, so that, *if and when* a specified market price is reached, then my conditional order becomes a firm order to buy (or sell) the shares at the market." To illustrate, an investor can telephone his broker to place a stop order to sell 100 shares of a listed stock at $15. The current market price is $18. If and when the stock price drops to $15, this triggers the order automatically to become a market order to sell 100 shares. Since stock exchanges encourage orderly, continuous markets, this market order is then likely to be executed at *about* $15, although the actual sale price of these 100 shares can be somewhat above or below this specified trigger price. Soon after the sale is executed, its outcome is communicated to the client by way of the broker. Without going into detail, the mechanics of the conditional market order basically are administered by the specialist making a market in the stock. Stop orders can be entered for specified time periods, such as a day or week, or until otherwise cancelled.

Whether an investor is long or short in a stock, the use of stop orders can be shown to automate the strategy of cutting losses and letting profits run. To illustrate, an investor today buys a stock at $30 estimating that, if the general level of the stock market remains about the same, then the price of the selected stock will be about $40 within several months. He further believes, however, that there is a small chance of a major market decline, in which case he estimates the price of the selected stock can rapidly start dropping toward $20. To avoid the possible loss of about $10 per share ($30 − $20), the investor can, when buying shares at $30, simultaneously enter a stop order to sell, say at $27. If events occur according to his best estimate, then the stock price will advance toward $40, providing him with a potential paper profit of

$10 per share. In contrast, if the price of the stock starts to drop from $30, then his stop order will be triggered at $27 so that the shares will be sold at about this price. In this way, the investor can use a stop order to automate his strategy of cutting possible large losses from stocks he buys.

To extend the illustration the stock price begins to rise from $30 so that the investor begins to have a paper profit. While he wants to implement the strategy of letting profits run, he also wants to protect his paper profit. Therefore, he can periodically revise the stop order, raising the specified price over time but always keeping it somewhat below the current market price. For example, when and if the market price is $35, he changes the stop-order trigger price to $32. Only if the stock price then declines to $32 will the conditional market order be triggered. However, by automatically selling the shares at about $32, the investor will have protected at least his profit of $2 per share ($32–$30). In contrast, if the stock price continues to advance above $35, he can continue letting the profit run, yet protect much of the growing paper profit by continuing to revise upward the stop-order trigger price.

Stop orders similarly can be used in conjunction with short sales. An investor sells short a selected stock expecting that its price soon will decline. Concerned, however, about the possibility that he may misjudge the situation and that the stock's price will rise sharply, he can simultaneously enter a stop order that will automatically buy back the shares if the stock's market price rises to a specified level. For example, 100 shares are sold short at $30 in the expectation that the price soon will fall toward $20. For protection, however, a stop order to buy 100 shares is placed at $33. Only if the stock rises to $33 will the conditional purchase order be executed. The short seller will thus lose about $3 per share, plus transaction costs; but this will be cutting possible losses if the stock price continues upward. Use of such stop orders in conjunction with short sales is another way of reducing "the risk of selling short" (Chapter 16). In contrast, if the price of the stock sold short starts declining from the sale price of $30, the short seller can let his growing profit run, yet protect most of it by periodically revising downward the initial stop-order price, keeping it always somewhat above the stock's current market price.

Before accepting conventional descriptions about how a stop order *might* be used to cut losses and protect profits, realistic investors insist on further examining the practicality of stop orders.

The use of a stop order to cut losses and protect profits does not enable an investor to avoid two major initial decisions: (1) Which stocks shall I buy (or sell short)? and (2) When shall I buy (or sell short) the selected stocks? As demonstrated in preceding chapters, such stock selections and initial timing decisions can require substantial time and resources without much assurance of consistent success.

Investors who choose to commit the time and resources to making these initial selection and timing decisions must make another key decision in using stop orders: At what price shall I enter a stop order? A stop order is automatically executed once a trigger price is reached, but it requires initial specification of the trigger price.[1]

Deciding *where* to set a trigger price becomes a key issue in using stop orders. Setting a stop-order price far away from the current market price reduces the protective feature of the stop order. Conversely, by choosing to set a stop-order price closer to the current market price, the protective feature increases, but so do the chances that the order will be triggered by a small price fluctuation, resulting in additional costs of being "stopped out."

Practical difficulties of specifying a stop-order price can be illustrated by examining the decision problem confronting an investor who bought some stock at $10 that now is selling for about $40. He wants to let run this current paper profit of about $30 per share. By setting a stop-order price of $20 per share (one-half the current market price), the trigger price is unlikely to be reached. Therefore the profit can continue to run unless the stock price drops sharply from $40 to $20. If this unlikely event occurs, the investor will have protected only $10 per share ($20 sale price − $10 cost) of his paper profit. To protect more of his paper profit, he can specify a trigger price of $30. When and if this price is reached, then his shares will be sold, protecting his profit of about $20 per share ($30 − $10).

Note, however, that by seeking to protect a greater proportion of his paper profit, the investor increases his chances of being automatically sold out. Toward the extreme, he can specify a stop-order price of $38 that is only $2 below the current market price of $40. Although this stop-order price will protect nearly all ($28) of his current paper profit of $30 per share, it will be triggered by a small price fluctuation (five percent) that is likely to occur "by chance." In this event, the investor protects most of his paper profit. However, he must now do the following: pay transaction costs for the stock sale; pay capital gains tax on the realized profit; probably search for a new stock in which to invest his after-tax proceeds; and pay the transaction costs to buy the new shares. Having been "stopped out" at about $38 per share, the investor can stand back and see whether the shares continue to fall below $38

---

[1] An investor also can use stop orders to trigger purchases or short sales of stocks in which he is not currently long or short. These additional uses of stop orders involve similar practical problems of deciding *which* stocks and *which* trigger prices.

and whether his stop order succeeded in cutting larger possible losses. He is as likely to find, however, that the stock's price remains around $38 for awhile, before "bouncing back" to resume its upward price climb, possibly passing beyond $40 per share. Whatever the subsequent price series, the stockholder, by being stopped out at $38, will incur direct transaction costs and tax liabilities for realized profits. In summary, there are costs to "insuring" profits by means of stop orders.

Use of stop orders in conjunction with short sales results in a similar need to decide which stop-order price to specify. An investor sells short 100 shares of a stock at $30 expecting the price soon to drop to $20. His expected profit on this 100-share transaction is about $1000. Which stop-order price should he specify to cut possible losses? A trigger price of $32 will limit the maximum loss to about $200 plus transaction costs. While this may seem a low "insurance cost" relative to the expected profit of $1000, there is the possibility that the stop-order will be triggered at $32, resulting in a $200 loss, only to be followed by the stock's subsequently falling toward $20 as expected. In this event the short-seller is stopped out at a loss and forgoes the subsequent profit opportunity, or else he again decides to sell short the stock, paying additional transaction costs. To reduce the hazard of thus being stopped out by small price fluctuations, the short seller can set a higher trigger price, such as $40. Although less likely to be soon reached, this price, if it is reached, will trigger a loss of about $1000 on the 100 shares ($40 purchase price − $30 sale price).

Execution of a stop order generally will be done around the trigger price because of exchange measures to maintain orderly, continuous markets in listed stocks. Once triggered, however, a stop order becomes a market order, so it is possible that an execution price will depart rather sharply from the trigger price, especially for stocks that are volatile in price. To illustrate, to protect part of a profit, a stop order to sell is placed at $30. If triggered, execution generally will be around $30; but heavy trading in the stock may delay execution of the triggered market order until the price has dropped further, say to $28. Thus not all stop orders are executed close to their trigger price.[2]

The use of stop orders is at times prohibited in specific stocks. Typically this occurs with a stock that has a substantial price rise in a short time period. Some investors are likely to begin placing stop orders to protect their newly won paper profits in this stock. In this way an increasing number of conditional sale orders are placed below the

[2] A *stop-limit order* is a variant of a stop order and a limit order. Instead of being a conditional market order, it is a conditional limit order. In practice, it requires specification of two prices: a stop (trigger) price and a limit price. Either the same price or different prices can be specified for stop and limit.

stock's current price. Therefore, if the market price declines somewhat, some stop orders to sell will be triggered, which can lead to a compounding process of lower prices, additional triggering of stop orders to sell at these lower prices, followed by still lower prices. Alert to such a potential compounding process of a stock's price decline, an exchange monitors its stocks for such emerging conditions. When judged appropriate, the exchange then announces a temporary prohibition of stop orders in specific stocks. For these stocks, stop-order prohibitions can not only ban placing of new stop orders but also cancel existing stop orders. Such prohibitions remain in force until subsequently rescinded by the exchange.

In conclusion, automaticity of stop orders to cut losses and let profits run rests on an investor's specifying stop-order prices. There is little practical difference between deciding on a specific price for triggering a stop order and deciding on a specific price at which directly to place a market or limit order to buy or sell a stock. Either decision involves the hazards of predicting future stock prices, whether by using fundamental analysis, technical analysis, charting, or some "art of judgment." There is no reason to believe that estimation of trigger prices for stop orders will be any more consistently successful than specifying prices at which directly to buy or sell stocks. Investors who measure the merits of investment opportunities against the general consistency-of-success standard are not very impressed with descriptions of how stop orders are supposed to work—if all goes well—or with some selected hindsight examples of stop orders that worked well. Therefore, unless presented with solid evidence demonstrating the *practicality* of using stop orders over time, realistic investors will turn to alternative investment strategies that are less dependent on predictions of future prices of individual stocks.

chapter 22
Dollar-Cost Averaging

Now skeptical of many procedures claimed useful for improving investment timing, investors can examine a strategy that enables them to avoid specific timing decisions and yet directly benefit from stock-price fluctuations. This strategy is dollar-cost averaging, key features of which are outlined in the following illustrative statements.

Dollar-cost averaging in a broadly diversified portfolio of common stocks is an appropriate investment strategy for investors who believe that stock prices in the coming decades generally will be higher than they are today.

Two years ago I bought 100 shares of what I thought was a growth stock. The price has since fallen from $40 to $20. Therefore I am now going to dollar average by buying another 100 shares of this stock.

Realistic investors want to know how dollar-cost averaging is supposed to work, in principle, and how it can be expected to work in practice.

Benefitting Directly from Stock-Price Fluctuations

Commitment over time is necessary for a dollar-cost averaging (DCA) *program*. Before beginning such a program, an investor must understand not only its objectives and procedures, but also must assess the likely future patterns of his behavior and resources.

A DCA program has three principal objectives. First, it enables investors systematically to accumulate funds to meet their individual goals, such as for future education costs or retirement. Second, it enables investors systematically to invest part of their income in common stocks. Broadly diversified portfolios of NYSE common stocks could have provided rates of return approximating seven to nine percent per year during the 40-year period from January 1926 to December 1965.[1] While past returns do not necessarily forecast future results, unless an investor believes that general stock prices will be substantially lower in 10 or 20 years, he should consider committing part of his income to a realistic program for investing in common stocks. Third, a DCA program enables investors to benefit from stock-price fluctuations by buying more shares when stock prices are comparatively low and fewer shares when stock prices are comparatively high. A consequence of this process is that the investor's *average cost* per share always will be at or below the average price paid per share. This objective is achieved systematically, without bothering to try to time individual investment decisions on the basis of predicted price changes.

Three principal procedures are necessary for achieving the objectives of dollar-cost averaging.

A DCA program should be developed around a *broadly diversified portfolio* of stocks. As demonstrated in Chapter 9, diversification can remove individual-stock risk so that only the general market risk remains. Furthermore the return on such a broadly diversified portfolio will approximate the general market return over time. An investor can directly create his own broadly diversified portfolio; but, in practice, most individual investors will find it more economical to diversify indirectly by purchasing shares in investment companies that typically diversify among many different stocks, none of which dominates the total value of the portfolio. Such indirect diversification usually involves lower transaction costs than is possible by directly accumulating a broadly diversified portfolio (Chapter 24).

The program requires investment of additional funds after *equal time intervals*, such as monthly or quarterly. A periodic interval should be determined before beginning a DCA program and then adhered to over time.

The program requires investment of an *equal dollar amount* of additional funds at the predetermined times. To illustrate, having decided to invest $100 at the beginning of each month, an investor regularly invests this predetermined amount instead of buying, for example, an equal number of additional shares each month.

Principal features of a DCA program can now be illustrated. A hypo-

---

[1] Estimated from figures reported in Table 1 of Lawrence Fisher and James H. Lorie, "Rates of Return on Investments in Common Stock: The Year-by-Year Record, 1926–65," pp. 296–301.

thetical investor decided to invest $100 in a broadly diversified port-
folio early one January, and he invested an additional $100 after each
subsequent three-month interval. This hypothetical investor's first
three years of experience are summarized in Exhibit 20–1.

Over the three-year period, the investor regularly invested $100 in the
DCA program. During this time the per-share price of the broadly diversified portfolio fluctuated so that the periodic investment of $100 re-
sulted in the purchase of more shares when stock prices were comparatively low and fewer shares when stock prices were comparatively
high. For example, 5.6 shares were purchased on April 5 of the second
year when the price was $18; and only 4.1 shares were purchased on
July 5 of the third year when the price was $24½. Such purchases of
more shares at comparatively low prices is an automatic outcome of a
DCA program.

At the end of its third year, the total value of the accumulated funds
in the illustrative DCA program is $1375 (column g), which is $175
greater than the cumulative sum of $1200 committed by the investor.
This result is only at one point in time. Losses would have resulted
from liquidation of the program at certain other times, such as a loss
of $6 around October 5 of the first year ($400 cumulative investment
− $394 total sale value). Larger losses similarly would have resulted at
the beginning of the subsequent two quarters. A DCA program is thus
no guarantee against losses incurred by selling stocks below their purchase price. A DCA program can avoid losses only if maintained over a
long period of time in which stock prices generally rise.

Effective commitment is necessary before beginning a DCA program.
This requires understanding and acceptance of its general objectives
and procedures and confidence that the longer-run general trend of
stock prices is upward. Moreover it requires an investor to assess his
likely future behavior and resources. *Will* he remain committed to a
DCA program under various market conditions? *Can* he remain committed under various conditions?

Commitment to a DCA program requires an investor to continue to
be willing to invest additional funds even when the stock market falls
to levels below the level at which the plan begins. To illustrate, an investor who is confident about the long-run merits of a DCA program
welcomes general market declines as opportunities to purchase more
shares for each dollar invested. Conversely, an investor who is easily
discouraged by general market declines may be unwilling to continue a
DCA program under such conditions. If he then sells, losses can result
from liquidating the portfolio accumulated up to that time. Instead of
liquidating under such discouraging conditions, he may decide to dis-
continue further purchases. Although this avoids then having to realize

Exhibit 20-1. First Three Years of An Illustrative Dollar-Cost Averaging (DCA) Program*

Equal Time Intervals	Equal-Dollar Investment	Price per Share of a Broadly Diversified Portfolio	Number of Shares Purchased (c)÷(b)	Cumulative Number of Shares Owned	Cumulative Investment in DCA Program	Total Value of Shares Owned (c)×(e)
(a)	(b)	(c)	(d)	(e)	(f)	(g)
First Year						
January 5	$100	$20	5.0	5.0	$ 100	$ 100
April 5	100	21	4.8	9.8	200	206
July 5	100	22	4.5	14.3	300	315
October 5	100	20½	4.9	19.2	400	394
Second Year						
January 5	100	19	5.3	24.5	500	466
April 5	100	18	5.6	30.1	600	542
July 5	100	20¼	4.9	35.0	700	709
October 5	100	21	4.8	39.8	800	836
Third Year						
January 5	100	21½	4.7	44.5	900	957
April 5	100	22	4.5	49.0	1000	1078
July 5	100	24½	4.1	53.1	1100	1301
October 5	100	24	4.2	57.3	1200	1375
December 31	—	24	—	57.3	1200	1375

*To simplify the mathematics of this exhibit, the following procedures have been followed:
(1) No provision has been made for reinvestment of cash dividends.
(2) It is assumed that the periodic investment is fully invested in a broadly diversified mutual fund having no sales charge.
(3) Number of shares is reported to *one decimal place*. While not generally feasible for direct investment, many mutual funds have investment plans that enable an investor to accumulate full and fractional shares to the third decimal place.
(4) No provision is made for possible taxes incurred.
(5) Total value of shares owned (column g) is to the nearest whole dollar.

221

losses, it also precludes the opportunity to buy greater numbers of additional shares at these lower prices. Thus, before initiating a DCA program, an investor must assess his probable willingness to remain committed to the program in various market conditions.

Even investors willing to remain committed to a DCA program can find themselves unable to continue because of resource limitations. Before initiating a DCA program, an investor should evaluate his current wealth position and probable future flow of funds. He must be confident of his ability to continue a DCA program for a long period of time without being forced to sell in order to meet other financial obligations. For example, his income subsequently may decline so that, not having adequate cash reserves, the investor has to sell his accumulated portfolio, possibly at a loss, in order to pay various expenses. In particular, a DCA program can be inappropriate for individuals who have limited cash reserves and uncertain future patterns of income and expenses. Effective commitment to a DCA program thus requires an investor to assess whether his resources will likely be adequate to continue investing over time.

In summary, strict dollar-cost averaging goes further than the features highlighted in the first illustrative statement.

"Dollar-cost averaging in a broadly diversified portfolio of common stocks is an appropriate investment strategy for investors who believe that stock prices in the coming decades generally will be higher than they are today."

It requires effective commitment to a systematic investment program. A participant in a DCA program basically is confident that his portfolio returns will be as high—and possibly higher—than general market returns over time. Because of broad diversification, his risk is basically the general market risk. By investing in a professionally managed portfolio, he is willing to avoid subsequent decisions about which stocks to buy, when to invest, and how much to invest. Strict adherence to a DCA program precludes subsequent judgments about such issues of investment selection and timing.

Variations of Dollar Averaging

Variations of dollar averaging now can be compared with the objectives and procedures of a DCA program.

Instead of building a DCA program around a broadly diversified portfolio of common stocks, a variation of dollar averaging involves investing in only one or several selected stocks. This *limited-diversification approach* differs from a DCA program in three principal ways.

The limited-diversification approach requires an investor to select one or several stocks for periodic purchase in a competitive market. The investor must decide *which* individual stocks to buy periodically, a decision he avoids by developing a DCA program around a broadly diversified portfolio.

Periodic purchases of selected stocks cannot provide substantial diversification benefits. Despite an impressive past record, any one company can be confronted by unpredictable events resulting in stagnation or decline of its stock price. Ideally such a decline provides an opportunity to buy more shares at lower prices. In practice, however, it can be frustrating and potentially unrewarding to continue dollar averaging in a stock undergoing an extensive price decline and an uncertain future. Imagine, for example, the dilemma confronting an hypothetical investor who began dollar averaging in Penn Central shares when the price was in the 60s, only to be followed by a prolonged decline toward under $10. In contrast, an investor holding a broadly diversified portfolio is likely to be reasonably confident of future recovery from declines in general share prices.

Frustration with a stock initially selected for periodic purchase is likely to result in subsequent selection of a different stock. For example, his confidence shaken when a selected stock has declined in price, an investor with a limited-diversification approach decides against continuing its periodic purchase. Furthermore he then decides to start dollar averaging in another selected stock judged to be a "better buy" at the time. The limited-diversification approach thus can easily result in an investor's having to make subsequent stock selections, a process that is avoided by commitment to a DCA program built around a broadly diversified portfolio.

Instead of investing additional funds after equal time intervals, a second variation of dollar averaging involves discretionary timing of subsequent investments. This *variable-timing approach* can be illustrated by an investor who has decided to invest $200 quarterly in a broadly diversified portfolio. His investments have been regularly made about the beginning of January, April, July, and October. His next investment is scheduled to be made tomorrow. Noting, however, that stock prices have been generally declining for three straight months and believing this trend will continue, the investor now decides to defer his next purchase for at least several days in anticipation of buying even more shares at expected lower prices. By so doing, the investor is trying to improve his investment timing, rather than adhering to a predetermined DCA program of periodic purchases.

Even if an investor is unusually successful in making additional investments at times when stock prices are generally low, this is unlikely to have much impact on his long-run return from a broadly diversified portfolio. Over time such portfolios will not fluctuate as much in value as many of the component common stocks. Timing of additional investments in such portfolios thus is not as important as it potentially can be for purchases of individual common stocks.

Instead of investing an equal dollar amount periodically, a third variation of dollar averaging involves altering the dollar amount of additional investments. Such a *variable-dollar-amount approach* usually is implemented by one of two principal procedures.

Instead of periodically investing an equal dollar amount, an investor decides to purchase the same number of shares after equal time intervals. Such a procedure automatically results in the investor's committing less funds when stock prices are comparatively low and more funds when stock prices are comparatively high. To illustrate, an investor who decides regularly to purchase 100 shares of a broadly diversified portfolio will invest $1000 when its stock price is $10 and $1200 when the price is $12. The average cost per share for these two transactions is $11, excluding commissions. In contrast, a strict DCA program of periodically investing an equal dollar amount, say $1000, will result in the purchase of 100 shares at $10 but only about 83 shares when the stock price is $12. By purchasing fewer shares at the higher price, the average cost per share for these two transactions is about $10.90 ($2000 total cost ÷ 183 shares), excluding commissions. Thus by purchasing the same number of shares, no matter what the price, the investor forgoes an opportunity systematically to buy more shares at low prices and fewer shares at higher prices. Furthermore periodic purchase of the same number of shares makes it difficult for an investor to plan his future investment dollar commitments that become dependent on future stock prices. For example, an investor intending periodically to buy 100 shares must invest $1000 when the price is $10 and $1500 when the stock price is $15. It is more difficult to budget for these varying future amounts than for a periodic equal-dollar investment program, such as $1000 quarterly.

Varying dollar amounts also can be based on investor judgment concerning estimated future changes in stock prices. Consider an investor who previously decided to invest $200 quarterly at the beginning of January, April, July, and October. His last investment was $200 in April. Since then the general market has declined sharply. Judging that the market is near its low for the future, he decides to "double up" his July investment to $400. By so doing, however, he is using the $200 previously scheduled to be invested in October. This "doubling up" decision will be vindicated if stock prices generally rise after his July investment; but, alternatively, what if stock prices continue to decline from July through October? Then he will be unable to buy even more shares for the $200 that was previously scheduled to be invested in October. The variable-dollar-amount approach thus reinstates the need to decide how much to invest at different times, a series of decisions that is avoided by commitment to a DCA program.

Combinations of the three principal variations of dollar averaging also are possible. However, an investor who varies selected stocks, time intervals between investments, and dollar amounts of purchases may as well recognize this as a continuing process of deciding: which stocks to buy, when to buy, and how much to invest. Not only does such a process have no resemblance to a DCA program, it contradicts the objectives and procedures of such a program.

Adherence to a DCA program need not be inflexible. Over time an investor committed to such a program can have some changes in a broadly diversified portfolio. Similarly, a DCA program is not invalidated because an additional investment is made on the fifth rather than the regularly scheduled first of a month. Also, as an investor's income grows over time he can decide to increase his planned periodic investment, say from $100 quarterly to $150 quarterly. Notably, such variations are based on convenience or a revised long-run commitment to the DCA program—not on attempts to "outguess the market" by frequently varying stock selections, investment timing, or amounts invested.

Rationalization of past investment decisions can lead to *after-the-fact dollar averaging*. Often heard are variations of the second illustrative statement.

"Two years ago I bought 100 shares of what I thought was a growth stock. The price has since fallen from $40 to $20. Therefore I am now going to dollar average by buying another 100 shares of this stock."

Although using the term "dollar average," such a statement arises in response to past events, instead of as a carefully determined commitment to the objectives and procedures of a DCA program. The speaker had no intention of "dollar averaging" when he first bought the stock at $40 per share. Now, apparently to justify the initial decision, he decides to purchase 100 shares at $20 per share in order to reduce the average cost to $30 per share, excluding commissions. In contrast to a DCA program, this after-the-fact decision involves: (1) a single stock, not a broadly diversified portfolio; (2) an arbitrary time interval; and (3) unequal dollar amounts, $2000 at $20 per share in contrast to the initial dollar cost of $4000. Alert to such after-the-fact dollar averaging, realistic investors now can recognize it as a rationalization—not as a rational investment strategy.

In conclusion, variations of dollar averaging involve additional costs —and possible frustrations—of making investment selection and timing decisions without providing any clear additional benefits for investors. In contrast, a DCA *program* can be suitable for many investors wanting systematically to accumulate funds and to participate in general market returns from common stocks. Therefore the objectives and procedures of a dollar-cost averaging program warrant thoughtful consideration by practical investors.

REVIEW OF PART FIVE

Question: How can I decide when to buy and sell stocks?

Answer: The conventional answer to such a question is to outline a variety of methods that *may* help an investor improve the timing of his investment decisions. These surveys rely on selected episodes of "successful" and "unsuccessful" timing methods. Acknowledging the difficulty of isolating one key to successful timing, they encourage an investor to learn more and more about various methods from which he can then distill a personal style of deciding when to buy and sell stocks. Conventional focus thus is on possible benefits, with little attention to the costs of trying to improve investment timing.

Dissatisfied with conventional portrayals of "what might have been" or "what might be," open-minded investors welcome more serious appraisal of popular methods purported to aid investor timing decisions. They want to know the logical credibility of such methods. Furthermore they are concerned whether these methods are as easy to implement in practice as they seem to be in principle. Insistence on reasonable evidence is a hallmark of serious investors. Therefore they welcome evidence whether various aids to investment timing are in fact "successful" in terms of the consistency-of-success standard.

Examination of the rationale underlying some popular timing methods finds them without clear logical support. Often such methods rest on the premise that total participation in the stock market is comprised of two principal categories of investors—the shrewd and the unsophisticated. Technical indicators such as the Confidence Index and charting rest on this presumed dichotomy of investors believed to behave differently over time. The logical credibility of this presumption is doubtful in a competitive marketplace.

What about the practical implementation of popular tools of investment timing? One level is to know procedures for constructing advance-decline lines and charts and mechanics of entering stop orders. A more advanced level is to understand how use of tools such as advance-decline lines and charts depends largely on subtleties of individual interpretation. If, as some claim, interpretation of charts is an inexact art, then there is no convenient way for proponents of charting to transmit their interpretative skills to others. Aspiring chartists must commit themselves to acquiring possible interpretive skills through personal experience. Similarly, the mechanics of stop orders are not complex. What is complex is deciding in practice where to specify trigger prices for stop orders in order, for example, to make operational the conventional dictum of cutting losses and letting profit run.

227

Few, if any, of the popular timing methods reviewed in Part Five measure up to the consistency-of-success standard. A growing body of evidence indicates that use of technical analysis and charts is not demonstrably effective over time. Supporters of popularized timing methods are likely to reject such evidence as inadequate. They will claim that such tests are inconclusive because they fail to capture the subtleties of using technical analysis and charts as part of a total decision process. For example, they will assert that technical analysis must be interwoven with comprehensive analyses of fundamental and behavioral aspects of selected stocks, the general stock market, and broad socioeconomic factors. This view of technical analysis, which requires intensive investor commitment, is incapable of direct testing. Its acceptance or rejection will depend on the indirect evidence of the portfolio returns over time of investors following such a total strategy. In summary, each individual investor must weigh the evidence offered to support or refute use of technical analysis. Investors unwilling to accept the evidence to date should ask themselves what additional evidence will satisfy them.

Positive results can follow from rejecting popularized techniques for timing the purchase and sale of selected stocks. Attention can shift from trying to learn more and more technical details to focusing on broader issues of specifying individual financial goals and identifying effective procedures for achieving individual goals. Investors with goals of building up their shareholdings will want to consider the relative merits of a carefully formulated *program* of dollar-cost averaging. Systematic accumulation of a broadly diversified portfolio is a hallmark of such a program. Effective ways for individuals to participate in broadly diversified portfolios will be presented in Part Six.

* * *

Now skeptical of the practicality of many popularized tools of investment timing, thoughtful investors will probably want to review further the cases for and against technical analysis and charting. In the spirit of further inquiry, serious investors are encouraged to review the case for investment timing as presented in recent textbooks, articles, and the following types of books.

Hurst, J. M., *The Profit Magic of Stock Transaction Timing* (Prentice-Hall, Inc.: 1970).

Lerro, Anthony J., and Charles B. Swayne, Jr., *Selection of Securities: Technical Analysis of Stock Market Prices* (General Learning Press: 1970).

PART SIX

USING THE NEW PERSPECTIVE OF THE STOCK MARKET

chapter 23
Reviewing Personal Investment Goals and Strategies

Accepting the risk that traditional views will be shattered, open-minded investors welcome an opportunity to examine how a new perspective can be relevant for reexamining personal investment goals and strategies.

Stock Market Opportunities: Logic and Evidence

Investors traditionally are encouraged to view the stock market as a forum of abundant opportunities. For too long, however, no logical basis has been provided for this market-opportunity viewpoint. Instead it basically rests on selected episodes of "investment success," with such hindsight evidence suggestive of future opportunities. While focusing on positive opportunities, proponents of the market-opportunity viewpoint generally acknowledge that some past investments have been unsuccessful and some future investments will be unsuccessful. Therefore they encourage investors to learn more details about the stock market in order to improve their skills in identifying opportunities and avoiding investment pitfalls. In sum, they encourage individuals to aspire to the level of part-time analyst and portfolio manager, basically by emphasizing possible benefits and by neglecting to specify the probable costs of individual resources.

Extreme critics occasionally attack the market-opportunity viewpoint. Basing their criticisms on a malevolent-market viewpoint, they view the market largely as a forum abundant with privileged participants, tipsters, insiders, manipulators, and fools. By searching through past records they can select sufficient episodes of past market abuses to build a plausible case to support their malevolent-market viewpoint. Based on such selected evidence, these critics typically reject the view that market opportunities are available to many investors. Extreme critics view the stock market more as a casino game loaded against nonhouse participants, whose principal choice is whether they want to lose funds quickly or slowly.

A fresh, new perspective on stock market opportunities is provided by a competitive-market viewpoint. This viewpoint recognizes that there have been—and will be—episodes of market opportunities. It also acknowledges that there have been—and will be—episodes of market abuses. Instead of focusing on selected episodes, however, a competitive-market viewpoint encourages broad examination of the general logic and evidence of stock market opportunities.

As developed in the introductory chapters of this book, in a market comprised of many skillful competitors, it is difficult for any investor consistently to identify opportunities enabling him substantially to outperform his skillful rivals. Furthermore, in a competitive-market environment, prompt actions by skillful investors responding to new information contribute to stock price movements that continually reflect adjustments to generally available information. Throughout preceding chapters a competitive-market viewpoint has provided new perspective about traditional views of stock market opportunities.

The competitive-market viewpoint is related to the *random-walk* (R-W) view of changes in stock prices. In recent years, especially since the advent of computer-assisted research, there have been extensive tests, leading to growing support, of the R-W hypothesis. Therefore practical investors want to judge whether the R-W view with its supporting evidence is relevant for them.

First exposed to the two words "random walk," investors may become defensive. The words sound technical, and they hint of events beyond individual control. Although the concept of randomness is prevalent in many everyday events, people readily associate it with games of chance, seen by many as trivial pastimes. Despite such barriers to its initial acceptance, the term "random walk" is becoming prevalent as a way of describing the process of stock-price changes over time.[1]

---

[1] A lucid early statement about random-walk theory is provided by Eugene F. Fama, "Random Walks in Stock Market Prices," *Financial Analysts Journal*, September–October 1965, pp. 55–59. Recently the same author provided a comprehensive, more advanced review in an article, "Efficient Capital Markets: A Review of Theory and Empirical Work," *The Journal of Finance*, May 1970, pp. 383–417.

There are two principal versions of the R-W view of changes in stock prices. The first is the *technical version*, which asserts that past trading information about a stock cannot be predictive of future price changes. For example, to know that a stock's price declined one dollar yesterday does not provide information useful for predicting whether today's closing price will be higher, lower, or unchanged. Yesterday's price change reflected the composite decisions of many investors responding to information about the stock relative to other investment opportunities. Today's price change essentially will reflect general investor evaluation of new information, or revised interpretations of generally available information, about this stock and alternative investment possibilities. On this basis a series of changes in a stock's price can be generally viewed as a random series of positive or negative price changes, with an occasional no price change between subsequent transactions.

Even in a random series of price changes there can be a "run" of similar outcomes, such as a sequence of several positive price changes. But such a run is as likely as not to be broken by a negative price change as the next outcome. A practical analogy is the flipping of a fair coin whereby, despite a run of five heads, the next outcome is equally likely to a head or a tail. The past run of heads is not predictive of the next outcome. Similarly a run of three fours on a fair die is not predictive of the outcome of the next toss. While the odds are 6 to 1 against another four, this outcome is as equally likely as any of the other five numbers on the die. All that can be known are such statistical probabilities of future outcomes. The past series of outcomes is not predictive of which one of the six numbers will appear on the next cast of the die.

A growing body of random-walk evidence directly challenges the position of those who view charts as valuable guides to future changes in stock prices. Charts generally show histories of past price changes. Emphasis is on trying to use trends and changes in trends to predict future price changes. As demonstrated in Chapter 20, realistic investors reject cases for charting that are based on selected past chart patterns that seem to have been predictive of subsequent events. The plotting of series of hypothetical price changes generated by series of random numbers can lead to some traditionally attractive chart patterns. Therefore a key issue is whether, compared to alternative strategies, the long-term use of many charts results in a sufficient number of profitable investment transactions to warrant the cost of purchasing or plotting charts of past price history. Tough-minded investors now await convincing evidence supporting the economic value of charting.

The technical version of the R-W view goes beyond information about past changes in stock prices. It similarly challenges the predictive value of many popular technical indictators such as stock trading volume, advance-decline relationships, odd-lot statistics, and short-sale indexes. All such past history is generally available at a price to competing investors. If one, or some combination, of such technical indicators is found to be of practical use for predicting future changes in stock prices, then the actions of investors competing to use this information are likely to result in rapid removal of the technical indicator's economic benefits. Results of extensive tests of the technical version of the R-W view continue to add support to its general validity (Chapter 19).

The *fundamental version* of the random-walk view is an even more total challenge to traditional accounts of stock market opportunities. Basically the fundamental R-W version rests on the view that the stock market approximates the standard of a competitive market. There are many skillful participants at any time, and potentially skillful new participants can readily enter the forum. Information is generally available to these competing investors. This information includes a comprehensive assortment of past information and extensive future projections—largely based on interpretations of past information. This information base is used by many competing investors to make investment decisions reflecting their assessments of alternative investment opportunities at a point in time. Thus today's market price of a stock is a best estimate of its current value. Tomorrow's price may be somewhat higher or lower in response to new information or revised expectations about alternative opportunities. However, because each new price change is unpredictable, a series of stock price changes can be logically described as approximating a random process.

The fundamental version of the R-W view is a tribute to the general efficiency of the stock market. It is consistent with the market's generally being a highly competitive forum operating in a legal and regulatory environment that encourages prompt, full, and fair disclosure of information to competing investors. In such a competitive forum it is difficult for any one security analyst to keep "picking winners" or for any one investment manager to keep "beating the market." The very efforts of many skillful participants attempting to outperform the market contribute to the market's approaching the competitive-market standard. Despite occasional episodes of abuses, which usually lead to legal or regulatory penalties, the competitive-market viewpoint seems to provide a realistic basis on which to evaluate market opportunities. It is this viewpoint that underlies this book's preceding evaluations of various investment strategies.

In conclusion, the R-W view cannot be lightly dismissed. It rests on a logical interpretation of the stock market as a competitive forum comprised of many skillful analysts, portfolio managers, and investors. Rejection of this logical basis must therefore rest on pessimistic views about the talents and resources of the many individuals and institutions professionally committed to the market. Furthermore extensive evidence supports both versions of the R-W view. Refutation of this R-W evidence now not only requires realistic counter-evidence, but also it requires suitable evidence to support the market-opportunity or malevolent-market views. Selected examples based on hindsight can no longer be accepted.

Investing in a Competitive Market

Any investor remains free to reject the competitive-market viewpoint and to dismiss the extensive evidence supporting the random-walk view of changes in stock prices. He or she can continue seeking new opportunities to beat the market, encouraged by the many commentators who cite past success stories and indicate how an investor might achieve above-average returns on certain future investments—*if* all goes well.

In contrast, what are some positive implications for investors now willing to consider that the stock market, in practice, approaches the competitive-market standard? Viewed in this way, the stock market can be said to approximate a "fair game" in which it is exceedingly difficult to outperform, frequently and substantially, the many other participants. Although it is thus difficult to beat the market, over recent decades returns from broadly diversified portfolios of common stocks have been superior to those available from many other liquid forms of savings, such as deposit accounts and bonds. Although future outcomes are uncertain, participation in the stock market will enable investors to realize future returns related to probable expansion of the general economy and individual companies.

Acceptance of the competitive-market viewpoint can thus result in revision of investment goals. Rather than trying to beat the market, a more realistic goal is to achieve, with reasonable confidence, general market returns over time. A related goal is to achieve such general returns at *low cost*, both of money and of personal time.

For most practical purposes, "general market returns" are the total rates of return on broadly based indexes of common-stock prices. While their technical construction can imply particular portfolio diversification policies, basically these indexes are representative of broad categories of stocks. For example, the return on the Standard & Poor's Industrial Index is a useful standard against which to measure the return from a portfolio of industrial stocks principally listed on the New York Stock Exchange. Similarly the return on the Standard & Poor's Composite Index of 500 stocks or the NYSE Composite Index can provide a useful standard against which to compare the return from a portfolio of NYSE stocks diversified among utilities and transportation companies, in addition to industrial firms. In a similar way returns from investment portfolios substantially comprised of stocks traded on other exchanges or in the over-the-counter market can be compared with total returns from indexes representative of such markets.

A strategy for achieving general market returns over time is to buy and hold a broadly diversified portfolio of common stocks. Such a portfolio is likely to be spread among upwards of 50 different common stocks, representing firms in diverse industries. In addition, none of the individual stocks accounts for an unusually large proportion of the total value of the portfolio. An investor holding such a portfolio recognizes that returns on individual stocks in the portfolio will diverge from general market returns at various times. However he can be reasonably confident that the portfolio return, which basically is an average of the diverse individual-stock returns, will approximate the general market return. To illustrate, a portfolio diversified among many stocks listed on the New York Stock Exchange will return approximately +20 percent in a year when the general market return is +20 percent, as measured, for example, by the total return on the Standard & Poor's Composite Index of 500 stocks. Similarly the portfolio return will be about −20 percent in a year when a −20 percent return is reported for an appropriate measure of general market returns. In addition to being confident that the portfolio return will approximate that of the general market in individual years, an investor following a broad-diversification strategy can be reasonably confident that his portfolio return will approximate the general market return over time. In essence the broad-diversification strategy involves "holding the market" in order to achieve market returns over time.[2]

The broad-diversification strategy is rejected by those who encourage investors to concentrate their holdings in only five to 10 selected stocks.

---

[2] The need to diversify broadly among many different stocks will be questioned by those acquainted with recent studies demonstrating that most of the benefits of diversification are achieved by holding around 10 to 20 different stocks. While this lower level of diversification does provide substantial benefits on the average, compared with only one or several stocks, there are continuing benefits from even broader diversification. (See R. B. Upson, P. F. Jessup, and K. Matsumoto, "Portfolio Diversification Strategies," *Financial Analysts Journal*, forthcoming). Therefore the practical question is whether the costs of broader diversification exceed its benefits. This question is answered in the next chapter.

This concentration strategy usually is based on the general observation that broadly diversified portfolios are unlikely to perform much differently than the general market. Therefore investors who want to outperform the market must concentrate their resources and attention on a few securities selected for their potential to provide above-average returns. Furthermore such concentration is said to enable investors to focus on improving the timing of their purchases and sales of the few selected stocks. Such a concentration strategy initially seems sensible in principle. In practice, however, practical investors now question whether any investor can be frequently successful in identifying stocks providing above-average future returns and in timing the purchases and sales of the selected stocks. Without such frequent success, returns from a concentrated portfolio can substantially exceed general returns in some years, but they are likely to be substantially below general market returns in other years. While the investor cannot be very confident where the portfolio return will be relative to the general market return for any one year, the return from the concentrated portfolio over an extended period of time is unlikely to exceed the general market return, a result similar to that from a broadly diversified portfolio. Proponents of the concentration strategy therefore must demonstrate the practical superiority of their strategy. They must provide more substantial evidence than hypothetical possibilities of substantially higher returns over time *if* an investor buys and sells "the right stocks at the right times."

In conclusion, in a competitive market a realistic goal is to achieve, with reasonable confidence, general market returns over time. A strategy appropriate for this goal is to buy and hold a broadly diversified portfolio. An investor who implements such a strategy at low cost will achieve higher net returns over time than another investor who follows a similar strategy, but at higher cost in terms of cash expenses and personal commitment. Therefore realistic investors will want to evaluate the principal costs and benefits of creating their own broadly diversified portfolios in comparison with indirectly participating in such portfolios by purchasing shares of investment companies. The principal elements for such a cost-benefit evaluation of portfolio diversification are presented in the next chapter.

chapter 24
Deciding Between Direct or Indirect Portfolio Diversification

Investors can implement a broad-diversification strategy either *directly* by owning a portfolio of many different common stocks or *indirectly* by owning shares of investment companies that hold broadly diversified portfolios. Realistic investors therefore want to examine the principal costs and benefits of direct versus indirect portfolio diversification.

Broadly diversified portfolios of common stocks are likely to achieve general market returns over time. Emphasis therefore shifts to participating in such portfolios at *low cost* in order to achieve a reasonably large net return, which is the total portfolio return minus participation costs. Whether to invest directly or indirectly in broadly diversified portfolios thus should be decided after examination of at least three principal cost areas: transaction costs, management costs, and taxes.

Transaction Costs

Transaction costs make it impractical for an investor to purchase his own broadly diversified portfolio unless his investment in common stocks is more than about $25,000. To illustrate, a broadly diversified portfolio should probably have more than 50 different stocks. Assume, however, that holding 25 different stocks is judged sufficient initial diversification, with the investor intending to diversify further in coming years. Spreading $25,000 equally among 25 different stocks

238

involves an investment of $1000 in each stock. The average price per share of stocks listed on the New York Stock Exchange at year-end 1971 was about $42. If $1000 were invested in each of 25 different stocks listed on the NYSE, the implied brokerage commission to buy an average-priced stock is about $26, including an odd-lot differential.[1] Therefore the total cost of purchasing the illustrative 25-stock portfolio will be about $650 ($26 × 25), which is 2.6 percent of the total investment of $25,000. Direct diversification of the same amount of money among more than 25 different stocks generally can only be done at higher total cost. Also, similar diversification of smaller initial amounts of money generally results in proportionately higher transaction costs.

In contrast, indirect diversification in a portfolio of more than 25 different common stocks can be achieved by buying shares of registered investment companies listed on the New York Stock Exchange. For illustrative purposes, at the beginning of 1973, the share price of Tri-Continental Corporation, the largest such company, was around $33, so that investing $25,000 in this one investment company would have involved a commission of about $290, or 1.2 percent of the total investment of $25,000. Even if $25,000 were spread among three or five different listed investment companies, the total transaction cost for such extensive indirect diversification is usually less than that of directly diversifying among more than 25 different stocks listed on the NYSE.

Investment companies listed on the New York Stock Exchange are *closed-end* investment companies. By "closed-end" is meant that these companies have a fixed number of common shares outstanding; and this number of shares is changed only infrequently, for example by stock splits or by rights offerings, in which a company offers, for a limited time period, to sell a proportionate number of new shares to existing stockholders. Thus the common-stock capitalization of these firms is similar to that of other listed firms in commerce and industry. In contrast, the assets of closed-end investment companies usually are comprised of diversified holdings of common stocks and some cash or near-cash assets. On this basis they differ from other listed firms with assets such as land, plant, and equipment.

Because the assets of an investment company are basically in cash and marketable securities, its *net asset value per share (NAV)* can be readily calculated. At any point in time, an investment company's NAV is the total market value of its portfolio minus any liabilities, which usually are relatively minor, divided by the number of outstanding common shares. The NAV for most major closed-end investment

---

[1] Calculated from schedules reported in the *New York Stock Exchange Fact Book*, 1972, pp. 56–57.

companies is reported weekly in *The Wall Street Journal* and several other sources of financial news.

Market prices of closed-end investment companies frequently differ from their net asset values. To illustrate, during the first week of 1973, the NAV of Tri-Continental Corporation was about $41½ while its market price was $33 so that the stock was trading at a discount of about 20 percent from its NAV. At the same time other listed investment companies were selling at various discounts and premiums relative to their NAV. Furthermore, for any one closed-end investment company, the difference between its market price and its NAV changes over time, resulting in changing discounts and premiums. Reasons for such variations among companies and for the same company have not been rigorously specified. Despite such variations, changes in the market prices of closed-end investment companies are generally associated with changes in their NAV, which reflect returns from broadly diversified portfolios of common stocks. In summary, for many investors the purchase of shares of a closed-end investment company is one major way to participate indirectly in a diversified portfolio at a transaction cost lower than that for directly creating a broadly diversified portfolio of common stocks.

Open-end investment companies—generally called *mutual funds*—can be contrasted with closed-end companies. Most open-end investment companies hold broadly diversified portfolios of common stocks. Their assets thus are basically similar to those of closed-end investment companies. Unlike the closed-end companies, however, the number of outstanding shares is not fixed. Each business day, a mutual fund stands ready to sell additional shares at a price directly related to its NAV and to repurchase (*redeem*) its outstanding shares, almost always at NAV. Thus the number of outstanding shares changes on a daily basis, in relation to new sales and redemptions. Furthermore daily share prices of mutual funds are directly linked to NAV.

From the viewpoint of an investor's transaction cost, there are two principal types of mutual funds: load and no-load. *Load funds* are sold at NAV plus a specified sales (or "load") charge that is basically a commission to the salesmen and sales organizations that distribute load funds. Generally, for small purchases the load charge is around 8 or 8½ percent of the total dollar amount of the purchase transaction, although the percentage is greater relative to the dollar value of the shares purchased.[2] Usually the percentage load charge is scaled down-

---

[2] For example a $1000 purchase transaction of an eight percent load fund involves an $80 load charge, such that the dollar value of the shares actually purchased is $920. Therefore the transaction cost of $80 relative to the dollar value of the shares actually purchased approximates 8.7 percent.

ward for large dollar investments. Because the schedule of load charges for any one fund is the same for all salesmen, an investor cannot "shop around" to find a lower-cost source of the fund. Load charges provide commission incentives for salesmen to sell mutual funds to potential investors who might not otherwise buy shares of funds. For this reason it is often said that mutual funds are not bought—they are sold.

No-load funds differ from load funds principally in that they do not have extensive sales organizations compensated largely through load charges. No-load funds stand ready to sell additional shares or redeem outstanding shares basically at NAV, as calculated at least once each business day. Thus an investor buying shares in a no-load fund can avoid the load charge associated with purchasing shares of a load fund with similar objectives and holding similar stocks. On this basis, purchase of a no-load fund involves a lower transaction cost than purchase of a similar load fund.

Lacking commission incentives for sales organizations, no-load funds are not *sold* in the same way as load funds. At times no-load funds have brief notices in financial newspapers inviting potentially interested investors to write for descriptive literature. An investor requesting such information will receive by return mail a prospectus describing the fund and its operations. (The Securities and Exchange Commission requires all mutual funds—no-load and load—to provide such a prospectus to potential investors.) However, no salesman will call. Therefore the investor must review the prospectus to become informed about the fund's history, stated investment policies, management, and recent stock holdings. Furthermore, since no prospectus provides information about a fund's operations compared to that of other funds, other prospectuses also should be reviewed, or else the investor should refer to books or magazines providing comparative information about mutual funds. One major source of such comparative information is *Investment Companies: Mutual Funds and Other Types*, published annually by Wiesenberger Services, Inc. Investors who thus obtain and evaluate information about various no-load mutual funds are in essence *buying* a mutual fund, not being sold one by a salesman. Willingness of people to buy mutual funds is demonstrated by the more rapid recent growth of no-load funds, without salesmen, as compared to load funds.[3]

In summary, from the viewpoint of transaction costs, direct purchase of a broadly diversified portfolio is impractical for most individual investors. Therefore the practical choice is between purchasing shares of closed-end investment companies, load mutual funds, and no-load

---

[3] Armon Glenn, "Bought, Not Sold," *Barron's*, May 24, 1971, pp. 3 ff.

mutual funds. Based only on the transaction costs, no-load funds generally are the least-expensive way of buying an indirect participation in a broadly diversified portfolio.

Management Costs and Tax Strategies

Direct diversification requires devotion of time and cash resources to two principal subareas of personal portfolio management: (1) obtaining and evaluating investment information, and (2) administrative details. Costs of personally managing a portfolio can vary widely among investors, but they cannot be avoided.

Obtaining and evaluating investment information (search costs) can involve various levels of cash expenditure and personal time. By choosing to obtain investment information principally from a brokerage firm and from occasional readings of financial columns in newspapers, an investor can keep his search costs at a comparatively low level. In contrast, another investor can choose to communicate frequently with his brokerage firm and to spend long hours reading various investment information available in libraries or received by paid subscription. Search costs of the second strategy can be high—both in terms of cash expenditures for investment information (even if tax deductible) and of personal time that can be devoted to other uses. Until credible evidence is forthcoming that high search costs will result in substantially higher portfolio returns over time, realistic investors are likely to focus on investment strategies involving comparatively low search costs.

Administrative details also involve management costs for investors who directly manage diversified portfolios. Such investors must be continually alert to financial events that require prompt decisions about stocks in their portfolios. Chief among these events are preemptive offerings, whereby a company issues to its existing shareholders rights to subscribe, on a pro-rata basis, to new securities of the firm. Because these rights usually have value for a limited period, a prompt decision is required concerning whether to subscribe to the new securities or to sell the rights. To do neither can result in the rights expiring without value to the holder. Merger and tender offers are other financial events that generally require shareholdrs to decide reasonably promptly whether to accept offerings of new securities or cash in exchange for a stock they own. An investor directly holding a diversified portfolio is usually informed of such events by the companies involved or by his brokerage firm. When thus informed, the investor must take time to evaluate the offer and make a decision. Furthermore such periodic subscriptions and exchanges of securities add to the bookkeeping costs of direct stock ownership.

Records of all transactions, income, and expenses involving securities are desirable for measuring investment results over time and are necessary for tax purposes. Record keeping can be costly, especially in terms of personal time; and the costs typically increase as the number of securities in a portfolio increases and as the frequency of stock purchases and sales increases. Furthermore, unless deposited in a brokerage account, there are storage and handling costs involved in directly managing a diversified portfolio.

Indirect diversification enables an investor to avoid many details and direct costs of personal portfolio management. Investment companies, by pooling funds of many individual investors, are generally able to achieve economies of scale in obtaining and evaluating investment information and in managing the portfolio. Full-time staff members can continually study diverse investment information, a process that most part-time investors will find too costly and time-consuming—especially in relation to the total dollar value of their individual portfolios. Similarly, staff members monitor and respond to financial events, such as rights offerings and merger offers involving stocks in an investment company's portfolio. Investment companies also administer diverse details of record keeping and periodically provide financial statements summarizing their operations.

Transferring many of the details and costs of portfolio management to the staff of an investment company involves a cost. Annual total expenses of many larger investment companies approximate one-half of one percent of the portfolio's total dollar value. To illustrate, the total expenses of a mutual fund with $100,000,000 of total assets is likely to approximate $500,000 in that year. An individual with an investment of $10,000 in this fund is thus effectively paying about $50 in indirect management costs. This amount is not charged directly to the investor but, instead, is subtracted from the fund's total revenues that come principally from dividends and interest received from the fund's portfolio. Thus, if the fund's revenues amounted to about $3,000,000 during the year, then the total expenses of $500,000 will be subtracted, leaving annual net income of $2,500,000 to be distributed as net income to the fund's shareholders. On this basis, the individual with the $10,000 investment will receive a distribution of $250 from the fund's net income. While a total expense level of about one-half of one percent is typical of many investment companies, the percentage varies —especially on the upside. Therefore investors evaluating the costs of indirect diversification through shares of investment companies will want to review various companies' expense ratios over preceding years.

With this information, they can assess whether the costs of some professionally managed portfolios are not often less than the costs—in cash expenses and time—of directly managing a portfolio of stocks.

Tax strategies are a third principal component in a decision on whether to diversify indirectly via shares of investment companies. Direct diversification provides an individual investor with reasonable flexibility to time his realized gains or losses from securities transactions. Such timing of realized income can be a potentially important element in strategies of total tax planning. In contrast, an investor who chooses to diversify indirectly via shares of investment companies basically must accept the tax consequences of portfolio decisions made by the professional portfolio managers, who are only able to consider the general tax consequences for most shareholders in an investment company.

In conclusion, many individual investors will find it less costly to diversify their portfolios indirectly instead of directly. Transaction costs make direct diversification essentially impractical for many investors. In addition, the diverse details and costs of directly managing a portfolio often exceed the management cost of indirectly diversifying a portfolio of similar dollar size. For many investors the typically lower transaction and management costs are likely to more than offset possible tax drawbacks of indirect diversification. Therefore there is a strong case for many investors to consider diversifying indirectly by owning shares of one or more investment companies.[4] Any investor is free to decide otherwise, but then he should be prepared to explain, at least to himself, why he chooses to depart from the general conclusion.

[4] Additional analytical evidence consistent with this general conclusion is provided by Keith V. Smith and John C. Schreiner, "Direct vs. Indirect Diversification," *Financial Analysts Journal*, September–October 1970, pp. 33–38.

chapter 25
Choosing from Among Diversified Portfolios

Choosing to invest in a managed portfolio enables many individuals to diversify at lower cost than by personally managing a broadly diversified portfolio themselves. Not only can indirect diversification lower transaction costs, it can reduce the cost of personal commitment required of a part-time security analyst and portfolio manager.

Investors can choose to diversify indirectly through intermediaries such as pension plans and investment companies.[1] Pension plans are not readily available to all individuals; and, where available, important features of a plan are determined principally by the corporate contributor and pension fund manager. In contrast individuals wanting to diversify indirectly can choose among various investment companies having differing goals, investment policies, services, and costs. At the beginning of 1973 there were about 500 different registered investment companies having their share prices reported daily in *The Wall Street Journal*.

To an individual about to choose from among 500 different investment companies, the selection process must seem formidable. In contrast, however, as a part-time analyst and portfolio manager he or she is confronted with daily decisions on whether or not to buy or sell one

---

[1] Investors can have their personal portfolios professionally managed by organizations such as investment advisory firms and bank trust departments. These organizations typically solicit personal portfolios exceeding $50,000, an amount that permits some diversification but not broad diversification among more than 50 different stocks.

of *several thousand* different common stocks traded daily in the nation's various stock markets. Therefore to choose among investment companies is more manageable than continually trying to decide *which* individual stocks to buy and sell, and *when*. Also, a new perspective of the stock market provides some guidelines for choosing among investment companies.

What to Expect from an Investment Company

Individuals can estimate future results from an investment company by three principal methods. Method one is to review an investment company's stated policies to answer the question: What results are the investment company managers seeking to achieve for the stockholders, and how? Method two requires a review of an investment company's past performance to answer the question: How well has the portfolio done in the past? Method three is to build on new evidence about competitive markets in order to answer the question: How well can this portfolio reasonably be expected to do in the future? Combinations of the three methods also can be used.

An individual can form expectations about an investment company by examining its stated broad policies (Method one, "broad policies," includes subcategories such as investment objectives, policies, and restrictions). Because they continuously stand ready to sell and redeem their shares, open-end investment companies (mutual funds) are required to provide current prospectuses to potential shareholders. These prospectuses present each fund's broad policies. Current prospectuses are not as available for closed-end investment companies, but many of the major ones outline their broad policies in reports to shareholders.

Broad policies vary widely among investment companies. For example, some companies specify aggressive capital appreciation as a principal objective, while others specify reasonable current income as a primary objective with capital growth as a secondary objective. Furthermore each investment company is likely to specify in general terms its intended strategy for achieving its stated objective. A fund focusing on aggressive capital appreciation will specify its intention, for example, to use margin and to invest in less-known companies believed to be in emerging growth industries. In contrast, a fund focusing on reasonable income and growth is likely to have a policy of avoiding margin and investing principally in large listed companies having histories of established earnings and dividends. While diversification among common stocks is the general practice of investment companies, some (balanced funds) diversify into other assets such as bonds and some, by stated policy, restrict their diversification by owning stocks only in specific industries such as insurance, petroleum, and utilities.

Informing himself about stated policies of some investment companies, an investor then can choose one or more companies having policies consistent with his personal investment goals. He expects that over time the portfolio managers basically will achieve their specified general objectives. For example, he expects that a portfolio focusing on current income will provide an above-average dividend yield with less capital gains than will a portfolio focusing on capital growth. Over time he can judge the investment company's results against its stated objectives and compared to other portfolios with similar objectives. Thus *judging* a portfolio's results is consistent with a traditional view that portfolio results cannot be precisely measured and directly compared because of their diverse objectives, strategies, and exposure to risk.

Emphasis on *performance* challenges many traditional views of portfolio management. As popularized in the 1960s, "performance" basically means appreciation of a portfolio's capital value. This measure is used to rank and compare results of various portfolios. Striving to rank high in the performance ratings, some aggressive portfolio managers adopt strategies such as investing in less-marketable shares of less-known companies, frequently buying and selling stocks, and using margin. In the late 1960s the publicized success of portfolios ranking near the top of the performance ratings received wide publicity that attracted large amounts of new funds for their management. This performance derby focused popular attention on *how much* the portfolio manager made your money grow, instead on *how* is the portfolio manager attempting to make your money grow in terms of general portfolio policies. Despite traditional opposition to comparing unlike portfolios, performance comparisons among funds with differing objectives and strategies thus were popularized.

An individual can form expectations about an investment company by examining its past performance (method two). This popular procedure involves major pitfalls for unprepared investors. Three pitfalls are: (1) *incomplete* performance measures, (2) performance compared to *selected* alternative investment opportunities, and (3) performance in *selected* time periods.

Performance, as measured by appreciation of a porfolio's capital value, is an incomplete measure.[2] It neglects the dividend component

---

[2] Some researchers are trying to develop combined measures of return *and* "risk" for evaluating portfolio performance. A useful introduction to such measures is provided by J. Peter Williamson, *Investments: New Analytic Techniques* (Praeger Publishers: 1970), especially, Chapters II and III.

in a portfolio's total rate of return (Chapter 5). To illustrate, in one year a portfolio appreciates 15 percent while a broad market index appreciates 13 percent. In popular terms, the portfolio outperformed the market. Measured by total returns, however, such a conclusion is incorrect if, for example, the portfolio provides a dividend yield of less than one percent while the market index provides an average dividend yield of three percent. Practical investors also must watch for comparisons using dissimilar measures, such as when a portfolio's total rate of return in one year is compared to only the price appreciation—excluding dividends—of a stock market index.

Past performance is often compared only to *selected* alternative investment opportunities. One such comparison involves showing how, in a recent decade, an initial amount invested in a particular investment company would have appreciated more than the same initial amount deposited in a savings account or invested in a U.S. savings bond. Another such selected comparison involves showing how an amount invested in a particular investment company would have appreciated more than the same initial amount invested in another investment company selected for the two-way comparison because of its relatively poor performance in that period. Alert to such selected comparisons, practical investors will insist on rate-of-return comparisons among many different investment companies.

Comparisons of past performance also are affected by selection of time periods. An investment company high in the performance rankings in one year can be relatively low in the same rankings another year. Similarly its record during 1963–67 can place it high in the rankings for that five-year period, while its record for 1966–70 places it very low in the rankings for this subsequent five-year period. Practical investors therefore will insist on comparisons of returns from various investment companies during several time periods.

New perspective and new evidence are useful to an individual wanting to know how well an investment company reasonably can be expected to do in future time periods (method three). In a competitive market no one investment company approaches a monopoly of skillful portfolio managers having consistent access to unusually timely and useful information. Therefore no one investment company can reasonably be expected to "beat the market" by frequently reporting returns substantially above those of other investment companies following similar policies. Furthermore comparison among investment companies with *different* portfolio policies is unlikely to uncover one or several that frequently outperform the other portfolios or the general market. By seeking to excel, the many competing portfolio managers create a marketplace in which no one of them consistently can excel. Their very actions contribute to a competitive market.

A mounting body of evidence supports the view that over time returns from investment companies approach general market returns and that no one investment company consistently outperforms the others. Thus the author of a comprehensive evaluation of mutual fund performance from 1945 through 1964 concludes that his evidence "indicates not only that these 115 mutual funds were *on average* not able to predict security prices well enough to outperform a buy-the-market-and-hold policy, but also that there is very little evidence that any *individual* fund was able to do significantly better than that which we expected from mere chance."[3] A different study analyzes mutual fund performance from 1948 through 1967, and its author concludes that "the issue of whether mutual funds outperform 'the market' depends, in large degree, on the *selection* of both the time period and market proxy" and that "past performance results for common stock mutual funds showed no *consistent* predictive value." [italics added][4] More recently another writer asked, "Of the 180 mutual funds for which published performance data are available over the decade 1961–70, how many funds did better than the Standard and Poor's Composite Index (the '500' Index) in each of the 10 years?"[5] His answer is none. "How many beat the index in any nine of the 10 years? Again, none. Any eight of the 10 years? One fund out of 180 beat the S & P 500 Index in eight out of 10 years." These conclusions about mutual fund performance are generally similar, even though the three studies vary somewhat in their analyses of "risk," a concept about which there is not yet general agreement (Chapters 8 and 9). Thus they provide broad perspective to an individual wanting to know how well any one investment company realistically can be expected to do.

Not only do investment companies find it difficult to beat the general market over time, reportedly so do managers of corporate pension funds. To illustrate, in disclosing for the first time how well 31 banks are managing about *$2.8 billion* of common stocks in its total pension fund pool of about $10 billion, the Bell System reported that the investment results lagged slightly behind market averages in the 5¾ years ending September 30, 1972.[6] Relative performance reportedly improved

[3] Michael C. Jensen, "The Performance of Mutual Funds in the Period 1945–64," *The Journal of Finance*, May 1968, p. 415.

[4] Robert S. Carlson, "Aggregate Performance of Mutual Funds, 1948–67," *Journal of Financial and Quantitative Analysis*, March 1970, pp. 22–23.

[5] J. Peter Williamson, "Measurement and Forecasting of Mutual Fund Performance: Choosing an Investment Strategy," *Financial Analysts Journal*, November–December 1972, p. 78.

[6] *The Wall Street Journal*, February 20, 1973, p. 10.

over the time period. An official of AT&T states, "If you look at it year by year, you find that the market averages were tough to beat for nearly all managers of large institutional funds in some years."[7] Also, results varied widely within years. For example the range of returns in 1971 was from 10.6 percent for one managing bank to 32.2 percent for another bank.

Additional evidence demonstrates the difficulty pension-fund managers have in beating the market. Studies by a major investment banking firm reportedly show that "stock investments of professionally managed pension accounts 'have generally underperformed' the Standard & Poor 500-stock composite index."[8] Reviewing the results, an official of the firm says, "The more people seem to reach (for results), the more similar the returns become. . . . And although professional management is being applied more aggressively, we do not see returns on these accounts moving away from returns in general."

Evidence that professional managers of mutual funds and pension funds find it difficult to beat the market is not an indictment of their skills. Instead such evidence supports the competitive-market view that in a forum of many skillful competitors, no one fund manager can have a consistent edge on his competitors. Relative success in one time period is not an adequate basis for predicting relative success in a succeeding period.

An individual investor now can relate this competitive-market perspective to his choice among investment companies. He will avoid popular fallacies and misplaced emphasis on trying to use a portfolio's past returns as a basis for predicting its future returns. His best estimate is that over time returns from a broadly diversified portfolio will approach general market returns. Unless an individual has sufficient resources to warrant direct management of a broadly diversified personal portfolio, then he will focus on the benefits of indirect diversification. Because many investment companies provide benefits of broad diversification and because they can be expected to provide similar (market) returns over time, they provide a useful—but seemingly similar—product to individual investors. Therefore what should an individual look for in choosing among investment companies?

What to Look for in an Investment Company

Instead of being *sold* shares of a particular investment company, practical investors want to make an informed decision before *buying* shares

[7] *Ibid.*

[8] *The Wall Street Journal*, March 13, 1973, p. 32.

of any investment company. Only after examining several different investment companies can an investor choose from them. Individual examination of alternatives requires some personal time and resources, but it can provide more confident financial decisions with longer-run benefits.

A responsible individual will appraise his personal financial goals and resources before deciding whether to own stocks at all. This same personal appraisal can be used in choosing among investment strategies. An investor managing a personal portfolio can choose from many different strategies or combinations of strategies. Nearly all of these possible strategies are similarly available to an individual choosing to participate in an investment company. As demonstrated in this book, few—if any—popular strategies provide a basis for beating the market. Some, however, are relatively costly for individuals to administer and some result in greater volatility of portfolio returns. Therefore practical investors turn their attention to portfolio expenses and portfolio volatility.

Dollar expenses of an investment company are reported in its periodic income statements and its prospectus. For comparative purposes, such expenses can be converted to ratio format, such as operating expenses to average net assets. This ratio ranges from around one-half of one percent to over one percent for some investment companies. Therefore cost-conscious investors will choose from among investment companies with low ratios unless convinced that those with higher ratios provide better opportunities or services. Practical investors welcome convincing arguments and evidence.

Probable future volatility of returns from an investment company can be estimated from its stated broad policies. For example, some investment companies are permitted by policy to use leverage and to invest in relatively volatile stocks. Others have policies that restrict such activities. Although more aggressive strategies are likely to result in more volatile returns over time, it is not as certain that aggressive strategies provide higher returns compounded over time. (Another way of estimating the volatility of a portfolio's future returns is to assume it will be similar to its past relative volatility, as measured by the portfolio's Beta.) Practical investors welcome additional evidence that higher risk strategies will enable their money to grow larger, faster, than is possible by a broad-diversification strategy (Chapter 9).

An individual also should examine the different services provided by investment companies. Descriptions of available shareholder services and their costs, if any, are provided in investment company prospectuses and are summarized in manuals such as *Investment Companies: Mutual Funds and Other Types.*

Automatic reinvestment plans are available from most investment companies. This service permits a shareholder to choose not to receive periodic cash dividends and instead to have the dividends automatically reinvested in additional shares of the investment company. Similarly, capital gains distributions, if any, can be automatically reinvested in additional shares. The cost of this service to the participant typically is zero or nominal.

Voluntary accumulation plans are available from most mutual funds and some closed-end investment companies. Basically this service enables an investor to open an account with a specified custodian that is usually a large bank. Whenever he wishes, the investor then can send additional money to the custodian, directing it to use these new funds to purchase additional full and fractional shares of the investment company. These additional shares will be credited to the investor's account with the custodian, and an acknowledgement of the transaction will be sent to the investor. When he wishes, the account holder also can sell shares; and he can direct the custodian to have his shares transferred from his account to stock certificates issued to him. Voluntary accumulation plans usually require minimum amounts for the initial purchase and for subsequent transactions. These minimum amounts vary among funds, but the initial requirement is generally between $100 and $1000, and subsequent requirements are between $25 and $500. This service is useful for investors who choose to build up their equity capital over time, for example, by periodic purchases as part of a dollar-cost averaging program (Chapter 22). Cost of participation in voluntary accumulation plans is usually zero or nominal.

Other services provided by some investment companies include retirement plans for self-employed individuals and withdrawal plans. By reading the prospectuses, an individual can begin to learn whether he is eligible for these services and whether such services are suitable for his personal financial program. Another service is the conversion privilege available from some distributors who offer a group of funds having different broad policies. A shareholder of one of these funds may transfer his investment to another one of the group's funds. For example, a holder of shares in the group's growth fund may decide near retirement to transfer his investment to the group's income fund. Such a shift within a group usually involves a modest transaction cost, if any.

Investment companies are not without potential problems. At least one mutual fund temporarily suspended redemption of its shares when it found its own assets to be very illiquid. Therefore before committing money to any one investment company, an individual will want to review its size, length of history, management experience, and advisory and custodial relationships as clues to the company's future operating stability. Before choosing to participate in small, new, untested port-folios, individuals will want to review the reported experience of hedge funds (Chapter 17).

An individual wanting to make an informed *choice* among investment companies must review several of them. Knowing what results he can reasonably expect over time, he focuses on how investment companies differ in their expenses, services, special costs, operating policies, and management experience. By thus personally preparing to make an in-formed choice, an individual finds less reason to be *sold* a fund. Instead he can focus on the costs of *buying* into various investment companies that he judges suitable for his financial program. For this reason no-load funds should be reviewed by individuals wanting to make in-formed purchase decisions. While no-load funds are not necessarily suitable for all individuals, investors who choose to inform themselves about different funds can reasonably ask what additional benefits they obtain from paying a sales charge.

Alert to fallacies of selected comparisons and knowing basically what to look for and expect from various mutual funds, informed investors welcome credible evidence that they should pay to be *sold* load funds in cases where they can *buy* similar "packages" of policies, experience, and services from some no-load funds. Informed investors also include the option of choosing to *buy* shares of closed-end investment com-panies. Furthermore individual investors choosing to diversify indi-rectly need not limit their final choice to one portfolio. Large pension funds and endowment funds sometimes choose to split their portfolios among several managers. Similarly, individual investors, while avoiding extensive fragmentation, can choose to accumulate shares in several diversified portfolios judged suitable for their goals.

REVIEW OF PART SIX

Question: How can new perspective about stock market opportunities be useful to me?

Answer: New perspective enables an individual to assess various ways to participate in the stock market. To be only *aware* of different ways is insufficient. An individual must *assess* the principal costs and benefits of various participation methods in order to choose a method suitable for personal goals and resources.

Directly managing a personal portfolio can be costly for many individuals. Costs include more than transaction costs. They include the personal time and expense spent to obtain and evaluate information about individual stocks and to manage administrative details. Valuing their time and money, practical individuals want to be reasonably confident that expected benefits from personal portfolio management will exceed the costs.

Many individuals who choose to manage their portfolios directly must apparently expect to do better than the general market. Stock market "success stories" encourage such popular expectations. It is always *possible* that some individuals will thus receive benefits that substantially exceed their costs of personal portfolio management. However, a growing body of evidence supports the competitive-market view that no one participant—professional, semiprofessional, or amateur—is likely to beat the market. This conclusion is not defeatist. It is a tribute to the skills of many participants in the stock market. Investors willing to accept this conclusion will logically shift their attention to other benefits available to an individual participant in a competitive stock market.

Knowledge of general benefits from diversification is not new to investors. Most conventional investment literature describes why and how investors should diversify. Modern portfolio theory provides newer, more rigorous demonstrations of why proper diversification pays and how to diversify efficiently. However, in a dynamic investment environment, obtaining, processing, and evaluating information basically necessary for efficient diversification is too costly for most individuals and many institutions. Any individual, however, can adopt a broad-diversification strategy whereby he or she can be reasonably confident of obtaining general market returns.

Individuals who choose to focus on diversification benefits can assess the relative costs of direct or indirect portfolio diversification. As shown in Chapters 24 and 25, there is a strong case for many individuals to choose to diversify indirectly by acquiring shares of one or more investment companies. With their new perspective, individuals choosing this method do so because they expect to achieve broad diversification at comparatively low cost. They do not expect to select one or two investment companies that will beat the market. Instead they expect their investment company shares to do about the same as the general market over time; and they look for investment companies that provide "packages" of policies, experience, and services judged most appropriate for their individual financial goals and resources. Practical investors who choose to examine alternatives thus become more informed *buyers* of investment company shares. Before paying to be *sold* shares of a specific investment company, they examine whether shares of other investment companies, judged suitable for their personal objectives, can be obtained at lower cost.

* * *

The case is strong for many individuals to diversify indirectly by buying shares of investment companies. Before choosing this method of participating in the stock market, practical individuals will want further to inform themselves by reading the following types of materials.

Books:

> *Investment Companies: Mutual Funds and Other Types.* This comprehensive manual is published annually by Wiesenberger Services, Inc.
>
> Mead, Stuart B., *Mutual Funds: A Guide for the Lay Investor* (D. H. Mark Publishing Company: 1971).
>
> *Mutual Fund Fact Book.* This booklet, published annually by the Investment Company Institute, provides a useful, timely introduction to the mutual fund industry and how it relates to individual investors.
>
> Springer, John L., *The Mutual Fund Trap* (Henry Regnery Company: 1973).

Other materials:

> Prospectuses of mutual funds provide informative reading material. Prospectuses of various funds are available from brokerage firms and mutual fund distribution companies. Because no-load funds do not have extensive sales networks, their prospectuses usually must be obtained by writing directly to the fund. Both load and no-load funds at times place notices in financial newspapers inviting interested individuals to send in a coupon for more information that will include the fund's prospectus. Sources such as *Investment Companies: Mutual*

Funds and Other Types provide the mailing address of many investment companies to which one can write for a prospectus. Similarly reports of closed-end investment companies usually can be obtained by writing directly to the company.

Among periodicals that regularly report about investment companies are *Forbes* and *FundScope.*

PART SEVEN
CONCLUSIONS

chapter 26
Making Individual Investment Decisions

A principal objective of this book is to provide individual investors with a new perspective. Although seemingly structured as a conventional stock market primer, the book challenges the logic, evidence, and practicality of many traditional approaches to stock market profits. In the process, readers learn how to sharpen their skills in asking tough questions and insisting on credible answers and evidence. Yet the book goes beyond challenging conventional views. Using the competitive-market view as its foundation, it builds logically toward practical conclusions relevant for open-minded individuals wanting to make informed decisions about their personal investment strategies.

Conventionally the stock market is portrayed as providing profit opportunities for investors willing to learn how the market operates and how to select individual securities. An individual interested in stocks thus is encouraged to become a part-time analyst managing a personal portfolio.

Seductive statements about investment opportunities are embedded frequently in popular descriptions of the stock market and in conversations about the market. Examples of such "opportunity statements" have introduced many previous chapters of this book. As demonstrated, however, most opportunity statements are unrealistic when subsequently dissected by the logic and evidence demanded by the competitive-market viewpoint. The statements typically rely on nothing more solid than selected past examples or conjectural future possibilities.

Directly challenging the conventional view, the competitive-market viewpoint demonstrates how the stock market can be visualized as a forum of skillful participants having similar access to generally available information. It follows that in such a marketplace it is virtually impossible for any one investor—amateur or professional—substantially to beat the market over time. Knowledge of this viewpoint enables realistic investors to ask hard questions about investment procedures purportedly capable of beating the market.

Now introduced to the competitive-market viewpoint, readers of this book can review three principal directions for their future stock market investments. Basically an investor can choose to:

1. Try to beat the market.
2. Participate directly in the market for purposes other than beating it.
3. Participate indirectly, in order to be confident of doing as well as the market over time—and at low cost.

Each investor ultimately must choose from these three principal directions.

Investors who choose to *try to beat the market* must either summarily dismiss or carefully refute the competitive-market viewpoint. Neither action will be easy. Summary dismissal involves an act of faith sufficiently strong not only to sustain the traditional view but also to overcome the persuasiveness of the competitive-market viewpoint. A reading of this book is likely to challenge past acceptance of traditional doctrine. Now exposed to the competitive-market viewpoint, readers no longer will be readily able to accept statements about "doubling one's money" or about "how well an investor has done"—with *some* stocks in *selected* time periods. In the future such typical incomplete statements are likely to be confronted by either hard questions or polite disinterest. Continued faith in the traditional view therefore will require buttressing by solid evidence supporting its credibility and refuting the competitive-market view. Realistic investors, characterized by their openness to new information, will welcome such new evidence.

Investors can choose to *participate directly in the market for purposes other than beating it.* Some find a certain joy in participating in financial transactions involving uncertain monetary outcomes. (After all, many people willingly commit funds to games of chance despite knowledge that the long-run odds favor the house.) To monitor each day's outcome, investors can read the closing stock quotations to learn —and possibly relate to others—how well some of their stocks did on a particular day. Then they can await the next day's price changes. Furthermore frequent telephone conversations with brokers willing to discuss investors' favorite stocks is also a potential source of satisfying involvement in day-to-day market activity. In the longer run, *some* of the individual stocks are likely to show substantial capital gains, providing not only personal satisfaction but also an opportunity to share this "success" with other stock market devotees. Also there is always a possibility—however remote—of somehow buying and holding one or more stocks that can literally "make one rich." That some people hold similar hopes—despite the odds—is indicated by those who willingly place funds on "long shots" in the belief that the amount of the possible win can more than offset the low probability of its occurrence.

Other motivations can lead investors to buy individual stocks without an explicit goal of beating the market. Some investors apparently buy stocks in individual companies with whose products or services they personally identify, such as a favorite airline, grocery chain, restaurant system, or the local utility. Conversely, in recent years, other investors have chosen to buy shares of some firms whose policies they oppose in order to attend meetings and confront management with proposed changes in corporate policy. Other possible explanations why some investors choose to hold selected individual stocks without intending to beat the market can be postulated, but it is sufficient to recognize the diversity of human behavior—not to catalog it. As well illustrated by "Adam Smith," for some investors there is apparent exhilaration in participating in—not necessarily winning—the stock market game.[1] Notably, the actions of some investors choosing this avenue need not invalidate the view that the stock market also consists of many skillful participants whose actions contribute to the market's approaching the competitive model.

Investors can choose to *participate indirectly, in order to be confident of doing as well as the market over time—and at low cost*. This choice is consistent with the competitive-market viewpoint and its conclusion of the virtual impossibility that any investor can beat the market. This viewpoint leads directly to consideration of a broad-diversification strategy (Chapters 23 to 25). Furthermore various costs of directly creating and administering a broadly diversified portfolio are prohibitive for most individual investors, for whom the practical alternative is indirect diversification by investing in shares of one or more investment companies that hold broadly diversified portfolios of common stocks. Choosing this direction thus results in dismissing the need to decide which of many *individual stocks* to buy and sell, and when, and sharply narrows the decision to which investment company shares (*portfolios of stocks*) to buy, and when.

Which investment companies are appropriate for individual goals ul-

---

[1] "Adam Smith," *The Money Game* (Random House: 1968).

timately must be decided by each investor. An informed decision is likely to require further reading of some descriptive literature, such as mutual fund prospectuses, and some objective manuals about various investment companies, such as *Investment Companies: Mutual Funds and Other Types*, published annually by Wiesenberger Services, Inc. Sources like these will provide information about factors such as:

Stated objectives
Stated investment strategies
Length of history
Size
Management
Current stockholdings
Custodial arrangements for securities
Accumulation and withdrawal plans
Administrative costs
Sales charges, if any

While thus learning more about various investment companies, realistic investors realize that, in a competitive market, no one investment company can be confidently *predicted* to outperform the market and most other investment companies. Therefore rather than try to identify or predict a "one best" portfolio, an investc. can choose to diversify among shares of several investment companies judged appropriate for personal investment goals.

When to invest indirectly in portfolios of stocks held by investment companies also is an ultimate decision to be made by each investor. There is, however, substantial evidence indicating how difficult it is to outguess market turning points through various timing techniques (Chapters 18 to 21). Such evidence strengthens a case for systematic investing, basically by a program of dollar-cost averaging (Chapter 22). Many investment companies provide services to facilitate systematic investment programs. In view of the logic and ease of systematic investing, many investors will want to review the appropriateness of such a program in relation to their personal financial goals and resources.

Investors who choose to participate indirectly in the stock market may be criticized for their willingness to accept general market returns over time instead of striving to excel. Such criticism rests on the traditional view of market opportunities. Until this view is solidly supported and the competitive-market view is refuted, then there is a strong case for many investors to adopt realistic goals and strategies appropriate for a competitive market. Achieving realistic goals at relatively low cost—both of time and money—can free many investors from the frustrations of striving to achieve the difficult—if not impossible—goal of beating the market and free their time and talents to devote to potentially more productive pursuits or to more pleasant pastimes.

More about the Competitive-Market View

This book is designed to build persuasively toward practical conclusions. Its intended style is that of challenge and inquiry. It draws on mounting evidence that basically refutes traditional views of stock market opportunities and supports the competitive-market view. To date, most of this evidence has been written technically, by using advanced mathematics and statistics, and addressed to professional audiences.

Individuals wanting to learn more about recent studies of capital markets are encouraged to review in full some of the articles cited in this book and to read articles personally chosen from recent issues of following journals:

Financial Analysts Journal
The Journal of Business
The Journal of Finance
Journal of Financial and Quantitative Analysis

Drawing principally from such sources, published collections of selected readings now are available. In addition to reading selected articles, interested readers will benefit from reading the following, more advanced books.

Brealey, Richard A., *An Introduction to Risk and Return from Common Stocks* (The M.I.T. Press: 1969).
———, *Security Prices in a Competitive Market: More about Risk and Return from Common Stocks* (The M.I.T. Press: 1971).
Granger, Clive W. J., and Oskar Morgenstern, *Predictability of Stock Market Prices* (D. C. Heath and Company: 1970).

Index

Accounting procedures, 100; and reporting of EPS, 49, 50–54; "generally accepted," 49, 62

"Adam Smith," 261, 261n

Advance-decline (A-D) line, 227; as technical indicator, 187, 189, 190, 234; questions concerning, 189; definitions of, 189; predictive qualities of, 189–190; provides only incomplete analysis, 190

After-the-fact dollar averaging, 225; not rational investment strategy, 226

Allied Chemical: Betas of, 87

Allocation process: distribution of oversubscribed new issues, 122–123

Aluminum Company of America, 75, 90, 91, 113

American Cyanamid, 167, 168

American Hospital Supply, 28; growth record of, 110

American Telephone and Telegraph (AT&T), 7, 19, 29, 144, 250; Betas of, 86, 87, 96; warrants of, 135, 138, 139; convertible preferred stock of, 140, 141, 142

Anaconda, 90, 91; Betas of, 87

Archer, Stephen H., 92n, 97n

Avon Products, 28, 56; growth record of, 108, 110, 114, 116

Bank trust departments: manage personal portfolios, 245n

Bar charts, 195; summerize daily price information, 196; portrays volume information, 197; compared to P-F charts, 200; construction of, 200

Barron's, 16, 121, 190; in stock market information system, 17

"Beating the market," 8–10, 260, 261; objective of many investors, 40; measurement of, 41–42; requirements of, 42, 43; difficulty of, 92, 234, 235, 260, 261, 263; and hedging, 177; and technical analysis, 193, 208, 210; and charting, 208, 210; investment companies' chances of, 248; and pension funds, 249, 250; and mutual funds, 250; most strategies do not provide basis for, 251; competitive-market view of, 254

Bell System: pension fund of, 249

Beneficiaries of revised environments, 131; as special-situation stocks, 127; identification of, 127, 128, 129; stock prices of, 129–230

Bernstein, Peter L., 109n

Beta, 73; measures relative volatility, 80–85, 87, 101; graphic example of, 82–84; defined as slope of the "line of best fit," 83, 84; calculation of, 85; variations in for same stock, 85–87; of selected stocks, 86, 87; unstable over time, 87; should be used with caution for individual stocks, 88; used to measure portfolio risk, 89, 94–95, 251; used to classify stocks into risk classes, 97; and "market sensitivity," 97

Blue-sky laws: prohibit sale of securities of doubtful potential, 118

Blume, Marshall E., 94n

Bohmfalk, John F., Jr., 113n

Bolten, Steven E., 76n

Bonds, 135, 136; alternatives to investing in stock market, 36, 40; relation to convertible securities, 140; compared to